THE DIVINE NATURE OF GOD

KNOW GOD: Be god

E. E. WISEMAN

Copyright © 2017 by E. E. Wiseman. All rights reserved.

No part of this publication may be reproduced,

without prior written permission from the author.

All Scriptural quotations are taken from the *Holy Bible, New King James Version*, Thomas Nelson, Inc. 1982 and *of the King James Bible, Pure Cambridge Edition*.

Book design copyright © 2017 by Wiseman Publishing. All rights reserved.

Published in the United States of America

ISBN-13: 978-0692888049

DEDICATION

He is like the rod you lean on when climbing a steep hill. He is like a life jacket that keeps you afloat in rough waters. To bump into an oasis in the desert is a wonderful thing. He didn't have to be that way, but he allowed himself to be just that and I am grateful to God that I have a true brother in you Vincent Lekeateh.

CONTENTS

Preface	i
Introduction	1
Chapter One: God the Creator	7
Chapter Two: God is Love	33
Chapter Three: God is Light	59
Chapter Four: God is a Spirit	77
Chapter Five: God the Judge	95
Chapter Six: God the King	129
Chapter Seven: God the Father	165
Chapter Eight: Divinity and the Promise	189
Reference	198

PREFACE

You take your hard-earned money, pay for a book like this and are excited to read it like a new story or a title that is worth reading. After that, you keep it on your shelf and it just becomes one of your collections. The question I ask is this: Did you learn anything or do you know the gravity or implication of not knowing God? In a generation like this, where the church is actually like tempted to sit in hell. When religion is taking over the church and the true value or meaning of spirituality has become like lines drawn in the sand. When good is mixed with evil and evil is mixed with good until even Christians are lost in daylight. In an era when pastors talk about the power of God, not because they all believe in it, but because it is one of those things that we must read from the Bible. Gradually the Holy Spirit has been removed from His church because rather than seeking God who convicts, many have gone out to study human philosophy, psychology and the art of deception and manipulation in which pastors treat Christians as clients.

Therefore, they please the members of their congregation rather than save them for the sake of the offering. For lack of faith in the One who convicts, they went out to convince people to come to church; baiting them with all types of candies. But in this generation, the right hand of God is lifted up against the backslidden city to turn them back to what is right or to cut them off. The choice, therefore, is yours because those who do not know God in the house of God don't know Him because they don't want to know Him. Do you truly want to know God? I do not mean singing the song titled, "I just want to know you more," I mean doing whatever it will take to know Him. God does not sell cheap in the market that is why those who end up knowing are those who diligently seek Him until they find.

Now even if you didn't seek Him if someone else seeks Him and comes to tell you something new about Him, will you even try to listen before you criticize or reject it? If you are like that, I want to speak to you. You go to the Word reading always but never learning any new thing as though God ran out of what to teach you. Yet you want new miracles in your life without learning any new thing. How is that possible? Even when God sends a man to talk to you about Him, you reject Him as it is said no one prefers new wine over the old wine. They always say old wine is better. Dear, if old wine is so better for you that you will not even entertain the possibility to learn something new or that you don't know, then you should embrace your life as is and not complain or cry because that life experience was and is being created by that "old wine knowledge" that you hold so dear. For I judge that if you love the Creator so much, you should also love His creation. I see a demon of pride or "stiff-necked-ness" that has taken over some in the church to crippling levels making Christians who do not know much about their God not wanting or desiring to know anything more about Him.

To you who think you have already known everything about God that you need not learn anymore, this is what I will say. Have you entered perfection? Are you free from all doubts? Are you free from all fears? If you answered no to any of the above, know that there is still something you have to learn because perfect love drives away fear and love also believes all things. Therefore, do not make this book a one-time read, but a book that you will hold close to you for the next few years until your knowledge and experience of God begins to change and a new door of revelation is opened for you in Him. For those who don't really care about knowing God, I warn you before the time for there is a wind already sent from the Lord against all who hate Him and handle His word with laxity to remove their lamps from its place until they are cut off. However, for those who want to know God, I want you to pray this prayer.

Oh God and Father of our Lord Jesus Christ who is also now my Father, according to Your Word by which eternal life is the knowledge of You, I hereby lay aside all that I know or might think I know about You, and pray that through this book, You will reveal to me Yourself as unto the child that I am presenting before You today. Grant that I will know You as You want me to know You in this era and establish me in the knowledge of You to the fullness of your grace and truth. Amen

With that mindset, I want you to dig deep into this word with an open mind expecting to accept to think new thoughts and accommodate new ideas about you and God. If you do that, God will reveal Himself to you and bless you at the end, let the adventure begin.

INTRODUCTION

Although some people do not believe it, there is no doubt that God is real. For in every man there is that desire to pay a tribute of worship to someone or something they believe is superior to them. But in all these forms of "gods," some have not been able to find the true God, seeing there are many false. Truth be spoken, some people don't even want to know the true God because they fear He will infringe into the evil desires they love. The reality is obvious; before there is any false, there is always the truth. So, there are many false gods (though to us there are no other gods) but one true God who created everything that we now see and us His sons and daughters.

In the circle of believers, there is no doubt that knowledge of our God has a lot to play on how we are going to spend the many years that God has given us here on earth and in eternity. Looking at Daniel 11:32, the Bible says *"...but the people that do know their God shall be strong, and do exploits."* Therefore, we who are the children of God, have the knowledge of our God as the only guarantee for our strength and success here on earth. The question one may be forced to ask is this:

How does the knowledge of God culminate to giving strength to do exploit?

This I think will be answered before the end of this write-up. II Peter 1:2 reads *"Grace and peace be multiplied to you in the knowledge of God and of Jesus our Lord,"* Another version says *"through the knowledge of God"* This also attests to the fact that even the grace of God that He gave us, together with His peace can only be accessed by knowing Him.

My people are destroyed for lack of knowledge, (Hosea4:6). Therefore, we see in this that even the very things that God has given us can only be enjoyed by us when we find the knowledge of our God.

"....that by these ye might be partakers of the divine nature...." (2 Peter 1:4); from this, it is clear that God wants us to share the same nature with Him. But how can we take part in a nature we know nothing about? Hence you will agree with me that there is a reason why we must all pin ourselves down to make sure we know our God so we can fully share in his nature.

For every tree is known by its own fruit. For men do not gather figs from thorns, nor do they gather grapes from a bramble bush. (Luke 6:44)
Come to think of it, Jesus Himself said that we cannot gather grapes from a bramble bush. If the baseline for the production of fruits lies in the nature of the tree. Then God cannot just be known for His acts only, but from what caused Him to act as He did and is still doing today. Thus, by knowing His true nature, we will be transformed to become that same nature.

And it came to pass, when the time was come that he should be received up, he stedfastly set his face to go to Jerusalem, And sent messengers before his face: and they went, and entered into a village of the Samaritans, to make ready for him. And they did not receive him, because his face was as though he would go to Jerusalem. And when his disciples James and John saw this, they said, Lord, wilt thou that we command fire to come down from heaven, and consume them, even as Elias did? But he turned, and rebuked them, and said, Ye know not what manner of spirit ye are of. (Luke 9:51-55)

Note that in the above scriptures, the disciples of Jesus were acting differently because they did not know the spirit they were made of. They were a cut out from God Himself, but they did not know it. Hence, they still desired to act like men. Thus, their problem was that they did not know who they were. Therefore, the day they know they will act differently.

Woe to you, scribes and Pharisees, hypocrites! For you cleanse the outside of the cup and dish, but inside they are full of extortion and self-indulgence. Blind Pharisee; first cleanse the inside of the cup and dish, that the outside of them may be clean also. (Matthew23:25-26)
If you check what is on the inside, and clean it, then the outside will be clean automatically. Real change comes from inside-out, not from outside-in. Hence by knowing who we are on the inside and ordering ourselves accordingly, we will build that divine nature which will grow to bear fruits in the open.

Before we continue, I think it will be good for us to explain the difference between Nature and Character per my understanding going forward. According to the Merriam-Webster Dictionary, "nature is the inherent character or basic constitution of a person or thing." However, by my understanding, I will define nature as the inherent potential attributes of a person or thing. On the other hand, I will define Character as the action and reaction produced by the nature of an individual or a thing as they relate with themselves, other individuals, circumstances and things. Basically, we can say that the character of an individual is produced by their nature while their nature is revealed by their character. Character is subjective to circumstances, place, and person, but nature remains the same. Now based on humans, you should note that both nature and character can be changed, but you can only change character by changing nature. Nature, on the other hand, is changed through knowledge, understanding (be transformed by the renewing of your mind) and by the willingness of the set individual.

For example, let's use both living and none living things to differentiate further. We know that inflammable liquids have the potential to easily ignite into flames even when they are not in flames. Thus, nature could be described as the potential of someone or something even when that potential is not manifesting. Now let's just say fire decides to relate with a piece of paper and a block of gold. After that experience, the paper will call fire a destroyer while the piece of gold will call fire a purifier. For us Christians, we are all commanded to be quick to listen; however, no matter the level of your listening ability, a foolish person will always say you don't listen. So, you see that to describe people from character could be very misleading and this is no different with God. We know from scripture that God is a consuming fire, but for those of us who love and obey Him, we will never know Him in the consuming fire capacity because it is one of His characters which are subjective based on whom He is relating with. However, on issues of love which is one of His natures, He has expressed how He loved the whole world and gave up His only Son. Therefore, as we move forward, I want you to keep this understanding in mind.

The Seven-Fold Nature:

"A good man out of the good treasure of the heart brings forth good things and an evil man out of the evil treasure brings forth Evil things" (Matthew 12: 35)

Looking at this scripture very keenly, I want us to draw something from it. There are two basic things that I want us to look at. We have "good treasure," and "good things." Firstly, the "good treasure" stands for the nature of the heart, while the "good things" signify the character traits that are produced by that nature. Secondly, we have to take note of the fact that, the good treasure is written in the singular, while the good things are in the plural. Therefore, every good treasure (nature) can or has the ability to produce many good things (characters). Now I do not want you to think that we are getting out of topic but want to stress here that, the character of God is basically different from His nature which is divine. I say so because many at times, we have been trying to describe God from the basis of what he has done. But I came to discover that trying to describe someone on the basis of what they do only, can be very misleading and with God, it is no exception.

Therefore, having understood this principle, I will like to make you take note that all the things which He has done that now we see and even those which we do not see, were done out of His sevenfold nature under which are embedded many characters. These we are going to see in the course of this text. I will, therefore, like to list the seven Natures of God that we are to discuss. Note that the listing is not done in order of importance, but just for the sake of order. The truth of the matter is that all the seven natures are of equal importance, making God perfect and complete and the perfecter of everything; especially us who are His children.

1) God is a Creator
2) God is Love
3) God is Light
4) God is a Spirit
5) God is the Judge
6) God is King
7) God is a Father and or Husband

The above mentioned seven natures of God make up the complete divine nature of the Godhead of which, we have been called to partake.

So, our perfect understanding of these will go a long way to enable us to know who we are and how we ought to behave ourselves on this planet earth.

Before I speak about us knowing God; we have to understand, however, that the kind of knowledge expressed here is not the ability to acquire or gather information about someone or something to gain understanding on what to do or say. Rather it is the ability to gather information about someone or something to gain understanding on what to say and become to the extent that it changes who you are as a person to the point where you become like the person from whom the knowledge originated: in our case the Almighty God Himself. When Jesus spoke about how we can know people, He said you shall know them by their fruits. However, speaking of God, He said He looks at the heart. The heart of people cannot be seen by men, but God can see what's in our hearts. Now our heart is like the warehouse of our personality. By this I mean everything you think, do or will ever do is stored up in your heart such that it is possible for God to know what you will become by just looking in your heart. Therefore, if God says you know Him, it means looking into your heart He has seen a lot of Himself in there. Would that not be wonderful to hear that God sees most of Himself in you? On our part, we know God as powerful, strong and able. He is all these and more not because we see Him like that but because that is what He is. The fact also that we see what He has done gives us confidence in Him.

The end of Christianity is not that we gain confidence in God for what he can do but that we gain confidence in ourselves for what we can do as we grow to become more like him.

    By now it should be coming clearer to you why knowing God gives us the strength to do exploits. To be frank with you, to know God is to become (god) like God. Up until now, some did not know that knowing the Bible is different from knowing God and that there is a difference between Christian religion and true Christianity. You can know a lot about what is written in the Bible. You might even travel all around the world to teach it, but when God looks at you, He does not check what is in your head He checks what's in your heart. And He knows that when a real stormy situation comes up since life does not emanate from the head (but from the heart), your heart will deliver and all that head knowledge will fly away leaving people wondering why this or that great teacher had to come to this.

    Therefore, our spiritual focus should not be on knowing about God but on becoming like God. This I say because when God looks at the universe, He sees two important people: Himself and all those who are like Him, period. Have you not heard the statement that 'he who does not have the son does not have the life?' And that 'he who has not His Spirit is none of His?' Beloved having the Son is to become like the Son and without this, we cannot enjoy the life God gave us. If the sons and daughters of men form the human race, then the sons and daughters of

God should form the divine or God race. As such every Christian should know that they are gods and the sons and daughters of the living God. Though I stress here about becoming like God and His Son, I do also want to stress here that the purpose of this book is not primarily to show you how to become like God (though you will learn some of that) because we cannot show you how to become someone for whom you have no information. Hence, our focus is to dissect the nature of God, break it down to the least and show you how God expects and has made room for you to also be like him. Let's dig into the nature of our Father and see how we are just like HIM.

CHAPTER ONE

GOD THE CREATOR

God is a supreme being, creator and ruler of the universe. He is the self-existent one, the "I am that I am" i.e. He does not require anything from anyone to be who He is or what He wants to be. So, God chooses what or who He wants to be; whenever He wants to be it. Just for your notice, when God saw that the world needed change, He became the Creator. When He saw that the children of Israel needed help; He became their Deliverer. When there was no one to save us from sin, He took charge and sent someone like Himself to be our Savior. When He wanted a lamb to cleanse us from our sin, He made someone like Himself a lamb for the sacrifice and when He saw that we needed life, He became our life. Like Paul, I will say I cannot say more about the "I am that I am" now.

Before the mountains were brought forth, Or ever you had formed the earth and the world, Even from everlasting to everlasting, You are God. (Psalm 90:2) In the beginning God created the heaven and the earth. (Genesis 1:1)

It is clearly written, "in the beginning God created." This makes us understand that God was the only person (and no one else was) present at the beginning. We do not want to ask the question about where He was when He created the things that we now see. The question we might want to ask is: How did God create the World? (Genesis 1: 3a) The Bible says, "And God said…" We know that the Spirit of the Lord was moving upon the face of the deep. The Bible also says, *"Not by might, nor by power, but by my spirit, saith the LORD of hosts..." (Zechariah 4:6).* Therefore, we can conclude that Papa God had in mind what He wanted when He said let there be. So, when He said it, the Word caused the Holy Spirit to take action, producing the required result.

During creation, we see that God only spoke the word. He said let there be and there was.

By faith we understand that the worlds were framed by the word of God, so that the things which are seen were not made of things which are visible. (Hebrews 11:3)

All things were made through Him, and without Him nothing was made that was made. (He here signifying the Word) (John1:3)

Thus, the worlds were framed by the word of God. If the world was created by the word of God, then it means the world is subject to the word of God. If the word of God framed the world, then God can still make adjustments in the world through His word.

Also, since God created everything, He (God) has claimed total ownership of everything, by right of creation.

I will not take a bull from your house, Nor goats out of your folds. For every beast of the forest is Mine, And the cattle on a thousand hills. I know all the birds of the mountains, And the wild beasts of the field are Mine. If I were hungry, I would not tell you; For the world is Mine, and all its fullness. (Psalm 50:9-12)

And God saw the light, that it was good; and God divided the light from the darkness. (Genesis 1:4)

God saw the light that He had made and said it was good. What was He saying? He was giving a guarantee that what He had made was as good as He wanted it to be and fit for the purpose for which He had made it. Looking very closely, we find out that there is another name attached to His creative nature. This is called the manufacturer. Come to think of it, when God had finished creating all the other things, the scriptures did not get to details on how He made them, talking only of His word. However, when it came to man's time, He did not just say let there be man, rather He said, let us make or manufacture man in our image. Brethren, by understanding, I truly think that; this is how God made all the other things that we see. Yet for reason of emphasis, He capitalized on what He said because that was the main tool behind creation. By this, I am saying that though the word was a principal tool during creation, it was not the only tool.

And God said, Let us make man in our image, after our likeness: and let them have dominion over the fish of the sea, and over the fowl of the air, and over the cattle, and over all the earth, and over every creeping thing that creepeth upon the earth. So God created man in his own image, in the image of God created he him; male and female created he them. (Gen 1:26-27)

So, we see that God created man, but for the sake of understanding, I will rather say He manufactured or made the man. Hence, He took His time to put His image into the fabric and instilled dominion in them. He was, therefore, a special creation to God. It is no doubt that man came up to be supreme amongst all of God's creation because God took His time to print His nature in him. When God was creating the other animals, He did define them; but not according to His nature as He did with the man.

For your Maker is your husband, The LORD of hosts is His name; (Isaiah 54:5a).

We see from above that God Himself is our Maker.

To Him who by wisdom made the heavens, For His mercy endures forever; (Psalm136:5)

The LORD by wisdom founded the earth; By understanding He established the heavens; (Proverbs 3:19)

Beloved if God established the heavens by understanding and founded the earth by wisdom, then it means there was more work in creation than just speaking and seeing. Don't you think so? If it involved wisdom and understanding, then it means before or after He spoke the word there was a lot of thinking on His part. Yet in Genesis for the sake of time and space like John in his closing remark said, the writer decided to cut it short. So, everything that God made, He took time to manufacture it step after step until He finished it and said it was good. God could have said it is good even before He started working because He is a God of faith calling things that be not as though they are. God still took time to work on every detail about what He was creating.

And God said, Let there be light: and there was light. And God saw the light, that it was good: and God divided the light from the darkness. And God called the light Day, and the darkness he called Night. And the evening and the morning were the first day. (Genesis1:3-5)

The question I will ask from the above scripture you just read is this: If that light just appeared the way we have been made to believe, then why did it take the whole evening and morning? We know also that a day to God is like a thousand years to us.

Hence calculating from that, a day in God's creation could easily mean one thousand years.

When we read that creation took seven days, we could from this time difference, deduce that all of creation took at least seven thousand years. If you even see the earth and the way it functions you will agree with me that it is not just a God said issue only; someone took the time to arrange everything in its place. The earth is naturally recycling itself.
One generation passes away, and another generation comes; But the earth abides forever. The sun also rises, and the sun goes down, And hastens to the place where it arose. The wind goes toward the south, And turns around to the north; The wind whirls about continually, And comes again on its circuit. All the rivers run into the sea, Yet the sea is not full; To the place from which the rivers come, There they return again. (Ecclesiastes1:4-7)

If you accept the geography of Solomon above, then you will agree with me that the world was made by a master planner. And not just by talking. Although His word formed one of the principal tools of creation. God was not just joking when He created the earth. The Guy took His time to make the earth with a plan that will last forever. See if you are asked to make a car, you will just put your ideas to work and come up with a car. Yet if you are asked to make a car that will last forever, you will not just do anything. That is the state of mind God had when He was making the world to last forever. With this understanding, you will say God really had to rest on the seventh day. With this understanding also, I want you to know that the theory of the big bang might actually be the way God created the world.

However, the only thing I think is wrong with that theory is that they say no one did it. This they say because they hate God and don't want to acknowledge Him, but cannot openly endorse the devil so they say no one. If the world created itself as they say, then the same process should continue today. Why then do people create things? They could have just said as the world created itself, if you need a car, just tell the car and it will create itself. Also, if the man just evolved from ape as they say, then why have humans not evolved to something else after such a long time? Maybe they should tell us what man will evolve to because they have told us what he came from. Foolishness in high places!

Christians do not believe anything.

"Is anything too hard for the LORD? At the appointed time I will return to you, according to the time of life, and Sarah shall have a son." (Genesis 18:14)

If you have had some experience walking with the Lord, you will know that the things of God all have a time tag on them. In the above scripture after God had mentioned the fact that nothing is too hard for Him, He still said according to the time of life. It means life has timing attached to it.

I, the LORD, will hasten it in its time."(Isaiah 60:22b)

So even when God hastens things, He only does it in its time. Wow! God does not just cause things to appear, He makes them with time.

Now talking of creation, there is one aspect that you have to note going forward: Creation in itself is the conception of a new idea about something you want to do and the planning to bring that idea into reality.

After this understanding, it will be good that we go on to see the three characters or abilities of God that are birth by this His creative nature.

The Character of Faith

At this stage, it is very necessary for us to know or note that God never asks us to walk in anything that is different from Him. Deuteronomy 13:4a says *"You shall walk after the Lord your God and fear him...."* This means that God only asks us to do those things that He himself does. In order words, God will not ask us to walk by faith when He himself is not walking by faith. If God actually took time to make all the things we now see, then how in the summary of His word did He come to the conclusion that mostly only what He said during creation should be written in the Bible? Come to think of it for example; Imagine that you just finished the construction of a great house and were asked to write a report on how you built the house. What you will want to do is break the project in stages and write how you accomplished each stage. Then if you are asked to reduce those report stages to just bullet points of at most three sentences, you will want to make sure you write down the most important and challenging part of that stage. On the foundation you could write something like this:

We filled the swampy area with dirt, separated the water from the site and raised 12 80ft. long circular pillars with a diameter of 10ft. with 25ft. below ground covering a total area of 2000sft. for a period of 2 months. To you, this might be the most important thing you might want people to know about the work you did at the foundation level of the house you built. Why will you say that? You will say that because that is the most important thing you want people to know about that foundation work. But when God had to write a point form of all that He did, the most important thing He wanted us to know about what He did was what He said. So, if you follow God's example literally, your report for the foundation will be like this.

We said let there be the foundation and there was the foundation and we saw that the foundation was good, and the beginning and the end was 2 months. Wow! If you want to get fired from your project management Job fast that's what you write as your report.

So, the question is how did God come to the conclusion that the most important thing He did in creation was what He said?

That from the principle of Faith and by faith, you will also understand that the operations of God are different from that of the natural man. In Hebrew11: 3, the Bible makes us know that the things that we see were not made of things which do appear. It is clearly stated that all things were created by the word of God and that without Him was not anything made that was made. Therefore, we see that God created the world and everything that we see by faith. The world was formless and void at creation. But God had the ability to see the change He wanted in the midst of the obscurity and opposition.

.... *God, who gives life to the dead and calls those things which do not exist as though they did; (Romans4:17b)*

We know that God is a God of faith because He calls those things that are not as though they were. Come to think of it, it means when God said, "let there be light;" the time it took for what He said to actually come to existence is unknown. But from the Book, we hear that the Evening and Morning was the first day. Hence God said let there be light. He then had faith that the light He spoke about was already in existence. If the light creation took place for a whole day, it means God spent that time describing and forming the light that He had created with His word. (i.e. being yet unseen).

THE DIVINE NATURE OF GOD

The act of calling things that do not exist as though they already exist is what I call "The Faith of Creation"

For as the body without the spirit is dead, so faith without works is dead also. (James 2:26)

The process of this as we see is that God said it and worked it because faith without works is dead. The reason why this character of God is so connected to creation is the fact that faith and creation both have to do with the present, the future and the ability to develop or bring something new into existence. We know that God has planned for every dispensation the things that He wants to do. So, since He cannot do it without His word, He starts declaring it before time i.e. calling it as though it already is. So, the reason we call it faith is not just the words but the way the word is said and God's mental disposition after the word has been spoken. God could have said I will make the light and the light will be good because that is how men speak. But He said, "let there be light," then He said again, "and there was light." On this there could be two periods when he said it:
 a) Immediately after He said let there be light or
 b) After the light was made.

There are also two main reasons why someone will make his word the most important aspect of his work.
1. That's if he is a king or president with people in place to do what he commands
2. That's if his word has the ability to make him or others do what he wants

In my understanding, I think both of the above are true in the sense that God always calls Himself as Lord. A lord is never without subjects who obey and do the commands of their master. Also, in the second case, I think God's word has the ability to make Him do whatever He says. If it were not so, then we will not call Him faithful because He always will do what He says. It means He is bound by His word. Also, as He has made His word higher than His name, it means His word controls His actions. Since all the hosts of heaven fear God, they, therefore, will not lift hand or foot without His command.

So, God speaks from who He is; then what He says dictates what He and everyone under His command do.

God's Creation cycle

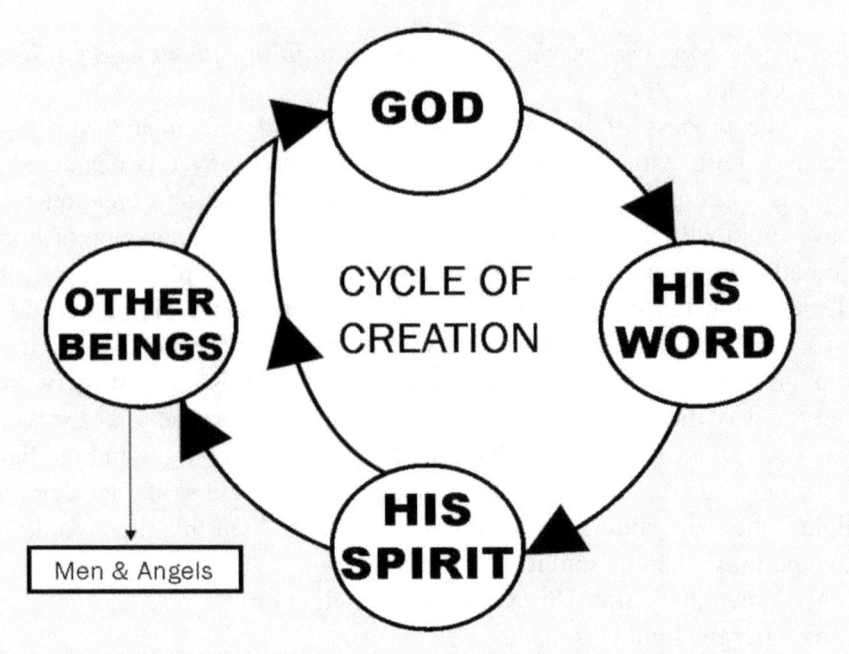

For God to also speak as though it is done means He has to believe either in Himself or the people that have to do or carry the responsibility. Hence in the spirit, if you do not speak as though something has been done, it is seen as though the responsibility has not been delegated or as though you do not believe in the person with the responsibility to do the job. That is why God believes in the Holy Spirit, the angels and men He sends and He expects all His subjects to also believe in Him. However, the most important Person God believes in after His word is the Holy Spirit and that is why He said, "not by might but by my Spirit."

It is well spelled out in scriptures that, with God all things are possible and it is worth noting that if there is the possibility of new things by God, it is because He has the driving force of creation. And the driving force of all creation is faith. Even those who have made things in the world of science had to believe. If not, they would have given up long before their discovery. Therefore, as faith is the substance of things hoped for, God had to speak what He believed and wanted until He finally had it.

It is therefore impossible to please God without faith because faith is the driving force that brings about the accomplishment of God's purpose in our lives and world. God has a dream for the world but that dream cannot come to pass unless we have faith.

But without faith it is impossible to please Him, for he who comes to God must believe that He is, and that He is a rewarder of those who diligently seek Him. (Hebrews11:6)

That is why you may have love, joy, peace, all that you can think of, but God has made the conclusion that without faith it is impossible to please Him. So, He commands us to walk by His character of faith from our adoption to redemption. If God had to say of Jesus "this is my beloved son in whom I am well pleased," it meant that He was pleased with him because of his faith. But God grieves when He has beloved sons who cannot please Him with their faith. When we look at the way God speaks about the future, we are tempted to think that He speaks like that because He just knows all things. God does not just sit and know things as you may think. I know that He is all knowing. Did He just get up in the morning and knew that you will go to Europe? No, only men know things like that when God shows, or tells them and even if they have to accept, it is because they have faith in the God that is speaking. But I want to shock you with this, God mostly knows His plans. And because He has faith in His plans for eternity, He declares it as though He just knows. Let's see proof of this. God knows you, but why does He yet put the things that will happen to you on the bases of Condition (IF)?

And it shall come to pass, if thou shalt hearken diligently unto the voice of the LORD thy God, to observe and to do all his commandments which I command thee this day, that the LORD thy God will set thee on high above all nations of the earth: And all these blessings shall come on thee, and overtake thee, if thou shalt hearken unto the voice of the LORD thy God. (Deuteronomy28:1-2)

But it shall come to pass, if you do not obey the voice of the LORD your God, to observe carefully all His commandments and His statutes which I command you today, that all these curses will come upon you and overtake you: (Deuteronomy28:15)

Hence, He says if you walk according to My will, it shall be well with you but if not, then calamity will befall you. God does not know what you will choose from that statement, but simply has two plans for you to choose from.

I call heaven and earth to record this day against you, that I have set before you life and death, blessing and cursing: therefore choose life,

that both thou and thy seed may live: (Deuteronomy 30:19)
By this, He also said, "I set before you this day life and death but I advise you to choose life so that you might or may live." Now I know that God has given us free will and He will not go against it.

For God sent not his Son into the world to condemn the world; but that the world through him might be saved. (John 3:17)

God did not say, "I have sent My son in the world that the world must be saved by him," instead He said, "...so that the world through him might be saved." The word "might", is a statement of probability and not of certainty. So, God gave up his Son Jesus while we were yet sinners to prove His faith. Also, Jesus Christ had to die while we were yet sinners to prove His faith. This I say because God did not know for certain those who were going to believe. But His action made it possible because by it, He proved His faith.

...for man looks at the outward appearance, but the LORD looks at the heart." (1Samuel 16:7)

Please do not misunderstand me. God knows what we think because He sees our hearts (spirits). If God declares that He will do above all that we ask or think, it means that He knows our thoughts. But just because He knows it does not mean that He can just change it any time any day. No. By the law of personal will, God can give you incentives to make you change but He cannot change you without your consent.

This decision is by the decree of the watchers, And the sentence by the word of the holy ones, In order that the living may know That the Most High rules in the kingdom of men, Gives it to whomever He will, And sets over it the lowest of men.' (Daniel 4:17)

It is clear, therefore, from above, that God knows all things and controls all things in the earth. But in the aspect of faith and the will of man, God knows your future by the wisdom of faith which is confidence in His plans and the faithfulness of His words. The only reason God is saying people will burn in hell is that He has planned for it and because He has said it, He cannot change it and it will not fail

The Character of the Manufacturer

Manufacturing is the process of work that took or takes place between creation and the actual manifestation of the created item. A typical example of this is seen in the process by which God created man and woman.

THE DIVINE NATURE OF GOD

Then God said, "Let Us make man in Our image, according to Our likeness; let them have dominion over the fish of the sea, over the birds of the air, and over the cattle, over all the earth and over every creeping thing that creeps on the earth." (Genesis 1:26)

Here the Bible makes us understand that God had made man in His own image and likeness. Then in verse 27, it says, *"So God created man in His own image; in the image of God He created him; male and female He created them."* The word *"created"* is written in the past tense; signifying God had created both of them. However, in (Genesis 2:7) *it says, "and the LORD God formed man of the dust of the ground, and breathed into his nostrils the breath of life; and man became a living being. And Adam gave names to all cattle, and to the fowl of the air, and to every beast of the field; but for Adam there was not found an help meet for him. And the LORD God caused a deep sleep to fall upon Adam, and he slept: and he took one of his ribs, and closed up the flesh instead thereof; And the rib, which the LORD God had taken from man, made he a woman, and brought her unto the man. (Genesis 2:20-22)*
The LORD God planted a garden eastward in Eden, and there He put the man whom He had formed. (Genesis 2:8)

God did not say let there be a woman. He simply took a rib from the man and used it to manufacture or make the woman. It also says above that God planted a garden. I am sure you saw that. So, God had to put some things together in order to make the man. We see that God created the world and everything that is in it for six days. The statement I want to make is; if these things that were created by God had taken place the way we are made to understand, then God would have used one day to create everything. What do I mean? The issue here is that the Bible evidently says that "and there was light". But it goes further to say that *"...And the evening and the morning were the first day."* What does that mean? It is suggesting that God took time to form the light He wanted. Also, it says,

"God planted." Hence the whole issue about creation is that creation is an idea while manufacturing is the processing of bringing that idea into reality.

It, therefore, means God actually took His time to work in His lab for six good days to produce what we now see on earth.

For every day He will come up with the objectives of that day and go to work day and night until He can say it is good. I know you or some have always believed that God just said let there be light and there was light or better still light just appeared. But if that was or is the case, then why will God put a whole day to rest when He did not do anything. The Bible even makes us know that God rested from all His work. So, you see that God was so tired that He had a sigh of relief on the seventh day and because He enjoyed the rest very well, He could not but bless that day, making it special.

Before any plant of the field was in the earth and before any herb of the field had grown. For the LORD God had not caused it to rain on the earth, and there was no man to till the ground; The LORD God planted a garden eastward in Eden, and there He put the man whom He had formed. (Genesis 2:5,8)

These scriptures make us know that God is a working God. Jesus even said that *"my father works and I work"* He said also that *"I must do the work of Him that sent me and to finish His work...."* In verse 5 we see that God had not caused rain to fall. In order words, the things that God had created were not yet operational. Because that statement is synonymous to a man who makes a TV but it is not yet showing any images because he had not switched it on.

So, we see that there was still something that God had to do to make creation operational. Verse 8 above states clearly that God planted a garden eastward in Eden. I know you understand what planting is all about, hence God planted seeds watered and watched them grow.

In John 6: 27b the Bible says *".... for on him has God the father set his seal."* Today in the world we have many manufacturing companies from electronic to mechanical and even nuclear equipment or apparatus. All these companies have a brand name which they put on their manufactured products. The seal tells us that though there are many TVs in the world, this particular one was made by SHARP Company. The fact that they put their seal on it is because they have qualified it for use or that it will perform every function that a good TV should perform.

For we are His workmanship, created in Christ Jesus for good works, which God prepared beforehand that we should walk in them. (Ephesians 2:10)

In Him you also trusted, after you heard the word of truth, the gospel of your salvation; in whom also, having believed, you were sealed with the Holy Spirit of promise, (Ephesians 1:13)

Likewise, we are sealed by the Holy Spirit, hence the Holy Spirit is God's brand name by which He has made us His workmanship. Hence only a manufacturer can put his seal on a product because he is sure of what he made. So also, because God made us in Christ Jesus, He has put His seal on us saying, "though there are many people in the world these ones are made by Me." So, then your existence is the very proof that God is a manufacturer just as SHARP TV is proof that the sharp company is a TV manufacturer.

Note that God had to make all these things because before he willed the earth to the man, he had total control of the earth. However, after he made the man, he officially handed the earth to man. Thus, there are some things he can no longer do on the earth without men.

The Character of the Guarantor

After establishing a good understanding of the fact that God is a manufacturer, it will be good that we now go on to see the last character of God's creative nature. Genesis 1: 4a says. *"And God saw the light, that it was good."* So, God was acting like a man who had the idea of a painting in His head. He spent a whole day on the board mixing colors until finally at the end of the day it paid off and He could say or appreciate His work by saying, *"it is good."* God was satisfied with what He had created. Until it was good in His sight, He did not stop working on it. Now the Bible says, *"let every man be a lie but let God be truthful."* Therefore, if God says something is good, it means that thing is good in all aspects of the word "good." This I say because He cannot lie. The issue is why will God be so sure about His work?

Since the word is the main material or instrument God used to create the whole world, let us take some time to examine closely the authenticity of this material that God used to create the world. It is good for you to understand that the durability of any manufactured product depends on the type of materials that were used to make it. Imagine a car made of gold and that made of aluminum, you will evidently accept with me that the car made of gold will be more expensive and even stronger than that made of aluminum.

As for God, His way is perfect; The word of the LORD is proven; He is a shield to all who trust in Him. (2 Samuel 22:31),

Every word of God is pure; He is a shield to those who put their trust in Him. (Proverbs 30:5)

In the above scriptures, the Bible makes us understand that the word of God is proven and pure. In the case of being proven it is declaring that

God has tested His raw material which is universal and has come to the conclusion that it is fit for whatever He will ever create or has created. Therefore, by this, He is saying that He did all the tests to check the authenticity of His raw material (the word) and found the test results sufficient and more for what He wanted to do with it. The purity of the material can be seen in two ways;

    a) As gold with impurities, He has purified it in the fire until all impurities have been removed, to the point that you cannot find any point of weakness in the materials.

    b) Secondly, the Bible says, *"Being born again, not of corruptible seed, but of incorruptible, by the word of God which lives and abides forever. (I Peter 1:23)* This makes us know that God's raw material is incorruptible, meaning God has so purified it that it is impossible for it to be contaminated again.

Also looking at those two scriptures one might be tempted to say coincidence but it is no coincidence at all that the two scriptures address the issue of trust saying that He is a shield to them that trust in Him. From all indication, we see that you can only give guarantee for things that you as the manufacturer are sure of (like I give Guarantee for this book). Hence because He is very confident of His word, He can boldly say, *"my word shall not return to me void but shall accomplish that which I please and it shall prosper in the thing for which I sent it." (Isaiah 55:11)*.

    This is the reason why God warns that people should not add to His word because His word has been proven. But anyone that will add to it will be proven as a liar because it will not work as it should if it were the pure word of God. Now, this is the reason why if God gives guarantee for something you should believe it because He knows the type of raw materials, He used to make it. When manufacturers bring a new product to the market, they tell you the new things that the new product can do better than the previous ones. Some will tell you their new brand of watches are waterproof because they know the build of the new product.

Whoever has been born of God does not sin, for His seed remains in him; and he cannot sin, because he has been born of God. (1John 3:9)

For whatever is born of God overcomes the world. And this is the victory that has overcome the world--our faith. (1John 5:4)

"And whoever lives and believes in Me shall never die. Do you believe this?" (John 11:26)

    Hence God after making us said, *"He that is born of God cannot sin!"*, "He that is born of God has overcome the world". Jesus said, "He that believes in me shall not die." In all these statements, God is saying or giving guarantee for His product or your life, even though you don't feel like it. Therefore, God can give guarantee for eternity because His word lives and abide forever. In all this, we see that God is the only living individual that gives eternal guarantee showing the degree to which He has proven His material (the word). However, note that the word was not the only material God used to create the things that we see. *Who being the brightness of His glory and the express image of His person, and upholding all things by the word of His power..., (Hebrews 1:3b)*

In the case of man, he formed him from the dust and breath in him and he became a living soul. So, we see dust and breath. Yet the superiority of the word is found in the fact that God holds all things together by the power of His word. So as a creator, God creates the picture of what He wants in His mind, uses faith to initiate the process, gets to work manufacturing what He said and then gives His seal of approval guaranteeing what He has made.

The Process of Creation

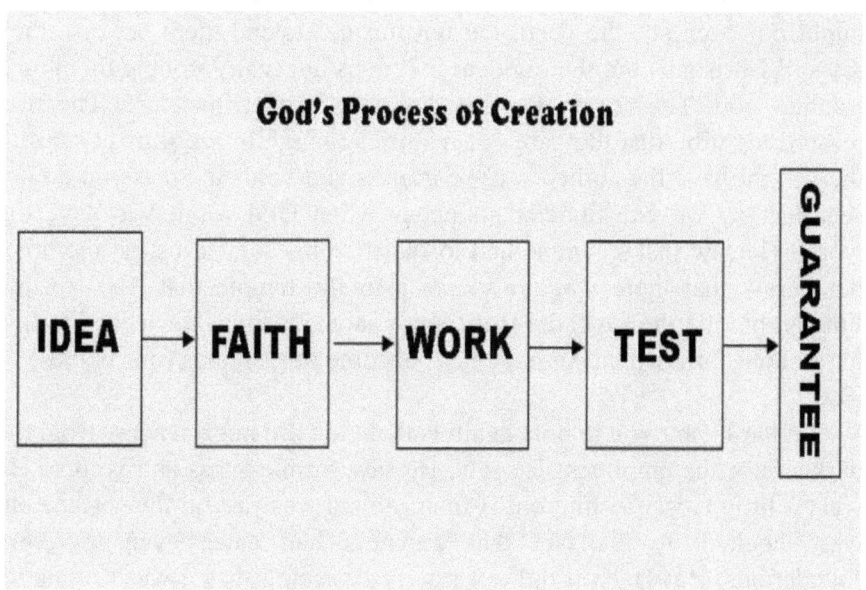

The Creator Connection

It was wonderful talking about the different characters of God that are related to his creative nature. *"...that by these you might be partakers of the divine nature..."* (2 Peter 1:4)
We see from this that God's original and present intention is that we should share His nature. Therefore, it will be of no use if the creative ability of God has nothing to do with the way we live our lives. It will also be good for us to establish an understanding of the relationship between our nature as Christians and that of God. The truth is we have our lot in divinity to a point where even if we deny it, we can't change it.

The earth was without form, and void; and darkness was on the face of the deep. (Genesis 1:2a)

Looking at that scripture very keenly leaves you with the impression that formlessness and emptiness might only have to do with God, but that is not true. If you are in the faith (because the Lord commands us to check whether we are in the faith) you will automatically realize that there is a degree of darkness or trouble either in your personal life or your environment or some form of emptiness that you don't like, want to change or think is the reason for your existence. The truth about this is the fact that some Christians might not even see it as you do and they might not even see the need. Do not misunderstand them because they are still Christians but the big deal is it does not really trouble them as it troubles you. The reason for this disparity is dual in nature. The first reason might be that they are not matured enough to see it or better still they might have the ability to see darkness and voids in areas you do not see. Just so we can understand better when God wanted to save the world, He saw that someone had to sacrifice his son. Jesus, on the other hand, saw that there was no sacrifice in the temple that was worthy. Finally, but not the least, the Holy Spirit saw that someone needed to live in the house, by which we have now become the temples (our bodies) of God.

What I want you to note again is that God did not run away from the darkness or the emptiness He saw. He saw formlessness and void so He went a little closer to find out if the problem was just on the surface but was shocked by the fact that darkness had eaten even the very foundations. But He still did not run away seeing that it was seemingly impossible to change. By His Spirit, He hovered still by faith, saying that it is still possible to effect the change He wants. So, know that you are a creator, do not allow the circumstances around you make you settle for less.

God didn't send us on earth to come and be weaklings that call on Him to fix everything in our lives. Rather He called and sent us to be as creative as He is. It is written in the beginning God created however, what He created was not good as He Himself stated it was void and darkness covered the face of the deep. Yet He decided to create and modify the earth better and better until it looks exactly like what He actually wanted.

So also, every Christian is called of God at Born Again and immediately you repent, your eyes open and the very first thing you see is how dark and void your surroundings or world is. You look at your family, there is trouble, you look at your marriage, there is void, you look at your career there is void, you look at your health, there is void, you check your mindset, there is void, as a matter of fact, it is trouble-trouble-trouble. At Born Again we all are reborn by God but what we do not understand is that the act of believing and repenting creates a new world for us which now stands as our personal beginning. As it is written, *"them that are in Christ are new creations: old things have passed away behold everything is become new."* (2 Corinthians 5:17).

So according to God, you are newly created and your world also is newly created and since Born Again marks the date of your new beginning, you can also say as God the creator said, "In the beginning I (your name) created my heavens and my earth, but my earth is formless and void and darkness covers the face of the deep but my spirit hovers over the face of the waters." Just a quick note; your heavens are all the plans and purposes of God for your life which all Christians expect. It is that ideal Christian life. But your earth or world is your present experience that is what you see, have, feel, relate with, do and put up with every day and it is that part that wants to make your heaven sound or appear as a lie. But as a son of God, He expects you to follow His example and not allow your spirit to be swallowed up by the negative circumstances in your life by causing your spirit to hover above the waters which represent His word concerning your life. For true creators do not allow their circumstances to dictate their mood or life rather, they take charge and control their circumstance until it changes and becomes what they want. The main reason why some suffer depression.

Child of God, who do you think is responsible for changing your life or world for the better? Until now you might be amongst those who still think God is responsible for creating a better life for them. Though it sounds good because it makes God a big superhero yet nothing is farther from the truth. God is not your superhero who delivers you and just carries you to safety. He is a superhero that makes all His sons and daughters as superheroes so that through Him, they can save themselves and others who are with them. Let's be clear on this. God said to Joshua, *"This book of the law shall not depart out of thy mouth; but thou shalt meditate therein day and night, that thou mayest observe to do according to all that is written therein: for then thou shalt make thy way prosperous, and then thou shalt have good success.." (Joshua 1:8).* Wow! It means Joshua was responsible for his own prosperity and God was just telling him how to make it work. We know to whom much is given much is expected.

Hence, we who are under grace are expected to be more creative and make everything new around us since God has given us much in Christ Jesus. For those who still think that it is God's responsibility to change or create the life that's best for them, listen to God's expectations of you: Resist the devil, walk not in the flesh, do not let sin rule over you, if you do these things an entrance will be opened for you into the kingdom of heaven, you will trample upon serpents and scorpions, the effective fervent prayer of a righteous man avails much, watch and pray that you will not be tempted, the violent take it by force, unto him who is able to do according to the power that works in you, the weapons of our warfare are not carnal but mighty through God to the pulling down of strongholds, etc. Check the last one, God is not our weapon of war but our weapon is only mighty through God which means God is not the one fighting but our fighting is only made lethal when it is through Him. Wow! Also, God is only able to do things according to the power that works in us. Therefore, even though God is Almighty, His manifest power only works in our lives based on another power called FAITH.

Therefore, to think that God will change every aspect of your life and make it good without your involvement is a deception from the high courts of the Devil

So, we by this must understand why just people like you and I should live by faith.
And again the just shall walk by faith (Habakkuk 2: 4) (For we walk by faith, not by sight:) (2 Corinthians 5:7)

THE DIVINE NATURE OF GOD

Having the mindset that life is a walk, makes us understand the reason why God cannot be pleased when we do not walk by faith. What then is God's mind of faith for us? It is like this: "Since I love your progress and wellbeing and know that you can only live a good life by faith (which creates), then I can only be pleased when you are enjoying the life that I gave you. So, your welfare is My delight as your faith is My pleasure." So, hear me and hear me well, it is not God who will create that future or life you want. You actually have to use your faith to change and create every new thing you want in your life.

When the Bible says the just shall live by faith you should understand that if the just do not use their faith they will die and not even live.

Since we share God's creative nature, He cannot establish new things on the earth without us and our faith. Hence, we must have faith to become our own very creators and create the kind of life He has given to us. If you don't still get it, I will explain a little more. The only thing that causes our spirit to hover above circumstances in life is our faith. Also, the only power that works in us and gives God the ability to do or accomplish much on our behalf is our Faith.
. *And this is the victory that has overcome the world--our faith. (I John 5:4)*
By this, we see that the Spirit of God moved over the surface of the deep by faith. Thus, the only thing that gives us victory over the world is our faith. I can talk on this for as long as long can be. I think what is established is established and if you want to be part of His nature, then you must learn to walk according to faith. Furthermore, we saw earlier that God took the time to work out the things that He called out by faith. So also, we ought to work out the faith life or work out diligently the things He has promised us in this life and that to come.
For as the body without the spirit is dead, so faith without works is dead also. (James 2:26)
Faith without works is dead and anything that is dead cannot produce fruits or results. So, then it is left for us to also act like the gods that we are to add works to our faith as God did. God spoke about the coming of a savior that He will send for a very long time. When the time came, He stopped talking only and stepped into action. The Son was born in the exact place where it was said that he should be born. Likewise, there are basically two things necessary to keep faith alive;

a) The art of speaking: Some people still think that their mouth was meant for eating, drinking, talking, and singing, but I want to show you more. The major reason why God gave you a mouth was so that you can use it as He did with His. God used His mouth to create and everything that He wants to do He starts by saying it hence, by His word He has established eternity.

So also, our mouth was given to us so that we can use it to create the type of life that we desire here on earth and after.

For by your words you will be justified, and by your words you will be condemned. (Matthew 12:37)

The condemnation Jesus is talking here is basically that for believers. It is not talking first about eternal judgment, though it can still be considered in that light. But we are made to know that God was saying that the children of Israel will die like mere men because they rejected knowledge even though He had said that they were gods. So also, we see a lot of born-again Christians today who are living as if God is dead. This is because by their own words they are refusing themselves the privileges of life. How do I mean? There are some people from various countries and tribes in the world who have a certain accent or way of talking that when you hear them speak, you can figure out or know their country of origin. Many Christians who do not yet have this knowledge spend their time speaking like people from their tribe or country. Although for us it is not much of the accent as it is the content of words. Many do not know that the citizenship of Zion is different from that of the people in the world.

And the inhabitant will not say, "I am sick" ;(Isaiah 33:24)
When men are cast down, then thou shalt say, There is lifting up; and he shall save the humble person. (Job 22:29)
For with the heart one believes unto righteousness, and with the mouth confession is made unto salvation. (Romans 10:10)
Beat your plowshares into swords and your pruning hooks into spears; Let the weak say, 'I am strong. (Joel 3:10)

Mind you that God did not say there shall be lifting up for you, it said you shall say it. But it really gets on my nerves when believers just speak anyhow about their lives and others around them. A born-again Christian will shout, "I am finished!" Because of a cockroach, it's really amazing.

The heart of the righteous studies how to answer, but the mouth of the wicked pours forth evil. (Proverbs 15:28)

Now that you know that what you say is what you get, train your mouth to say only those things that are good for you, your environment and the change that you want to see.

For this is what connects you to the character of faith manifested in God by which you will overcome the world.

b) The art of working: It is very easy to say in this our time that I am not a Pharisee because we all know that right now there are no Pharisee titles in our Churches today. What I want us to see is a small description of Pharisees given by Jesus, when He charged His disciples not to follow their example. By this statement, Jesus was also saying that it is possible for Christians to copy the example of the Pharisees.
Saying, The scribes and the Pharisees sit in Moses' seat: All therefore whatsoever they bid you observe, that observe and do; but do not ye after their works: for they say, and do not. For they bind heavy burdens and grievous to be borne, and lay them on men's shoulders; but they themselves will not move them with one of their fingers. (Matthew 23:2- 4)

One important statement about the character of the Pharisees was that Jesus never wanted them to do according to their works: for they say and do not. Jesus addressed the aspect of work. The work of the Pharisees had two things the saying and the doing. So, saying is part of working as we have discussed above but the next one (which is doing) is what I want us to focus on now. The Pharisees where experts in binding heavy loads and putting them on people's shoulders but could not carry any or do any. Are you that kind of a Christian? You know how to say what should be done but you never do it, when it's time for the work. Some have come to the conclusion that since our election was not according to works, it means that work is not necessary. The truth is, we cannot work to be accepted in the beloved because if you work for a gift, then it is a wage and not a gift. However, after obtaining the gift, you need to work to grow and to establish yourself in it. So, it is very important for us to now work out our salvation with fear and trembling as God is working in us both to will and to do of his good pleasure. Jesus said, *"I must work the work of him that sent me while it is day...." (John*

9: 4) In another place he said, *"my meat is to do the will of him that sent me and to finish his work" (John 4:34).*

If Jesus had to work, it means that we also have to work in order to create the life that we want and/or establish the purpose for which he sent us on Earth. A servant cannot be greater than his master. Some believers do not see the results of their faith because they do not know how to work it out. James told us that in order for us to have faith that is active; we need to work it out. So, after speaking our faith, we must set up a vision with clear goals and deadlines for their accomplishment if we really want to effect change.

A little sleep, a little slumber, A little folding of the hands to sleep-So shall your poverty come on you like a prowler, And your need like an armed man. (Proverbs6:10-11)

For even when we were with you, we commanded you this: If anyone will not work, neither shall he eat. That if any will not work, neither should he eat. (2 Thessalonians 3:10).

We must, therefore, eradicate spiritual laziness from our lives as Christians and put our hands to work so as not to tempt the Lord. In school, some Christians do not study but say they have faith to succeed. Some do not work hard but are trusting God for houses they did not build. Things do not just work like that so therefore if God has told you about you being a soul winner, then draw up a plan and start acting on it. If He said He will give you a job, then write your applications and drop them at the offices. You do not expect God to reveal your curriculum vitae to the CEO, do you? The conclusion of the matter is therefore very simple: God planted a garden eastward meaning He did not just speak; He acted. We must, therefore, learn to also plant our own gardens if we want to be co-manufacturers with Him. Hence if you really believe in something you will say it and if you have faith, then you will spend time to prove it with good works. Don't get me wrong God does miracles. However, these miracles were not made to replace work, rather they are meant to promote and encourage it.

But by the grace of God I am what I am, and His grace toward me was not in vain; but I labored more abundantly than they all, yet not I, but the grace of God which was with me. (1Corinthians 15:10)

Do you now realize from above that Paul's ministry was outstanding because he labored more than others? This he did despite the grace that was on him. Grace does not cancel labor. I do not think we have been graced more than God who gives it to us. So, if He still works, then we should get up and prove our faith by our works like James. When I talk about work you should know it's more than a physical job that you do. For many, these days are abandoning their spiritual responsibilities for physical jobs that take all their time and destroy their spiritual lives. As a result, spiritual responsibilities such as prayers, fasting, bible study, meditation, church fellowship, building a good relationship with the Holy Spirit have all suffered loss of importance or been completely abandoned by some who are now totally religious. But in all this, you must note that all these spiritual exercises are what connects you to the manufacturing character of God and you should do everything to maintain and grow them in order to create a better life for yourself.

As a matter of "faith", God gives guarantee for things before they even appear. In the world, people give birth to children and watch them grow to say whether they are good or bad. But as Christians, we call our children good and great even before they are born so as to give guarantee for their lives. The spiritual guarantee has to do with continual confession of what you believe while in the process of work or in the time of patience.

Who against hope believed in hope, that he might become the father of many nations; according to that which was spoken, So shall thy seed be. And being not weak in faith, he considered not his own body now dead, when he was about an hundred years old, neither yet the deadness of Sara's womb: He staggered not at the promise of God through unbelief; but was strong in faith, giving glory to God; And being fully persuaded that, what he had promised, he was able also to perform. And therefore it was imputed to him for righteousness. (Romans 4:18-22).

We are told in Genesis how Abraham left Haran to Canaan because God had promised that he was going to give it to him. We are also told that God promised to give him a child through his barren wife Sarah. Abraham left Haran at the age of seventy-five and had that child at the age of one hundred; which implies he had to believe God for twenty-five good years. After the child grew up, God tested him to kill the child as a sacrifice. He did not disobey but went to kill the child with the belief that God who gave the child could raise him up from the dead. For those who are not in touch with the spirit today, they will quickly quote the scriptures saying test all things, cleave to that which is good. Also, you will say it is not God; Satan, get thee behind me, but not Abraham. He did not even have the Bible to read from like we do today.

In Romans, we get a clear picture of what really happened with Abraham. Against hope, he believed in hope. This means that everything that could give a man the hope of having a child was gone. Abraham was too old and Sarah the wife was first of all barren and had crossed menopause. So, from every indication, it was impossible to have children by Sarah. But the Bible says though his situation was hopeless, he still believed in hope. By the fact that he was not weak in faith, he did not consider the deadness of his body or the deadness of Sarah's womb. Now I want us to look at the word "consider" for a moment

And truly if they had called to mind that country from which they had come out, they would have had opportunity to return. (Hebrews 11:15)

This makes us understand that if the fathers of our faith had decided to consider the countries from which they came from; they would have had the opportunity to return. The difference between some of us and them is that we like to put into consideration things that God is taking us away from. Better still some are too mindful of where they come from. Hence, we should not doubt why some are having the opportunity to remain spiritually poor, blind and naked.

So, if you want to be a guarantor as God you must not consider where you come from and must put on your most holy faith standing against all odds. Abraham did not stagger at the promises of God through unbelief but was strong in faith, being fully persuaded. He did not say at one time God can do it and again in another maybe if it is His will, He will do it or better still maybe we should just accept the situation. After all, I am not the first man to have a barren wife and Mr. Joe is already 120 years old. So, my case is even better. No! Abram did not do that. He did not stagger, meaning he did not change his confession and action. He even changed his name from Abram to Abraham, telling all his mates he is now a "father of many". He also changed the name of his wife from Sarai to Sarah, saying she is a mother of many children. See! Brethren Abraham had faith. One truth about guarantors I have noticed is that they never change their confession about their products. Even when you don't think so, they will still tell you this is the best.

Beloved, you have believed God for that thing until now and we know that your salvation is closer now than when you first believed the word of God. So, give guarantee for your life, your children and your generation by not changing your confession of faith and the truth.

If thou faint in the day of adversity, thy strength is small. (Proverbs

24:10)
It is said if you fail in the day of adversity it means your strength was weak. So, we should not be weak in faith postponing our victory or even denying it all together with unbelief. Fulfill therefore the will of God for your life by being co-guarantors with Him. So, while you are working and waiting, if you keep your confession you will keep the blessings and obtain the promises of God for your life.

The Creator Connection

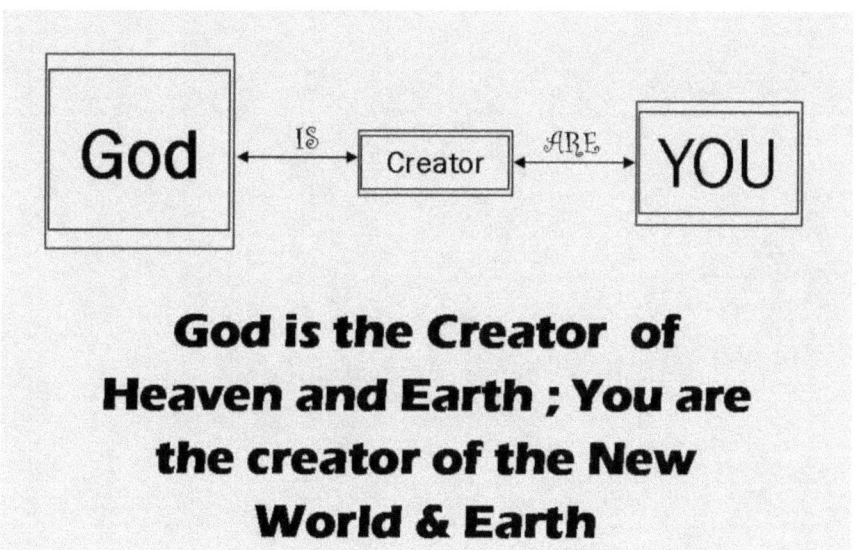

CHAPTER TWO

GOD IS LOVE

The world and everything that is in it is still intact today because God is love. We are not saying that the world looks good because God looks lovely. We do not even know exactly what He looks like so let's not delve into that. By the scriptures, we also understand that there was nothing on Jesus that will attract us to Him. Hence, He was just as any other man upon the face of the earth. Though I know God is lovely. If you go through the scriptures you find one outstanding thing: Man has always been on God's nerves. God has always been angry in His relationship with men but for a few exceptions. We all know that God has the power to destroy the whole world if He wants, but in the midst of all that His power to destroy is another power that programs His actions contrary to His anger and that power is love. If the world is still in one piece today, it is because there is somebody in it called man. Many do not understand why. For you to understand, I will like to take you to the very beginning.

In the beginning when God had created all the other things, He came to the time of man's creation and said, *"Let us make man in our image, after our likeness........"* verse 27 says *"So God created man in his own image, in the image of God created he him, male and female created he them" (Geneses 1:27)*
Why did God stress the image idea? He was making us see what He was seeing when He created man and put him in the garden. Before I declare it unto you, I want us to see another scripture.

"And God formed man of the dust of the grand, and breathed into his nostrils the breath of life, and man became a living soul" (Genesis 2:7)

The New Testament clearly makes us understand that what God formed out of the dust was not man it was his body: tabernacle as Paul puts it, saying "As long as I am still in this tabernacle..." After God had formed man's body, He now took the man out of him and put him in that body so that man could function on earth like him.

He took the spirit of His own life or a cut out of Himself and put it in the formed dust, then the man from that time became a living soul. In other words, man became another individual that was like God in nature and attributes but separate from God. All the people that are upon the face of the earth today at one time did not have the right to go to where they want or make their own decisions because they were in the loins of their father. I say father because the seed of every child is in the sperm of the father while the body forms in the womb of the mother. The relationship between man and woman can help us to better understand. We are told that no man ever hates himself or treats himself badly when in his right senses. So, a man in his right mind will not hurt his wife because his wife is himself. How did this come about?

And the LORD God caused a deep sleep to fall on Adam, and he slept; and He took one of his ribs, and closed up the flesh in its place. Then the rib which the LORD God had taken from man He made into a woman, and He brought her to the man. (Gen 2:21-22)

The above scripture states clearly that God caused the man to fall into a deep sleep, then He took one rib from him and closed it with flesh. The reason is that the life of God transformed the dust into the flesh. That is why if you remove the man out of the body it is just a matter of time the transformation will take place from flesh to dust again (as in death). That scripture is conveying a great truth which is: God opened a door in the man and took a rib from him and then closed the door so the spirit of the man does not come out (as in death). Hence, he stitched the flesh back together. However, there is a more profound truth in the rib that God took out. Now if the rib that God took out of the man is what we call rib today, then it means that women in the world today would have only one rib in their chest. But biology has proven that not to be true because men and women have the same number of ribs. So, what then is God talking about? God said He took "one rib." Now we do not know how many ribs where there but we know that if there are 10 things originally and you take one of them, the percentage of that one will be

10% of the original. By this, we could say that the woman is ten percent of all that man is. However, we can do a bit of mathematics to find out with the help of some assumptions.

For a man indeed ought not to cover his head, since he is the image and glory of God; but woman is the glory of man. (1Corinthians 11:7)

We know the Bible says that the man is the glory of God while the woman is the glory of the man. By this God is saying that man is to Him as the woman is to man. Hence this gives us a better understanding that God created man out of Himself the way He created the woman out of the man. Therefore, we can say that God took one rib from Himself and formed the man with it. When the time to create woman came, He took one rib from the man and made the woman. Now that you see the connection, I want us to see some mathematical expressions. Don't mind me, ok!

If God has a seven-fold nature as we have seen in the introduction, and we knowing that God is perfect, we can assume that perfection means 100 for each of God's nature, then we can say that God is 700G (G= God) altogether. Please don't go and tell someone that the preacher said God equals 700G. But when God said He took one, He meant that He took one of everything. Hence if God took one of everything in Him it signifies that:

$$God = 700 \text{ as Man} = 7$$

Now calculating the %
We will have: $7/700 \times 100 = 1\%$
Hence man is assumed to be 1% of everything that God is. Also, since the man in himself is not yet perfect (I say yet because he is still growing), we can assume that he has 10 of every nature that is in him as a man. By this $10 \times 7 = 70M$ (M = Man)
Now if we take one of each nature that is in man, we see that; woman = 7M
Calculating the percentage
$= 7/70 \times 100 = 10\%$ of M.

I have not said that the woman is 10% of all that man is. But the Bible makes us understand that women are the weaker vessels and that the woman was made for the man. So, do not be mad at me if I use figures for the purpose of understanding. I guess I am just happy with Mathematics.

Now looking at chemical reactions, if we say that a certain amount of g/mol solution is needed for a particular reaction, if you reduce or increase the concentration of that solution by 0.01% you can never have the same result because 0.01 is a very significant value when it comes to reactions. I know you are asking the question; reactions too?

I am just making you know that although you are just one percent of all that God is, the truth is God cannot do without you. Hence from the time God created man, He will always remain 99% without your existence. I want to conclude with this.

And GOD saw that the wickedness of man was great in the earth, and that every imagination of the thoughts of his heart was only evil continually. And it repented the LORD that he had made man on the earth, and it grieved him at his heart. And the LORD said, I will destroy man whom I have created from the face of the earth; both man, and beast, and the creeping thing, and the fowls of the air; for it repenteth me that I have made them. But Noah found grace in the eyes of the LORD. (Genesis 6:5-8).

The Bible says it clear that God regretted why He removed man from Himself and put him upon the face of the earth and said that He will destroy man for He was sorry that He had made him. Yet verse 8 has a big controversy, because it says, "But Noah found grace in the eyes of the Lord." It did not say that Noah was not like the rest of the others because even after the flood the Bible makes us understand that Noah was a drunkard because after God saves you from such a death, the last thing you want to do is get drunk. However, he planted his vineyard and was drunk of it and so when his son saw and laughed, he remembered his ability to curse.

The reason for this was that God said if I destroy man completely; it means I have destroyed 1% of My own self. So, He came down to Noah and said to Noah, "please I want to destroy the whole world but I want you to build an ark so that you and your family will be saved; by this save part of Me from complete destruction." Note that it was after this that the Bible says that Noah was moved with fear and built the ark.

By faith Noah, being divinely warned of things not yet seen, moved with godly fear, prepared an ark for the saving of his household, (Hebrews 11:7)

I believe many people in the world heard the announcement but God's grace was not in them to act, so they didn't fear and did perish. Do not disagree. Did you not read how it is written that the sons of Eli did not listen to their father's advice because God had purposed that He will punish them?

If one man sins against another, God will judge him. But if a man sins against the LORD, who will intercede for him?" Nevertheless they did not heed the voice of their father, because the LORD desired to kill them (1 Samuel 2:25)

So, God was patient with Noah until he finished building the Ark, then He sent the rain. After the flood, Noah made a sacrifice to God and He made by oath a covenant with Noah that He will never destroy the earth with water again. Then He said that when man sees the rainbow, He should remember the covenant but He went and put a rainbow all about His throne so that he does not forget.

And it shall come to pass, when I bring a cloud over the earth, that the bow shall be seen in the cloud: And I will remember my covenant, which is between me and you and every living creature of all flesh; and the waters shall no more become a flood to destroy all flesh. And the bow shall be in the cloud; and I will look upon it, that I may remember the everlasting covenant between God and every living creature of all flesh that is upon the earth. And God said unto Noah, This is the token of the covenant, which I have established between me and all flesh that is upon the earth. (Genesis 9:14-17)

And Noah builded an altar unto the LORD; and took of every clean beast, and of every clean fowl, and offered burnt offerings on the altar. And the LORD smelled a sweet savour; and the LORD said in his heart, I will not again curse the ground any more for man's sake; for the imagination of man's heart is evil from his youth; neither will I again smite any more every thing living, as I have done. (Genesis 8:20-21)

And He who sat there was like a jasper and a sardius stone in appearance; and there was a rainbow around the throne, in appearance like an emerald. (Revelation 4:3).

When God wanted to destroy the world with flood, He saved Noah and His house. When He wanted to destroy Sodom and Gomorrah, He saved Lot and his family. Now that He is planning to destroy this wicked generation, He has sent Jesus to save you and your family. Why does He do this all the time? It is because God will never remain without a representative on the earth.

So also, if a man's wife annoys him, sometimes the reason why a true husband (true because there are false husbands) will forgive the wife is not that the wife asks for forgiveness. The sole reason is that wisdom will ask the question can one be angry with himself forever? You know that this cannot be. What then was the rib that was taken out of the man to make the woman? If you understand how He created man you will understand how He created the woman. It says He formed the dust and breathed in it the breath of (His) life and he became a living soul. So, the man was a child of God because he was born by God though immature. When the time came for God to make woman, He took the man's breath of life and introduced it in the body He made from dust. That which is called rib in the Bible is not literal rib as it has been declared to be.

For man is not from woman, but woman from man. Nor was man created for the woman, but woman for the man. For this reason the woman ought to have a symbol of authority on her head, because of the angels. Nevertheless, neither is man independent of woman, nor woman independent of man, in the Lord. (1Corinthians11:8-11)

Ye are of God, little children, and have overcome them: because greater is he that is in you, than he that is in the world. (1John 4:4)

From the above scriptures, the Christian is from God as the woman is from the man. But a Christian is from God because his spirit is from God. So also, the woman is from man because her spirit came from the man: and not a rib. Therefore, as the man is not complete without the woman, even so, God is not complete without the man.

The Origin of Man and Woman

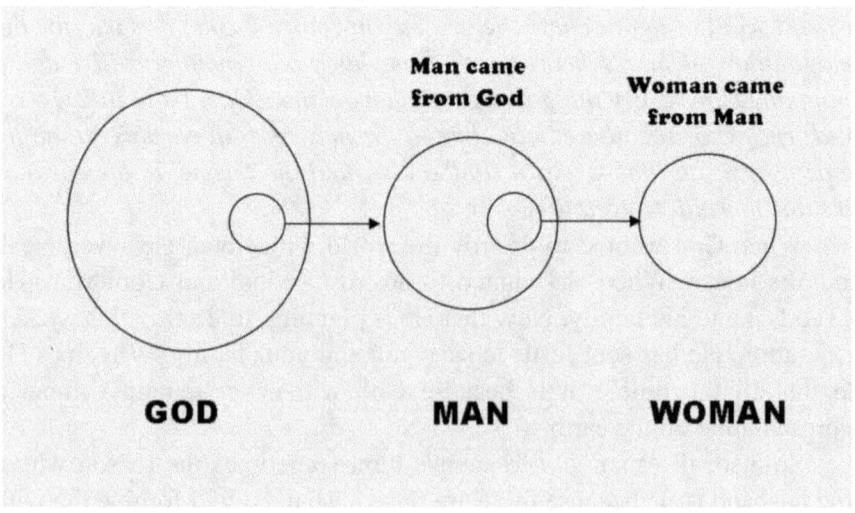

Finally, love might start with want but it is only perfected when it becomes a need. So, God does not only want us He needs us. Do not get me wrong. Even when Love needs; it needs you first for your sake because love does not seek its own. Therefore, when He says I love you, you should know that He needs you to be complete in Himself.

Therefore, if God is in love with you; He is saying, "loving you, is loving Me."

The Character of Mercy

As we have seen in this chapter, God is love and one of the major ways by which God proves His love toward us is through the character of mercy. Mercy is the election of God according to His purpose (which is) without qualification and by it He commands love. If God was not merciful then by now none of us will be alive and better still, we would not have had a place in His glory.

Mercy is the driving force behind forgiveness.

And the LORD said: "I have surely seen the oppression of My people who are in Egypt, and have heard their cry because of their taskmasters, for I know their sorrows. So I have come down to deliver them out of the hand of the Egyptians..., (Exodus 3:7, 8)

It is good for us to start by clarifying this issue first. Note that God wanted to bring justice to the oppressors of Israel but before God both the Egyptians and the Israelites were criminals. Hear me well, God was not dealing with the children of Israel because they were so perfect before Him. How then do you punish one criminal for treating another criminal bad? Sometimes we need to understand that God is not above His laws. He is the first to obey His laws. So, for this to be possible, God must forgive one person for the sake of another person. So, for the sake of His promise to their father Abraham, He decided to have mercy on them for His name's sake. I say for His name's sake because He made a vow to Abraham concerning his descendants and could not change or fail.

Now if He does not do it, then He becomes a liar. Proof that the Israelites were not free is the circumcision He asked them to do as a symbol of their repentance: which was a shadow of things to come. In line with this, I think to an extent, it is this mercy that is unmerited favor because it is for everybody; though the condition for this mercy is required from another person and not waived.

But God demonstrates His own love toward us, in that while we were still sinners, Christ died for us. (Romans 5:8)

For God did not send His Son into the world to condemn the world, but that the world through Him might be saved. (John 3:17)

When God demonstrated His love in Christ Jesus, He did it for the entire world. So, by the death of Christ, anybody in the world can be reconciled to God either Jew or Gentile. In the scriptures above, you realize that He died while we were yet sinners; all of us excluding none in the world. So, in Christ, God has secured life for the whole world. But what made Jesus die?

For God so loved the world, that he gave his only begotten Son, that whosoever believeth in him should not perish, but have everlasting life. (John 3:16)

Notice this statement; God loved the world. He did not specify anyone; the whole world was on His agenda. However, it was the character of mercy that made Him give His Son. And just as He delivered the Israelites for Abraham's sake; He had to forgive and deliver us for someone else's sake. In this case, Jesus was the one. So, mercy pushed God to give up His son for our sakes. By this, He created means to forgive us from our sins and free us from the oppressor. So, God's mercy created means for our salvation by transferring the punishment for our crime on someone else, (as with Christ for us who believe) or by extending a hand of kindness to another based on the good promise he made to another. As it is said *"Blessed is the man to whom the LORD does not impute iniquity…, (Psalm 32:2).*

In another case, God's mercy can create room for your forgiveness on the basis of something you did. In this case, it is still unmerited but the unmerited-ness is on a lesser percentage than the first one. It's this way because you might be a criminal but because you did something that pleased the judge, he decides to cancel or waive your crime on the basis of what you did. This happened to father Abraham.

For what does the Scripture say? "Abraham believed God, and it was accounted to him for righteousness." (Romans 4:3)

Abraham was not perfect before God, but he so believed God that God decided to forgive all his sins and pronounce him righteous. However, God determines who He shows mercy according to His will. Also, we see how Jesus said, "if you forgive those who trespass against you, your heavenly Father will also forgive you." This means that even though God is merciful, there is a criterion for that mercy.

And not only this; but when Rebecca also had conceived by one, even by our father Isaac; (For the children being not yet born, neither having done any good or evil, that the purpose of God according to election might stand, not of works, but of him that calleth;) It was said unto her, The elder shall serve the younger. As it is written, Jacob have I loved, but Esau have I hated. What shall we say then? Is there unrighteousness with God? God forbid. For he saith to Moses, I will have mercy on whom I will have mercy, and I will have compassion on whom I will have compassion. So then it is not of him that willeth, nor of him that runneth, but of God that sheweth mercy. For the scripture saith unto Pharaoh, Even for this same purpose have I raised thee up, that I might shew my power in thee, and that my name might be declared throughout all the earth. Therefore hath he mercy on whom he will have mercy, and whom he will he hardeneth. (Romans 9:10-18).

The Bible makes it very clear here that before Jacob and Esau were born, (i.e. before they had a chance to do anything), God had said that the older (greater) shall serve the (lesser) younger. Because He said, "Jacob have I loved but Esau have I hated." Before we continue, I believe God wants me to explain a misconception about His mercy here. First, why did God say the greater will serve the lesser? You have to note that God looks at the heart while Man looks at the outward appearance. Hence, if you understand the nature of something, you can determine how that thing will behave in a circumstantial future. How? You may ask! If you know someone is a hydrocarbon, you can predict they will float in water. That has nothing to do with your decision on them. It is just your conclusion on how their nature within can produce an outcome of character in their future. Talking of hate, I do not think God hates people for no reason.

The Bible makes us know that God hates two major classes of people: the wicked and the foolish. God hates the wicked because they do not deal with Love. He hates the foolish because they despise knowledge. So, if God said He hated Esau, in my judgment, I will conclude that it was because he grew to become foolish and despised spiritual things until finally, he sold his birthright. Now if God hated him from the womb, I will say it could be because he saw foolishness in his heart. In the world, we always find out that there are always people in the world that God hates and those that He loves. However, if God hates people for no reason, then He is out of his mind. God loves people for a reason, He hates them for a reason and if you read His Word, you will see that people are always responsible for the hate or love of God towards them. Now what makes God's mercy powerful is that God has mercy on you based on the nature of your heart and the nature of every heart is based on the level at which you guard it. Looking at the above scripture, the Bible makes us understand clearly that God was the one who hardened the heart of Pharaoh because He wanted to use him for His glory. The preacher asked the question. Why does God still find fault in them since He is the one who chooses whom to honor and whom to dishonor? For me, I do not think it's a matter of finding fault rather it's a matter of which criminal has hope of change and which one doesn't.

However, I want you to understand that no law is complete until it is applied to both sides. If God could free the Children of Israel for the sake of Abraham, then would it not be logical that He could also punish Pharaoh for the sake of his wicked fathers? Because I think he had also vowed to punish that generation for the crime of their fathers. Also, you must note that God will never harden a good heart to do evil because He does not tempt anyone with evil, (James 1:13). By this, I mean God can only harden your heart based on the state of the heart which is actually your choice. Please note that to harden someone's heart is different from determining the contents of the heart. For example: if I had the key to your house and you asked me to close the door of your house that does not mean I am responsible for the content in your house. That is if the only thing I did was to key the door.

So, God has the ability to close up your heart to maintain the content you decided to put in it. This He does for both righteous and wicked people. For the righteous, it is called establishment of the heart but for a wicked person who has hardened their heart against God, it is called hardening of the heart based on the fact that God cages them in their hardness of heart in such a way that they cannot change anymore. Watch this: before the brothers of Joseph sold him, they had been planning evil against him a long time so God hardened their hearts to carry out their plans. Also, before an evil spirit entered Judah to sell Jesus, he had hardened his heart toward money and was stealing from the evangelism coffers of Jesus. Therefore, God's mercy excludes qualification because nobody qualifies for God's original mercy. This is so because when you commit a crime you deserve your punishment, period. If the judge decides to forgive you, it is his sole decision, not yours. And the person who is not forgiven does not have the right to say you must forgive me.

Mercy, therefore, is a gift to some criminals and not a right.

For he who is free from crime does not have need of mercy. That is why God has the right to decide which crime He will pardon and which crime He will punish. Yet you must understand there is still some truth behind God's person of choice for mercy. *And we know that all things work together for good to them that love God, to them who are the called according to his purpose. For whom he did foreknow, he also did predestinate to be conformed to the image of his Son, that he might be the firstborn among many brethren. Moreover whom he did predestinate, them he also called: and whom he called, them he also justified: and whom he justified, them he also glorified. (Romans 8: 28 -30)*
Some people think that by foreknowledge, God knows those that are His before they were even born. Hence, He planned their lives from the place of foreknowledge to the place of glorification, passing through predestination, calling and justification. Nothing could be farther from the truth. Predestination is not a force for repentance. The force for repentance is a conviction, not predestination.

Also, predestination does not determine who is saved, rather it is the glorification plan or process of God for those who are saved already. So, no one can say God has predestined me to go to hell. Rather people refuse to believe because they love their evil deeds and hence refuse to repent. Also, Paul explained that the Word does not benefit some based on the fact that they did not mix it with faith. Though there are other laws that apply to conviction, none of them has to do with the fact that God has chosen some people and denied some. If that were the case, why does He say preach to all the worlds or nations; to punish the preachers? No. it's because He wants to give everyone the chance to believe. God may reveal Himself to some based on the fact that they have a good heart or are looking for Him already like Cornelius. Or based on the fact that someone related to that person is close to God and is interceding for that person. Or through the anointing of a man of God to convict people.
In (John 15:16) it says, *"You did not choose Me, but I chose you and appointed you that you should go and bear fruit, and that your fruit should remain*

When Jesus says we didn't choose Him but He chose us, you should understand that the choice is not based on who gets saved by God. Rather it is based on who is fit to do what. That is why He did not say I chose you to have everlasting life but instead said to bear fruits. Also, before God has ever called people from birth, it has always started from the faith of the parents as God said to Jeremiah, "before I formed you in your mother's womb, I knew you and had ordained you as a prophet unto the nation." Jesus was born out of Mary's belief, Isaac was born out of Abrahams faith, etc.

So then it is not of him who wills, nor of him who runs, but of God who shows mercy (Romans 9:16).

So then, we cannot boast that we are in God because we were more willing than others and did all the right things. It is clear that because God had shown mercy on us: we are forgiven from our sins giving us room to be able to come close to Him and benefit from Him those things that without His mercy, we would not have had. Hence, we were all guilty before He blotted all our sins. So, what is the conclusion? God has chosen to use the foolish things of the earth to confound the wise by which He has perfected praise in the mouth of babies as it pleases Him to reveal Himself to babes. So, therefore, no one was free from his judgment until He decided to make room for us in Him through Christ Jesus. So, by God's mercy, we all have a place at the table of blessings instead of a curse. But note that God loves the wise, but the wise think they are too wise for God, so He ends up working with the foolish, who are humble enough to submit to Him. Yet you must know that God's mercy does not continue without recognition or gratitude. And to show gratitude for the mercy He showed you, you must also be merciful to others.

For God will be merciful to the merciful.

The Character of kindness

The next character of love is the character of kindness.
Love suffers long and is kind; (1Corinthians 13:4) Just as we see from above it is written that love is kind. So, kindness is a character of love. But what is kindness? Kindness is the character that makes God our Helper. Thus, kindness is that state of heart in which an individual will want to do the impossible just so he or she can be of help to someone else. It is this kindness that made God feel sorry for us and volunteered to be our Helper. This God's kindness gave birth to what we all know

today as Grace. So, through kindness, God made grace available.
That in the ages to come He might show the exceeding riches of His grace in His kindness toward us in Christ Jesus. (Ephesians 2:7)

From above it is clear to all that the grace He now shows us, is in His kindness toward us. So, God in His kindness created grace to help us in time of need. Please permit me to use grace and kindness interchangeably whenever necessary. With that in mind, let us now talk about grace since grace is the manifestation of God's kindness. Some define Grace as unmerited favor. However, I differ from this definition because I do not think grace is completely unmerited. By my understanding, it is the foundation on which we obtained the grace that is unmerited; and this foundation is Mercy. So just as the death of Jesus on the cross was the accomplishment of mercy, so also is His resurrection the accomplishment of grace. Before we continue, I want to explain why I say that grace is not completely unmerited favor.
But as many as received him, to them gave he power to become the sons of God, even to them that believe on his name: (John1:12)

First off, note from above that everybody has a chance to receive Christ because of God's mercy. However, when you receive or believe in His name, you are given the power to become the son of God. This power is called Grace. Yet at this level, the power is in the form of a seed which has to grow. Note also that this power was not given to those who did not believe; but only to those who believed. Hence, even this seed of grace is gotten by belief. Thus, without belief, this seed of grace cannot be yours. At this level do you see some merit in grace? Is it not only for those who believe?

Therefore, no belief; no power to become!

From above, I think belief is a prerequisite for grace. Let's continue.
For by grace are ye saved through faith; and that not of yourselves: it is the gift of God: (Ephesians 2:8)
But without faith it is impossible to please Him, for he who comes to God must believe that He is, and that He is a rewarder of those who diligently seek Him. (Hebrews 11:6)
So then faith comes by hearing, and hearing by the word of God. (Romans10:17)
Grace and peace be multiplied unto you through the knowledge of God, and of Jesus our Lord, (2Peter 1:2)

...and be clothed with humility, for "God resists the proud, But gives grace to the humble." (1Peter 5:5) "If you keep My commandments, you will abide in My love, just as I have kept My Father's commandments and abide in His love. (John15:10)

Analyzing these verses will give us greater insight into the understanding I want you to have on this matter. We see clearly how it says we are saved by grace through faith.

The Question I ask is whose faith is he talking about: Our faith or His faith? If you agree with me that it is your faith, then that statement will read thus: "For by grace are you saved through your own faith." It goes further to say this is not of our selves rather it is the gift of God. This does not mean we do not have a responsibility in it. Rather it simply makes us know that it was a gift from God that we now can be saved by grace through our faith. Note that before it was not so. But to have faith, you have to give yourself to hearing the Word of God. Also, without this faith, you cannot please God. From this, you can also deduce that you get more grace by pleasing God. Again, it says grace be multiplied to you through the knowledge of God. However, we all know that the knowledge of God brings faith. What I want you to understand is that grace will not just come to you. You have to seek God with all your heart to get it. See, God will not give grace to just anyone. Please understand He says He resists the proud but gives grace to the humble.

So, if you are not humble, there is no grace for you brothers and sisters. Last but not least, Jesus says, "obey my command and abide in my love as I obeyed my Father's command and remained in His love." What I see in this verse is the possibility to even walk out of God's love. Wow! This is strange. Can one truly walk out of the zone of God's love? The answer is yes; Jesus will not lie to us. He had to obey to abide. We too must obey to abide for we are not greater than Him. Dear, right now, you must please God. You must draw near to Him if you want Him to draw near to you. From this, I base my reason why I think Grace is not unmerited because grace has a responsibility tag on it that we must fulfill. For me, I think this "unmerited favor" definition of God's grace undermines the fact that it is written that we should follow the examples of those who through faith and patience obtained the promise. We also help Christians to become lazy thinking that you just have to sit and wait for grace because it is unmerited.

I also define Grace as God's ability replacing human weakness. Whom He called, them He also justified..." Many at times when people go for an employment interview, they go with the CV to state their qualification so that their employer can see their qualification in order to accept them for the job. But I really see in it that God recruits people into His own vineyard without seeing their CV. Instead, God calls the people He wants in His own company and just trains them. He just gets up one morning and announces that, "owing to the fact that you all do not have CVs, I have said by my loving-kindness that you were accepted by My mercy and you will be qualified or made everything you have to be and given everything that you need to make you become the manager or the secretary I want you to be by My Grace."

Therefore by the deeds of the law there shall no flesh be justified in his sight: for by the law is the knowledge of sin. But now the righteousness of God without the law is manifested, being witnessed by the law and the prophets; Even the righteousness of God which is by faith of Jesus Christ unto all and upon all them that believe: for there is no difference: For all have sinned, and come short of the glory of God; Being justified freely by his grace through the redemption that is in Christ Jesus:Whom God hath set forth to be a propitiation through faith in his blood, to declare his righteousness for the remission of sins that are past, through the forbearance of God; To declare, I say, at this time his righteousness: that he might be just, and the justifier of him which believeth in Jesus.
(Romans 3:20-26)

We are justified by God's grace. In the world, we may think that justification means pleading not guilty. But in the kingdom of God, justification makes you qualified for God's purpose. Let's look at this closely. Truly, no one shall be justified by the deeds of the flesh. In order words, worldly wisdom, because they think that if you are not negative, it means you are qualified for the positive. But this is not true. We sometimes think that when God talks of justification, He means forgiveness (which is redemption) this also is a misconception. With God, justification is all about qualification. Wait a minute. We are establishing something here. Let's look at these two words closely. When a man has done something bad or has sinned, he asks for forgiveness but when a man wants to employ people, he asks for qualification. But how do these two words relate to what we are talking about?

Note that the part of God's love that forgives has to do with His mercy. The truth about mercy is that once God has already had mercy on you, He cannot have mercy again on you for the same thing. Have you ever gone to someone who forgave you for speaking rudely to them and say please forgive me again for that same crime you forgave me for already? Or do you put the stuff behind you and try not to do the same thing as you relate with the person. I do not mean that when you ask for forgiveness, He will not forgive you. But I am saying that in Christ Jesus, God has forgiven all your sins so that you should know that God is not forgiving you at that time that you are asking for the forgiveness. The only thing that makes us think that God is forgiving us at that time is the fact that it is at that time we are feeling guilty.

Hence, He said because I have already forgiven you, sorrow for sin, therefore, is acceptable. If you are a child of God, understand that the issue of sin has been dealt with. But in the case of qualification, the Bible says we are saved by grace and not mercy. What then does He mean? If justification was counted from the viewpoint of who is obeying the rules then many would have boasted. But the religious guys have not been saved because it is not by mercy that we are saved. When you go for a job interview and do not qualify for it, they will not send you to jail for not being qualified because it is not a crime. Hence it is, therefore, possible that you are not guilty yet still not qualified for a job or with God. Therefore, God's grace qualifies you for that which He wants you to be and to accomplish.

For you know the grace of our Lord Jesus Christ, that though He was rich, yet for your sakes He became poor, that you through His poverty might become rich. (2Corinthians 8: 9)

This scripture states it clearly that the grace of our Lord Jesus was made available to us by the act of His kindness which made Him choose the lesser that we might have the greater. His grace given to us enables us to manifest His will. For example, when you see a beggar by the road, you will most likely turn to have compassion as a Christian, which is very normal. In the case of Peter, it is no different. You might desire to give the person money or remove the person from that predicament. But if you do not have money or the faith that is needed to help that person, then we will conclude that you had compassion on the beggar, but did not have the ability to perform it. So, you lacked the grace.

So, grace can be looked upon as the ability of God to manifest His Kindness toward us and also the ability He has given us to accomplish the things He requires us to do.

And God is able to make all grace abound toward you, that you, always

THE DIVINE NATURE OF GOD

having all sufficiency in all things, may have an abundance for every good work. (2 Corinthians 9:8)

By this God is able to do whatever He desires. If not for grace, God would have been in heaven now feeling sorry for all of us, but would not have been able to save us. And the Bible says His hand is not too short to help. I do not know about you, but sometimes you really see people who want to help you saying I would have done something just that my hands are short. But God is not like that because His hands are always able to perform His will and hence by it, we are saved.

And He said to me, "My grace is sufficient for you, for My strength is made perfect in weakness...." (2Corinthians12:9)
God qualifies by giving you His qualities and then He energizes you with the ability to do that which He said about you. God Himself said of us that they that are born of God cannot sin because they are born of God.

Moreover the law entered that the offense might abound. But where sin abounded, grace abounded much more, (Romans. 5:20)

He says where sin abounded, grace, did much more abound. Hence, He causes His ability to perform His will to remain in us and grow to the extent that we cannot but act the way He created us to act. That is to be conformed to the image of His dear son, so He can be the first-born amongst many brethren. However, note that the grace of God does not come from the outside. Rather it is the power of God working from within you. For example, if you ask someone to edit a document for you, there are two major things that will apply for the success of that project.

The first one is the means. The "means" simply talks of all the materials the person will need to accomplish the required task. Say a computer, software like Microsoft word, the power to run the computer on, etc. Now ability is an entirely different aspect as it is based on whether the person asked to do the job is skillful enough to do the job. If you give an editing Job to a guy who does not even know how to turn on a computer, it is a waste of means or resources. That is why through God's kindness, God provides both the means and then takes time to give or train us on the skills that will be needed to accomplish the task He requires.

The Character of Goodness

Beloved from the way we see things in the world in which we live, it is no doubt that God is a good God. We know that Satan is in this world, but God has not just left all in his hands if not then he would have wiped us (who fear God) out completely by now. Come to think of it, the fierceness with which the devil has come to this world if God was not good, then we would not have been alive today. I know you might be saying it is true but how can you be so sure.

So He said to him, "Why do you call Me good? No one is good but One, that is, God. But if you want to enter into life, keep the commandments. (Matthew 19: 17)

Jesus made a very sharp statement there making us know that there is none good except God hence Jesus was saying that if you are looking for good then go to God because he is the epitome of goodness. But the very next statement in the same verse states that if you want to enter life keep the commandment. If God is as good as Jesus said why did he not just give all of us life? Why does he still want us to keep the commandment? In order to live, by this scripture, therefore, I came up with a definition of good according to Gods point of view:

God's goodness is His ability to do good and to plan good.

By the above definition, we see that there are basically two types of goodness when it comes to God. Take note that good produce goodness which is the manifestation of good qualities.

A good man out of the good treasure of his heart brings forth good things, and an evil man out of the evil treasure brings forth evil things. (Matthew 12: 35)

So, we see that it is the good nature that brings forth the good things. Now the good things Jesus was talking about are what we now call goodness. (Being good Actions). We know that it is possible to do an act that is good but which is not from a good treasure too, but that is not the type of goodness we are talking about. We would talk about that later. After this understanding, it will be necessary for us to talk about the two types of goodness.

a) Goodness: The Ability to Do Good.

Before we even begin, I will want you to remember that we are talking about the character of goodness which stems up from God's loving nature.

For God so loved the world that He gave His only begotten Son, that whoever believes in Him should not perish but have everlasting life.

(John 3:16)
God in the above scripture was making us know that He so loved the world such that by His goodness, He gave His only begotten son for their salvation. Note that when God was doing this, He did not consider whether the people are good or bad. He just gave without consideration.

That you may be sons of your Father in heaven; for He makes His sun rise on the evil and on the good, and sends rain on the just and on the unjust. (Matthew 5: 45)

Jesus made us understand that in the world there are two kinds of people, the evil and the good and/or the just and the unjust. But God makes the sun to rise and the rain to fall on all of them. Therefore, God's goodness reaches everybody without any discrimination. He will do to A, what He did for B irrespective of who they are or have done. This is the part of God's goodness that goes before His mercy and His grace. What I mean is that God cannot have mercy on someone that He has not first of all shown this goodness to. Also, He cannot give His grace on someone He has not shown mercy on.

Or do you despise the riches of His goodness, forbearance, and longsuffering, not knowing that the goodness of God leads you to repentance? (Romans 2:4)

It is evident in this scripture that God's goodness is related to His forbearance and longsuffering. Hence, He will forbear and suffer long because of the goodness of His love. In the "b" part of that verse, we are made to understand that the goodness of God leads us to repentance. Now repentance is the place of God's mercy. So, God uses this goodness to sensitize people and bring them to the place of His mercy. It is by this goodness that God sent out His servants in the parable of the wedding banquet to invite the people in. We all know that some people did not go. So, despite God's sensitization, some people will never see the place of God's mercy because other things are more important to them. Jesus describes such people like people whose friend sing songs to them and they refuse to dance.

In the book of Jonah, we are told that God sent Jonah to Nineveh to warn them of the coming danger. But he fled because he knew that if he tells them, God might change His mind. God has never done any destruction without warning; this is done by His goodness too. Therefore, by His ability to do good, He gives good warning before destruction so that He can have the opportunity to show mercy. If you are of the household of God, then know that your Father is good. For if your Father warns the wicked before destruction how much more will He do for you?

b) **Goodness: The Ability to Plan Good**

This goodness of God actually has some controversy with the other; in the sense that this goodness has considerations for whom it is dealing with. The truth is God is good to all or better still, God can do good to everyone, but He is not planning good for everyone.

For I know the thoughts that I think toward you, says the LORD, thoughts of peace and not of evil, to give you a future and a hope. (Jeremiah29:11)

God was talking to His people saying that He had good plans for them to bring them to an expected end. He said His thoughts were good and not evil, so God has planned good for us who are His children

Blessed is the man whom You instruct, O LORD, And teach out of Your law, That You may give him rest from the days of adversity…… (Psalms 94:12-13)

God chastens them that He loves so that He can spare them in the day of adversity. So, we see that God chastens us because of His plans of goodness on our lives. Note that chastening here means everything will not feel good but everything will turn out good and God is so faithful. So, the goodness of God provides you with all that you need for your personal livelihood or plans to prosper or increase that good in the future. It is therefore based on this attribute of planning good that promises are born. God said to Abraham, "leave your family; I will make your name great. Also, I will make you a father of many nations." God's goodness ensures that we grow and increase in status as well as in material prosperity as we walk with Him.

Finally, we should see the goodness of God and understand how the world system works. In the beginning, God will by His goodness invite everyone. Those that accept God will through His mercy and grace obtain the reward of obedience which is glory. Those who reject His goodness will through sin obtain the reward of disobedience which is death. So, for those who repent, God prepares them for His second level of goodness while those who reject Him, He prepares for destruction even though this is not by goodness but by His wrath. Hence, the goodness of God's plans works together with His grace in our lives to bring us to an end that is no doubt good and glorious. Joseph said, "you meant evil, but God meant it for good."

The Love Connection

If God has called us to be part or to share His nature, then it is clear that all He is, He wants us to be. So, He has made it possible for us to also share His love by giving us the spirit of Love.

Now hope does not disappoint, because the love of God has been poured out in our hearts by the Holy Spirit who was given to us. (Romans 5:5)

The hope of God cannot make ashamed because the love of God is poured out in our hearts by the Holy Spirit. Thus, God has ravished our hearts with His love meaning our hearts are socked in His love.

For the love of Christ compels us, because we judge thus: that if One died for all, then all died; (2 Corinthians 5:14)

The love of God in our hearts constrains us or puts us in a tight corner such that we cannot but go by it; since we judge that He died so we should no longer live for ourselves. You know love is the exact opposite of self-centeredness. Hence, the love of God stops us from being selfish in this world. As it is written, "if we love not, then we have not known Him (God). The proof of your knowledge of God is seen in the level of His nature evident or manifest in you. Based on the mercy connection, God being merciful has commanded all His children to also be merciful as He is merciful.

Therefore be merciful, just as your Father also is merciful. (Luke 6:36)

If God asks us to be like Him, it means that what we are; He is. God has shown us mercy by snatching us from the world. But it is left at this time that we have mercy on others so that He can also by that be able to reveal to us the full measure of the mercy He has for us in Christ Jesus.

Blessed are the merciful, For they shall obtain mercy. (Matthew 5:7)

This states clearly that the merciful are blessed because they shall obtain mercy. Yet how many people do we have in churches today who are not merciful? It is really becoming amazing. However, it is expected that we should show the world the mercy of our God by our mercy. If you are therefore merciful, you shall obtain more mercy.

For if you forgive men their trespasses, your heavenly Father will also forgive you. (Matthew6:14)

Therefore, if you want your own sins to be forgiven, just learn how to forgive others. We have in our midst some who call themselves

Christian leaders who do not know how to show mercy. For them mercy is punishment. You see leaders who will send someone to an isolated place of the church or hand the person to the devil just because the person told them they did something wrong. I am in no way by this implying I am against punishment or discipline in the church for the purpose of fear. However, if this is not done with the character of mercy in love, it could quickly escalate into punishment that does not produce good for its bearers thereby leading to the destruction of their faith and the sinning of those inflicting the punishment. If someone tells you he did something wrong, he just obeyed the word that says, "let us confess our sins to one another so we might be forgiven not so we should be punished." But if you cannot show mercy for people who have sinned against God, how much more will you not show mercy toward those that have sinned against you? Maybe you would have them excommunicated or incarcerated in your heart. The question then remains. How many people have you forgiven since you became His child? He says that if we do not love, then we have not known Him.

So, the sign that you have known the Father is the proof of His mercy that you manifest. I say, therefore, count it all joy when people offend you because it gives you an opportunity to qualify for more of God's mercy. In line with this, some apples truly fell far from the tree. This I say because some have come up with a selfish philosophy that teaches Christians to forgive one another based on the fact that their unforgiveness will end up hurting them more. Do you truly think that's the reason God wanted us to forgive? Though that philosophy might be true, it has no value before God since it's another expression of selfishness. Brethren lets forgive people from the heart because we love them and don't want harm to come against them; and not because we want to save our own skin. For on that Jesus will say; even the Tax collectors can forgive for their own sake. Let's love: let's forgive. The truth is you do not know where God's mercy can take you. Even though all this is written it is amazing that some Christians pray and ask God to kill their enemies without first showing them some mercy (i.e. the same people He said we should love). I do not blame them. The issue is, some are so afraid that they have judged that the only way for them to be at peace is by the death of their enemies or witches and wizards. Others are just outright angry that they don't consider mercy for anyone that hurts them. They have quickly forgotten that they are saved (that is if they will even see salvation with such evil hearts) because God decided to show them mercy. But now they go nuclear on anyone who offends them without the same love.

Even though God has made us like Himself and/or requires we become like Him, we still have the choice to decline or accept.

And sadly, some are choosing to decline. So, they are praying seriously for the death and destruction of any fly that passes by. I wonder why even though God has not answered they are still praying. In Acts of the Apostles, witches were giving their lives to Jesus so we should trust God for that in our days. You can never wipe all the witches and wizards in the world instead you can snatch some from the danger of hell. So, do not be foolish, be perfect even as your Father is perfect.

Secondly, talking of the grace connection, we have to be an extension of God's grace to the people of the world. Most people in the world have good plans but sometimes the ability and the means to perform them is not always present. But this is different for us because in salvation there is complete freedom from limitation or at least we have the hope that one day the limitation will be dealt with by faith. Hence, we have the ability to come to a point where we never are limited in no way whatsoever, when we want to do something good.

And God is able to make all grace abound toward you, that you, always having all sufficiency in all things, may have an abundance for every good work. (2 Corinthians 9:8)

God is able to make all His divine ability increase towards us, thus making us sufficient and able to increase our good works. This is clear in the fact that the manifestation of the spirit is given as a gift for our profit as children of God. So, then all the gifts were given to us by God so that the saying that He has given us all things that pattern to life and Godliness might be true. So, He has given us physical cash so that we can meet the physical needs of people and ours and He has given us spiritual manifestations so that we can meet the spiritual needs of people and ours.

And he said unto them, Go ye into all the world, and preach the gospel to every creature. He that believeth and is baptized shall be saved; but he that believeth not shall be damned. And these signs shall follow them that believe; In my name shall they cast out devils; they shall speak with new tongues; They shall take up serpents; and if they drink any deadly thing, it shall not hurt them; they shall lay hands on the sick, and they shall

recover. So then after the Lord had spoken unto them, he was received up into heaven, and sat on the right hand of God. And they went forth, and preached every where, the Lord working with them, and confirming the word with signs following. Amen.
(Mark 16:15-20)
And as you go, preach, saying, 'The kingdom of heaven is at hand.' "Heal the sick, cleanse the lepers, raise the dead, cast out demons. Freely you have received, freely give. (Matthew 10: 7-8)

The act of preaching the gospel is our method of extending God's grace to the world. It is by the preaching of the gospel that the world might know and experience what we have experienced and obtained in Christ Jesus. Hence the grace of God cannot get to the people of the world without our preaching.

For I am not ashamed of the gospel of Christ, for it is the power of God to salvation for everyone who believes, for the Jew first and also for the Greek. (Romans 1:16)

Paul was not ashamed of the gospel because it was and still is the power of God unto salvation to everyone that believes. Therefore, we should not relent in our efforts in the preaching of the gospel. We know that by it, God has given us the ministry of reconciliation. So, we should do the work of an evangelist. Jesus said, "as you go heal the sick, raise the dead..." I like this one. Jesus said one time if the people did not believe Him, they should at least believe His works. God said if they do not hear the voice of the first sign, then they will hear the voice of the second. Therefore brethren, at this time as never before we should seek to give to the people of this world and extend the grace of God toward them so they can speak in the places where our words cannot be heard. Let us not be greedy for gain as some do but let us give according to the grace that is accorded to us. Freely we have received, freely we must give if His likeness is our priority.

No temptation has overtaken you except such as is common to man; but God is faithful, who will not allow you to be tempted beyond what you are able, but with the temptation will also make the way of escape, that you may be able to bear it. (I Corinthians 10:13)

God also being faithful will not allow us to be tempted beyond the ability He has given us. Hence, He will always make a way for us through the same temptation. He said to Paul "my grace is sufficient for you" so we cannot say that we lack grace because where sin abounds grace abounds much more. By this, we should not only see lying and stealing because they are not in the kingdom. But God is saying that where there is poverty the grace to create wealth abounds and where there is sickness the grace to heal abounds so that we cannot complain but believe that Christ is our sufficiency. Hence, we ought to be strong in grace saying we can do all things through Christ who strengthens us.

Lastly, we should understand as children of God, we are connected to His character of Goodness because we were created for good works hence goodness is our nature from creation. If God is saying to us, be good, He is not commanding us to be good. He is just saying be who you are (i.e. He made you good). Therefore, we are partakers of His good nature but there is always this temptation to go back to Egypt as the children of Israel wanted to do. But I exempt you from that, trusting God that you are counted amongst the wise that have a sure reward.

For he that puts his hand on the plough and looks back is not fit for the kingdom. But I say to you, love your enemies, bless those who curse you, do good to those who hate you, and pray for those who spitefully use you and persecute you, (Luke 9:62; Matthew 5:44)

It says we should not do good only to people who treat us fairly. Note that I said that we should not only do good to them that treat us fairly, I did not also say we should do good only to our enemies. Paul concluded the whole matter in a better way;

See that no one renders evil for evil to anyone, but always pursue what is good both for yourselves and for all. (I Thessalonians 5:15)
But as for you, brethren, do not grow weary in doing good. (2Thessalonians3:13)

We should follow that which is good both in and out of the house. So, brethren it is left for us to add to brotherly kindness, love (goodness, mercy, and kindness) so that we can be fruitful in the knowledge of our Lord Jesus Christ

The Love Connection

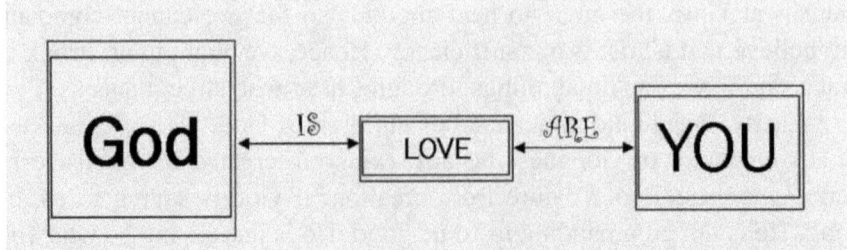

CHAPTER THREE

GOD IS LIGHT

This is the message which we have heard from Him and declare to you, that God is light and in Him is no darkness at all. (I John I: 5)

There is no doubt that God has a light personality from this verse. Come to think of it, what is light when describing its nature? When looking at the light it can mean a lot of things such as daylight, sunlight, electric light, to bring something to light, to clarify something, to have knowledge, enlightenment, etc. all the above talk of light as can be seen from different points of view. However, I want us to focus on one of these in order to understand the personality of God as light. The electric light bulb is an invention of science, which has greatly changed the lives of humans all over the world. When you come back from an evening meeting upon entering into the house you find every place very dark, the next thing you will do is switch on the light. I have a question for you. Do you really turn on the light? Though that is correct in conventional English, in order to explain my understanding, I will differ a bit from the status –quo. The truth is you only turn on energy to the bulb if you have to look at it keenly. The bulb is the light producer. Hence when you turn on the electricity, the bulb comes on and starts producing the light. Think about this again. Why is it that when the bulb is bad you don't still have light? It simply states that the bulb is bad and therefore cannot produce any light. So, you say the bulb is bad (not the light). Therefore, the light is never bad but the bulb is; which is the producer of the light. With this understanding in mind, I want us to look at more important things. The

Bible says that God is light. Meaning He is shining very bright.
The city had no need of the sun or of the moon to shine in it, for the glory of God illuminated it. The Lamb is its light (Revelation21:23)

For the glory of God lights it up and the lamb is its light. We all know that for us to have light from a lamp there are many things that come into play. You talk of the lamp made up of the wick, the oil, the burning flames, etc. We have seen that God is light and the light producer. We should note that the Lamb is Jesus Christ and Jesus Christ is of God. In the above scripture, we see that the glory of God is the produced light. In other words, the glory is the flame or the fire itself. Talking about flame you see that every flame has two components: the heat and light that is produced by it.

For behold, the darkness shall cover the earth, And deep darkness the people; But the LORD will arise over you, And His glory will be seen upon you. (Isaiah 60:2)

The reasoning that quickly comes to mind is this. The only thing that can be seen in the darkness is light. So, if God says that His glory shall be seen, then He is saying that His flames shall be seen on us. The Bible confirms that by saying He (Jesus) will baptize us with the Holy Spirit and fire. The flame of God is His glory. I do not want us to over labor this point. God willing, we will talk about that in detail later. In Revelation, the Bible says that Jesus is the lamp. We all know that the lamp carries the light. So, it stands that God is the light producer. In other words, God produces light in Himself because he is the father of lights

And after six days Jesus taketh Peter, James, and John his brother, and bringeth them up into an high mountain apart, And was transfigured before them: and his face did shine as the sun, and his raiment was white as the light. (Matthew 17:1-2)

The light did not come from someplace else. It was not a reflection of light shining on Him. Of course, anybody can recognize a reflection if they see one. All the time that Jesus was with His disciples they never knew Him in that dimension. The fact that they did not know Him in that facet does not signify that Jesus was not like that all along. Jesus wanted to show His disciples that He was a bundle of light locked up in His flesh or body. It is, therefore, no doubt that God is the light and the light producer (Jesus only does what he sees the father do). Note that you can never separate light from its producer.

That was the true Light which gives light to every man coming into the

world. (John1:9)

With all these, it is clear enough for us to believe that God is light and the producer of light.

The Character of Holiness

One of the three characters of God which stem from His light nature is holiness. To start with; what is holiness? According to Holman's dictionary, holiness tends toward separation and uniqueness. Holiness is a characteristic unique to God's nature which becomes the goal for human moral character. We have to note that holiness is a spiritual attribute. All the above definitions are acceptable, but in my understanding, they do not address or give us an understanding of what God's holiness means. These definitions talk of holiness only at the level of man. Yet we know God need not be separated from the world because He has never been one with her. Also, God cannot be perfected more than He already is. Though we will talk more about these definitions later, I want us to address the issue of God's holiness which is our priority for this sub.

'For I am the LORD your God. You shall therefore consecrate yourselves, and you shall be holy; for I am holy. Neither shall you defile yourselves with any creeping thing that creeps on the earth. (Leviticus11:44)

Every time God commanded us to be holy, it was mostly in relation to the fact that He Himself is holy. In Leviticus 20:26, God says, "you shall be holy unto me because I have separated you from other people that you should be mine." If God commands our holiness based on the fact that He has separated us from the world or because He has made us different from the people of the world, we can predict that holiness, is that character of God that perpetually keeps Him separated and different from the world. Hence, God's holiness keeps Him increasingly separated from the world and its systems.

Having been born again, not of corruptible seed but incorruptible, through the word of God which lives and abides forever, (1Peter1:23).

It states clearly that the Word of God is the incorruptible seed by which we are born again.

Now the parable is this: The seed is the word of God. (Luke 8:11)

Now by Jesus' statement in the parable, the incorruptible seed is the

Word of God.

In the beginning was the Word, and the Word was with God, and the Word was God, (John1:1). From these, we can conclude that if the incorruptible seed is the Word, and the Word is God, it means God is incorruptible.

Incorruptible seed Mathematics

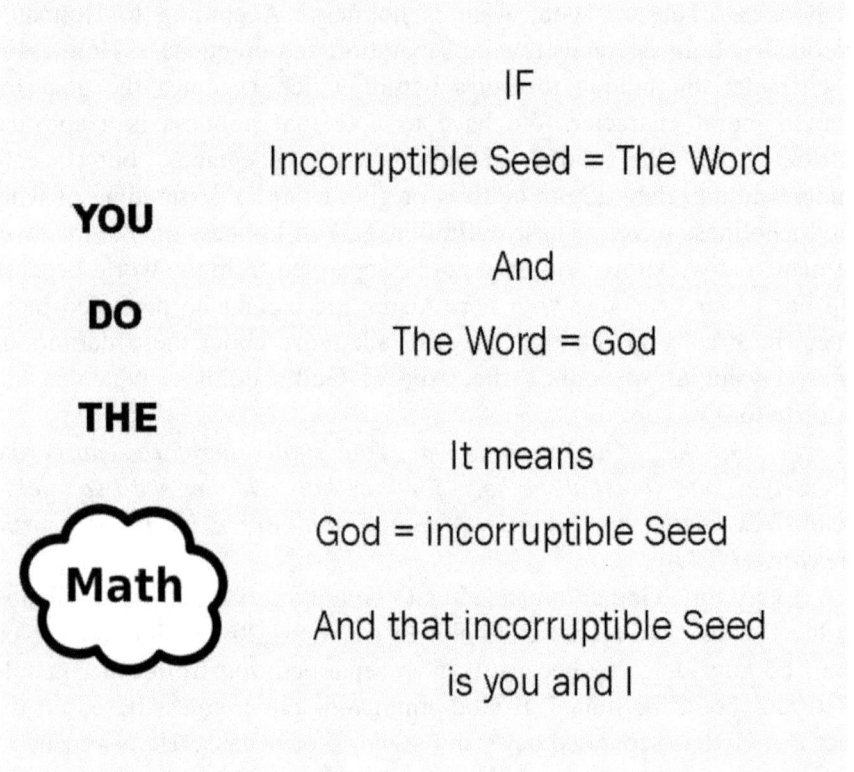

Now, this is the word that perfectly describes the holiness of God.

God's holiness, therefore, is that attribute of God that keeps Him perpetually incorruptible.

By holiness, God is separated from sin and the world. Last but not the least, it is by holiness that God says, "My ways are not your ways," or "as far as the east is from the west, so are My ways different from

your ways." Therefore, when God says, "I am holy," in simple terms He is saying, "I am incorruptible." Therefore, God will remain the same today and tomorrow and He will not change by the influence of another.
"that you may be sons of your Father in heaven; for He makes His sun rise on the evil and on the good, and sends rain on the just and on the unjust. For if you love those who love you, what reward have you? Do not even the tax collectors do the same? (Matthew 5:45-46)

God never reacts, He acts on the basis of who He is irrespective of what people do or do not do.

The Character of the First Teacher

He who has My commandments and keeps them, it is he who loves Me. And he who loves Me will be loved by My Father, and I will love him and manifest Myself to him. (John14:21)
The teaching character of God is two folds. These two teaching abilities come from two different aspects of His nature. The first comes from His light nature while the other comes from His Spirit nature. Right now, we are going to concentrate on the teaching ability of God that originates from His light nature. Jesus Himself from above said that He will love those who love him and will reveal Himself to them.

The word 'reveal' means to unveil or disclose something that was hidden.

It talks mostly of the teaching ability of God which shows new things or throws new light on any particular issue.
Your word is a lamp to my feet and a light to my path. (Psalm 119:105)
The Psalmist states clearly that the Word is a lamp and a light. Hence the Word is the ingredient by which God brings new directions into the life of His child or the believer.
The entrance of Your words gives light; It gives understanding to the simple. (Psalm119:130)
This also states clearly that the entrance of God's Word brings light. Thus, if God wants to start a new thing in your life, He begins by throwing the light of His Word on that new aspect. This He will do so that at the end you will be able to see the new horizon of His will and then go by it.

Behold, God is exalted by His power; who teaches like Him? (Job36:22)
Here it says clearly: who teaches like God? In other words, God is the best teacher there is.
But there is a spirit in man, and the breath of the Almighty gives him understanding. (Job32:8)

Therefore, we can trust the teaching ability of God because He knows how to bring you to the place of understanding. You do not have to be of any age to understand, with God at any time He can give you knowledge by revealing it to you. Revelation knowledge is the knowledge that you get by faith. Sometimes it could take a long time to actually even explain them, but they will be working for you. When Paul was exhorting Timothy to study to show himself approved, he was saying take your time to better understand the unveiled knowledge that God has given to you. Jesus was thanking the Father that He chose to reveal Himself to babes. So, no one can know God except He reveals Himself to that person. When God, therefore, chooses to reveal Himself to you, He will inspire you by throwing light into your spirit concerning His Word. As you believe so also you will understand.

The Character of the First Sanctifier

To sanctify simply is the process of transforming something from an impure state to a pure state. It also is the process of transforming something from an unacceptable state to an acceptable state and maintaining it in that new state. According to Holman's dictionary, Sanctification is the process of being made holy resulting in a changed life-style for the believer. The English word *sanctification* comes from the Latin *"santificatio"*, meaning the act/process of making holy, consecrated. In the Greek New Testament, the root *hag-* is the basis of *"hagiasmos"*, "holiness," "consecration," "sanctification (which brings about the revelation of our righteousness; hence improving our acceptability before God).

'Hagiasmes' means holiness; consecration and sanctification while the Hebrew "qadosh" means separate, contrasting with the profane. God determines that things and people dedicated to Him and to His use are separate from the rest. You may want to ask why I am taking all this time to define holiness again in this section. It is simply because Holiness and sanctification are different but closely related terms. Hence if these terms are close then the persons involved or possessing them must also be

THE DIVINE NATURE OF GOD

closely related. There are people in life who have certain abilities in them. However, there is no guarantee that they can transfer these abilities to others. The famous story of a dead man rising from off the bones of Elisha is proof of the fact that he was anointed. Yet he went to the grave with that anointing without transferring it as his predecessor did. Therefore, it is one thing to be something and it is an entirely different thing to be able to transfer that thing to another man. Thus, God is a sanctifier not just because He is holy, but because He knows how to make any other thing, place, and people holy as Himself.

Therefore, by sanctification, God can transfer His holy nature to others.

For whom He foreknew, He also predestined to be conformed to the image of His Son (Romans8:29a)

By this verse, we see clearly that even though justification and sanctification are all processes that believers go through for transformation, sanctification talks of transformation, to become like God (i.e. qadosh (separate) like God) and acceptable, while Justification talks of transforming to responsible levels and capacity. Because God had predestined us to be His express image, He becomes our sanctifier to make us separate and holy even as He is, in the inner man as in the body which is His temple.

That I might be a minister of Jesus Christ to the Gentiles, ministering the gospel of God, that the offering of the Gentiles might be acceptable, sanctified by the Holy Spirit. (Romans15:16)

Therefore, the offering up of ourselves to God is only acceptable before God by the sanctification of the Holy Spirit who is himself, Divine. Hence because we are constantly being sanctified by God, it makes it possible for us to continually remain acceptable and justified before Him. He by this maintains our acceptability and justification before Him. Talking of the sanctification process, there are two levels of a believer's sanctification.

The first level is the sanctification from an unbeliever to a believer.

In whom we have redemption through His blood, the forgiveness of sins. (Colossians1:14)

The process that transforms you through the washing of His blood and gives you His Spirit so that you can become born again is the first

level of sanctification.
Sanctify them through thy truth: thy word is truth. (John17:17)
That He might sanctify and cleanse her with the washing of water by the word, (Ephesians 5:26)

The second level is the one that goes on through the entire life of the believer by faith in Christ until perfection.

Jesus said, "Father I do not pray that you should take them out of the world, but that You should keep them from the evil one," (John 17:15). The process by which God keeps the believer from the evil of sin, sickness, oppression is called the second level of sanctification. It is a wonderful thing to know that God is your sanctifier, isn't it?

The Light Connection

The Psalmist wrote, *What is man, that thou art mindful of him? and the son of man, that thou visitest him? For thou hast made him a little lower than the angels, and hast crowned him with glory and honour. Thou madest him to have dominion over the works of thy hands; thou hast put all things under his feet: All sheep and oxen, yea, and the beasts of the field; The fowl of the air, and the fish of the sea, and whatsoever passeth through the paths of the seas. O LORD our Lord, how excellent is thy name in all the earth! (Psalm 8:4-9)*
You are the light of the world. A city that is set on a hill cannot be hidden. (Matthew5:14)
Let your light so shine before men, that they may see your good works, and glorify your Father which is in heaven. (Matthew5:16)
We all see from the scriptures that the blessing and inheritance of the son of man (Christ) have come to us who are called in the same order as Him. So even as Jesus was the light of the world, Matthew 5: 14 says it clearly "you are the light of the world", and goes ahead to say in verse 16 of the same chapter that we should let our light shine, because it is possible for you to be light yet you do not shine. If we have the nature of light, it, therefore, means we also have the characters of God that proceed from this light nature. So, as we increasingly experience the nature of His light that is in us, you can only be lighted up to the degree to which you have known God.
We talked before of the character of God's holiness or of the fact

THE DIVINE NATURE OF GOD

that God is holy. We went as far as explaining that God's holiness depicts His incorruptibility.

But as He who called you is holy, you also be holy in all your conduct, (1Peter 1:15.)

But you are a chosen generation, a royal priesthood, a holy nation, His own special people, that you may proclaim the praises of Him who called you out of darkness into His marvelous light; (1Peter2:9)

We are a holy nation and as He that called us is holy so we should be holy in our conduct. Conduct being our way of life expresses clearly our level of holiness. But before we explore that, let's see our character of holiness. Knowing that we are born of an incorruptible seed even the Word of God, it is therefore clear that every believer has an incorruptible nature. Hence, we all are holy by nature, thus that is the only reason why God commands us to be holy.

Do not misunderstand God here. God did not command us to be holy because we are not holy. Rather God commands us to be holy because we are holy.

God cannot say to an unbeliever 'be holy' because it is impossible for them to be holy. It is like saying to a dog 'be a man.' So because we have the holy nature, He demands that we grow in that nature. Therefore, it is like saying to a male child 'be a man.' Hope we are clear on that?

Note, that the ability that enables light to shine in darkness is its incorruptibility (holiness). Therefore, as children of a Holy Father, we are required to grow in our holiness until this corruptible put on incorruptible.

The first step by which God will replace the temporal with the permanent is by you, growing in your incorruptible nature. Until the corruptions of the world such as sickness, sin, infirmities, iniquities, deformation, limitation, weaknesses, fears and worries are all replaced by the incorruptible nature of your holiness. I said 'your own holiness' because, if God is holy and you are not, it makes no difference since the evil in this world will still consume you. Also, by the Word, we know that God's ability to change situations around you is based on/or limited to the power that works within us. Talking of conduct, our holiness manifests itself in our ability to be good in the midst of wickedness, rich in the presence of poverty, pure in the presence of sin, triumphant in the presence of evil, etc. and not in dressing style and facial appearance as some may think. People, who have defined holiness as looks rather than character, go all day cursing people and twisting their faces, making the atmosphere very tense for those around them. Know you are not a prophet because your face looks twisted. You are a prophet because God called you (that's if He called you indeed). The reason why some prophesy only evil is carved out on their faces. Maybe you will have the chance to explain to us the type of God who called you with such an evil eye. Is God evil? Some ascribe holiness to the type of ugly dress they put on which finally makes them not presentable and unfit for the society. I do not say believers should dress according to the pattern of the world; as some are already doing, trying to correct one misconception with another. Some, on their way to church, still have the notion they are going to appear before God. Hence when going to church, they dress like church and when going for work or school they dress like the world. When God said He is in the midst of two or three gathered in His name, He did not say that is the only place He can be found.

Maybe you should ask yourself this question: When does the temple of a Deity ever go to the presence of the set Deity (in our case; God being the deity)? Do you not know that God is ever present with you seeing that He lives in you by His Spirit? Therefore, anywhere you find yourself, know that you are in His presence because God lives in you. I will not close this section without saying this. Jesus said, "when you fast wash your face let your countenance be good" meaning holiness does not mean ugliness and dirtiness. So as a Christian, dress well and look good like God because it is a conduct of holiness. Leaving this outward stuff we should grow in holiness which is the ability of a Christian to imitate God, loving those who hate you and doing good to those who despitefully use you.

It is this light of Holiness that shines in darkness until darkness can no longer comprehend it.

Because they cannot understand the fact that evil is done to you and only good comes out all the time. Talking of the teaching connection, Paul said, "I am not ashamed of the gospel for it is the power of God unto salvation to them that believe." He was not ashamed even though circumstances around him wanted him to be; because he knew that the Gospel in the mouth of the believer has the power to save mankind.
For I am not ashamed of the gospel of Christ, for it is the power of God

to salvation for everyone who believes, for the Jew first and also for the Greek. (Romans 1:16)
Now then, we are ambassadors for Christ, as though God were pleading through us: we implore you on Christ's behalf, be reconciled to God. (2Corinthians 5:20)
But you shall receive power when the Holy Spirit has come upon you; and you shall be witnesses to Me in Jerusalem, and in all Judea and Samaria, and to the end of the earth. (Acts 1:8)
No one has seen God at any time. The only begotten Son, who is in the bosom of the Father, He has declared Him. (John 1:18)
All things have been delivered to Me by My Father, and no one knows who the Son is except the Father, and who the Father is except the Son, and the one to whom the Son wills to reveal Him. (Luke 10:22)

Hence, God has called us to save the world making us ambassadors of reconciliation to give the revelation of salvation to them that are in darkness. In order words, there is nothing as powerful as the gospel in the mouth of a believer. We have all received power because we all have the Holy Spirit in us.

By the scriptures above, you know that when Jesus was in the world He was the only light but now that He has gone, we (collectively) are the only light the world has.

Therefore, the world will only know God if we reveal God to them by the preaching of the gospel. God has given us the power to reveal Him to the world making us His witnesses. So, do not be ashamed to shine the light of the gospel of Jesus Christ because, with all the light that God has, He can only save your world through your own light. If you do not speak out and shine your light, the people will not be saved. In case you refuse to shine your light, I will shine mine to save you.

This is because any light that is not shining is in danger of darkness itself.

Together with this, we will say that's the reason why we should study the Word and pray for revelation because it's the way by which we get the knowledge of the gospel to give others
Let your light so shine before men, that they may see your good works and glorify your Father in heaven. (Matthew 5:16)

The next way we can shine the light of God is through our goodness. Let the world see the difference between you now and that which you were before and praise God. If you do not shine the light, God's name will be mocked because of you. Therefore, choose to set a good example to the believers so that God's name will be praised. As it is said, *"let him that names the name of the Lord depart from evil,"* *(2Timothy 2:19).* Do this and God will reveal Himself to you more and more.

Talking on the connection of sanctification, I will jump straight to saying that God did not just sanctify us but gave us the sanctifying ability.

Do you believe? It will be shocking to find out how many believers live in fear because they do not understand their sanctifying ability. I will define sanctification at two different levels because to us it operates at two levels.

    a. The sanctification of one's self *"You shall also make a laver of bronze, with its base also of bronze, for washing. You shall put it between the tabernacle of meeting and the altar. And you shall put water in it, for Aaron and his sons shall wash their hands and their feet in water from it. (Exodus 30:18-19) And Joshua said to the people, "Sanctify yourselves, for tomorrow the LORD will do wonders among you. (Joshua3:5)* In the days of old, whenever the children of God had to encounter God or were preparing for His move, He will ask them to sanctify themselves. In accordance with the laws of Moses, sanctification had to do with circumcision and washing of hands and feet.

        i. **Circumcision:** Was a law in which the foreskin of every male was cut by the priest on the eight days. It was, therefore, the responsibility of the parents to present the child before the priests for circumcision. So, just as it was in a way the responsibility of the priest, so also our High Priest, Jesus Christ has sanctified us with the circumcision of the heart through His death on the cross. This washing, therefore, is called the washing of regeneration and renewing. *But when the kindness and the love of God our Savior toward man appeared, not by works of righteousness which we have done, but* *according to His mercy He saved us, through the washing of regeneration and renewing of the Holy Spirit, (Titus 3:4-5).* We have to note that now our circumcision is of the heart and not of the flesh as it was in the old.

    ii. **Washing of hands and feet:** This washing was done by all Israelites to prepare themselves whenever they wanted to encounter God or touch any holy thing. It is the responsibility of the individual concerned. Therefore, as Christians, we also have to sanctify ourselves. However, the sanctification is no longer the washing of hands and feet, but a spiritual cleansing of the mind by the washing of the Word. Therefore, scripture states; *If you return to the Almighty, you will be built up; You will remove iniquity far from your tents. (Job22:23) Therefore, having these promises, beloved, let us cleanse ourselves from all filthiness of the flesh and spirit, perfecting holiness in the fear of God. (2Corinthians 7:1)* Let's be clear on this; God did not say, "I will remove iniquity from your tent," He says, "you will do it." Thus, by giving yourself to the Word, God will build you up so you can put iniquity out of your tent. So, child of God, you must cleanse yourself from all the works of the flesh by renewing your mind. Note that iniquity is what the scriptures refer to as the works of the flesh (which is in your tent or body). However the cleansing of a Christian goes beyond the works of the flesh (witchcraft, fornication, covetousness and all forms of sin) to cleansing from sicknesses, infirmities, limitations, setbacks, etc. if you have cleansed yourself from all works of the flesh and are still sick, know that your cleansing process is not yet complete.

So, keep cleaning until you are sickness free, infirmity free, limitation free, fear free and lastly (if you can take it) death free.

    b. **The sanctification of others:** All Christians have the ability to sanctify others and their surrounding environment. This ability is clearly written in the Word of God in an indisputable way. *Therefore let no one boast in men. For all things are yours: (1Corinthians3:21). Fools and blind! For which is greater, the gold or the temple that sanctifies the gold? (Matthew 23:17).* According to the law of ownership, if you own something you have the right to decide what happens to it and not the other way around. So, if you have a car; you decide when to use it and how you want to use it. With this understanding, I want us to discuss the above scriptures. As a Christian, you are the owner of everything that is on earth; people and things alike. By this, you are the one who decides what happens to them as the example of the car and not them on you. Also, because you are the temple of God, you have the authority to sanctify everything that comes on your path. The character of sanctification is an addition to the incorruptible nature.

This ability makes it clear that adding to your holy nature, if you come in contact with an unholy person or thing, it is the other unholy person or thing that will be affected by your holy nature and not the other way around.

He that has ears to hear let him hear what the Spirit is saying to the churches, (Revelation 2:7). Wow! If you do not believe read the scriptures below. *They will take up serpents; and if they drink anything deadly, it will by no means hurt them; they will lay hands on the sick, and they will recover. (Mark 16:18)*

Brother, God will not joke with us (not with serpents) and He will not lie to us seeing that He is our only hope. Jesus Himself said these words. Hence, a serpent in the hand of a Christian becomes as harmless as a dove. Wow! He did not end there but stated clearly without mincing words that if you drink poison you will not be hurt. He did not say the cup will fall from your hand if there is poison in it. Did you not read how Elisha sanctified food when they told him there was death in the pot? So, if there is death in the cup, your presence will sanctify or purify instead of it contaminating you. Child of God, this is the greatness of your life as a Christian. Some Christians do not play around sick folks because they have a long list of all transmissible diseases. They are afraid of being contaminated. But I bring you good news; Jesus did not see you like that. Stop believing a lie, it will limit you. See yourself the way God sees you. If you come in contact with HIV rather than it contaminating you, it will die and not prosper in your presence. You can name all the other diseases in the world the same law applies. I think this is the reason why God said a thousand shall fall by your right and ten thousand at your left and nothing shall come near your dwelling; because if they come they will die *So they said, Believe on the Lord Jesus Christ, and you will be saved, you and your household. (Acts 16:31) For the unbelieving husband is sanctified by the wife, and the unbelieving wife is sanctified by the husband; otherwise your children would be unclean, but now they are holy. (1Corinthians 7:14)*

There are a group of people that I do not think were sent by my Father judging by their fruits. These guys go on teaching Christians that their lives are affected negatively by their family background. Note: there is a difference when people are taught the fact that the devil will want to trouble them from their family background and actually teaching them to fear the corruption that could come from there. So, time and again they call Christians to come for family deliverance. This is very wrong and do not believe anyone who teaches this doctrine because they will deprive you of the liberty that you have received in Christ. The scriptures state above that rather than you being cursed by your family they will benefit from your salvation and be sanctified or saved. Is this thing not clear? Do not be blind to the scripture being deceived by your senses. Even in the case of a marriage between a Christian and an unbeliever, the scriptures declare that the children are clean because the unbeliever is sanctified by the believer. Let those who are spreading this bad doctrine repent. I imagine that if we are cursed from our families according to the flesh as they say, of what use is the exaltation of God concerning us which states that we are new creations in Christ and that old things are passed away? *If you forgive the sins of any, they are forgiven them; if you retain the sins of any, they are retained, (John20:23).* Child of God, you also have the authority to forgive sins upon the earth. Please understand that this goes beyond forgiving someone that wronged you to forgiving someone in the stead of God. Thus, if a man needs God's forgiveness, he can come to you and if you forgive him God will forgive him. Also, if you do not forgive him, God, too will not forgive him.

Think about this for a minute, the unbelieving husband can be a wizard, killer, thief, a magician, an idol worshiper, name the rest. The Bible says so long as it's an unbeliever the believer sanctifies him/her. So, if you believe, fear will leave you and you will touch the sick and they shall recover. When sinners come into your presence they will go informed on righteousness because God has given you the ability to sanctify them. Next, even your environment is waiting to be sanctified by your presence.

Then to Adam He said, "Because you have heeded the voice of your wife, and have eaten from the tree of which I commanded you, saying, 'You shall not eat of it': "Cursed is the ground for your sake; In toil you shall eat of it All the days of your life. (Genesis 3:17)

For the earnest expectation of the creation eagerly waits for the revealing of the sons of God. (Romans 8:19)

If you have been reading your Bible, these scriptures will not be strange to you. Above we see how the earth was cursed because of the fall of Adam.

But we must understand that the fate of creation is dependent on the spiritual state of the men in the world. (that is; carnal for worse and righteousness for better)

Because man had fallen, every increase in sin on the earth led to increased levels of curses on the earth. This is why it is written that the world will grow old like a garment; all this because of sin. However, after the appearing of our Savior Jesus Christ, creation will now be blessed by our righteousness. That is the reason why creation is waiting eagerly for the manifestation of sons of God and you certainly are one of them.

The Light Connection

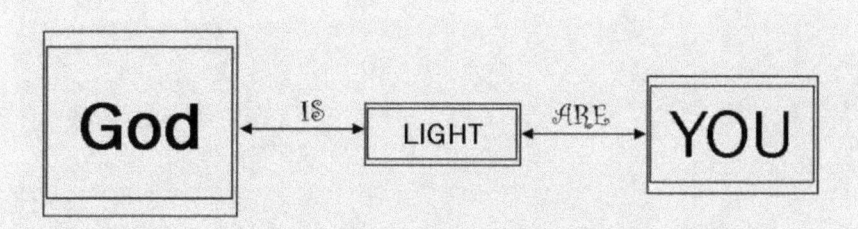

CHAPTER FOUR

GOD IS A SPIRIT

God is a Spirit: and they that worship him must worship him in spirit and in truth. (John4:24)

From the above verse, there is no doubt that God is a Spirit. But looking keenly at the rendering "a spirit" as it is rightly stated; God is a Spirit. Note that when God was talking about His nature of love, He said, God is love. He did not say God is love. So, what makes this different to the point that God refuses to be absolute in stating His Spirit nature? The truth simply put, is that God is Spirit because He is life. Because everything that is spirit has life in it. So, it is impossible to have life without being a spirit. Hence everything that is alive has a spirit or is a spirit. Therefore, God is not the only spirit being. You are a spirit, Animals are all spirits, Angels are all spirits and even the devil and demons are all spirits. So, it should not surprise you when God does not claim spirituality as a singular characteristic, though everyone else obtained this attribute from Him. So, it is important that we now understand what it means to be a spirit.

The Bible says .... *for a spirit hath not flesh and bones as ye see me have. (Luke24:39)* From this scripture, it is very easy to conclude that spirits don't have a body. Which if we do, we will be sincerely mistaken. Why is that? It is because Jesus meant that a spirit's body is not made up of flesh and bones. Hence, the way a spiritual body is, it cannot be handled by flesh and bones. This, therefore, means that by nature you wouldn't expect God to have flesh and bones. Based on the fact that we are establishing an understanding of who God is, I want us to focus on how to relate to the fact that God is Spirit in nature.

Jesus said to her, "Woman, believe Me, the hour is coming when you will neither on this mountain, nor in Jerusalem, worship the Father. You worship what you do not know; we know what we worship, for salvation is of the Jews. But the hour is coming, and now is, when the true worshipers will worship the Father in spirit and truth; for the Father is seeking such to worship Him. (John4:21-23)

If we look at the conversation of Jesus and the woman from Samaria before He said God is Spirit, you will see something profound about God. First, we understand from their conversation that there had been a dispute between the Samaritans and the Jews on the place of worship. From the foundation of Israel as a nation, God had chosen that a temple is built for Him in Jerusalem in the days of David the king. History tells us how Solomon the king built the temple of God in Jerusalem and dedicated it to God with great sacrifice. So, God made a promise saying his eyes shall be open and his ears attentive unto the prayer *that is made* in this place (the temple). So, anyone who came and prayed in the temple in Jerusalem knew God was going to answer because that is what he said. But Solomon sinned against God and it led to the division of Israel into two different countries. So, one was called Judah, consisting of two tribes under Rehoboam the son of Solomon, while the other was Israel made of ten tribes under Jeroboam whose capital was Samaria.

However, Jeroboam being afraid that the citizens of his new country will go back to Judah decided to stop them from going to worship in Jerusalem where God had commanded; hence, they sinned against God for generations. By the time Jesus came, they had been captured and separated completely from the culture of worship in Jerusalem which was called the holy city because of the Holy temple that was within it. So according to the law, Jerusalem was a holy city and that was where people had to go for worship. Yet when the Samaritan woman brought up the argument about the place of worship Jesus used that opportunity to teach us something about God we didn't know. Immediately Jesus said the time is coming when this or that mountain or place will no longer be necessary for worship. When you will no longer have to go to Jerusalem to worship the Father. Then again He said the time is now when the true worshipers will worship the Father in spirit and in truth. What was Jesus trying to signify? Did He now mean that those who worshiped the Father in Jerusalem were not true? But we know that everything that was done in the old was a shadow of the reality that was to come in Christ Jesus. Therefore, it is clear that God was attached to a place of worship that did not meet His actual expectations for worship based on His nature. So, by the appearing of Jesus, He was now looking for people who will worship Him based exactly on His nature and actual expectation. So, Jesus said the Father has been seeking such to worship Him. It means God was bearing the place of worship but was seriously seeking those that will worship Him in spirit and in truth. Why? Because He is a Spirit!

So, God was unable to connect with the people of old in the spirit because they were carnal hence the only option He had was to institute a place of worship. In Christ Jesus however, He now has people who can actually deal with Him at the level of the spirit as He has always wanted. Hence in Christ Jesus, there is no holy place to God only holy people. And a holy man in Cameroon will have the same attention from God as a holy man in Spain. Secondly, talking of truth, Jesus said to the woman, "you know not whom you worship." So, God was also fed up with worshippers who did not have the right knowledge of who He was. In other words, they were worshiping a God they did not even know. So, God wants to be known by those who worship Him. And so He sought for people who will worship Him in truth (the right knowledge of his personality). If you've ever been represented by people you thought knew you, then you will understand how God feels when people misrepresent Him because they lack the right knowledge of Him. By this God is saying He is a person who wants to have a spiritual connection with those who worship Him. Also, He is a person who can be understood if we seek to know His person. That said, I want us to look at the main characters of the spirit.

The Character of Life

It is the Spirit who gives life; the flesh profits nothing. The words that I speak to you are spirit, and they are life. (John 6:63)
Jesus said to him, "I am the way, the truth, and the life. No one comes to the Father except through Me. (John14:6)
Jesus said: "The words that I speak to you are spirit and life". Again He said, "I am the way the truth and the life." The Bible also says, "in the beginning was the word and the word was God." If the spirit is life, then

it is no trouble to say that God is life because Jesus even said He is life. Now if God is life then what is life? To better understand life, it is good that we start from the opposite of life, which is death. In this, we will conclude that anything that is not death is life. From the very first mention of death, it means separation of oneself from his body. In other words, when the spirit is separated from its body or separated from God and exposed to His wrath. But note that we are defining life at God's experience. Since He cannot be separated from Himself or exposed to His own wrath, we will not take these definitions seriously. Looking at the first definition of death Jesus said: *"I am the life."* He also said: *"I and the father are one."* Again he said: *"...baptizing them in the name of the father and of the son and of the spirit."* Therefore it is impossible to ever separate God from Himself seeing that He remains the same forever. But we cannot just derive the meaning of God's life from the fact that He is one. Note again that Jesus said, *"I came that you might have life and have it abundantly."* From this statement, I can't find a word that describes a person to be abundantly one. Therefore, for me, there are other attributes that make for an abundant life.

For the word of God is living and powerful, and sharper than any two-edged sword... (Hebrews 4:12)

More so, looking at the Word of God which is living and active, the Bible says we were born of an incorruptible seed even the Word of God. If the Word is life and the Word is incorruptible, it means the life of God knows no decay or depreciation. Just saying that it is incorruptible does not make it clear as it is supposed to be because the life of God knows no decay but it is not stagnant.

But if the Spirit of him that raised up Jesus from the dead dwells in you, he that raised up Christ from the dead shall also quicken your mortal bodies by his Spirit that dwelleth in you. (Romans 8:11)

It says; "he shall quicken your mortal bodies." The word: quicken; means to renew or bring back to life or to revitalize. So, the life of God is constantly improving and growing. Note that decay is a form of growth in the negative direction.

So instead of God saying He is life, He could have said, "I am constantly improving." (growing)

Furthermore, the Bible says the Word of God is living and active. This means that if the Word is life, life is active. Jesus said, "my Father

works and I work." So, for God to be alive it means He is actively working as it is said: *Behold, He who keeps Israel shall neither slumber nor sleep. (Psalm 121:4)*
... but the word of God is not chained. (2Timothy 2:9)
Now the Lord is the Spirit; and where the Spirit of the Lord is, there is liberty. (2Corinthians 3:17)

To add to that, Paul in the epistles said that he was bound but the Word of God was not bound. If that Word cannot be chained, it denotes that life itself is freedom.

So, when God says He is life, He is saying God is free and He is freedom personified.

So, it is very clear that God is freedom because if you are looking for liberty, just go to where the Spirit of the Lord is.
The Bible says that God respects His words more than His name; it means God honors His life.

Therefore, when God says He is life, He is saying, "I am honor personified." So, it is impossible to dishonor life successfully.

Lastly, Paul said the Word of God is sharper than any two-edged sword. Hence the Word of God is more powerful than any weapon of war. Therefore, life is power or dominion according to God.

So, when God says, "I am life," He is declaring that He will never be dominated by anyone.

But for these four main attributes, we can say that even the devil is life. Thank God he is not. Note that God is a spirit, the devil also is a spirit, God is one, the devil also is one (Jesus even said a kingdom divided in itself cannot stand. The devil cannot cast out the devil). God is everlasting, the devil too is everlasting but the Bible states it clear that he is busy because his time is short. Therefore, he does not have freedom, and he is not in dominion. Also, he has been stripped of all his power and honor.

So, the life of God is free, constantly improving, commands respect and honor and has power amongst others.

Life is; therefore, the sum of all what God is, what He is able to do, the influence He has on Himself and others and the circumstances He experiences based on who He is.

The Character of the Second Teacher

But if the spirit of him that raised Christ from the dead dwell in you.... shall also quicken your mortal bodies... (Romans 8:11)

In the character of life, we talked about the fact that God is growth. But looking at his ability to quicken from the dead or resurrect, the only way God can quicken us is through His ability to teach or His character as a teacher.

...But be transformed by the renewing of your mind, (Rom12:2).

So, quickening, transformation or revitalization is only possible, through the renewal of the mind. The Bible also says: how can they believe if they have not heard? Hence, someone must teach them for their minds to be renewed before transformation can take place. Jesus said, *"I still have many things to say to you, but you cannot bear them now. However, when He, the Spirit of truth, has come, He will guide you into all truth..." (John16:12-13)*

Take note that Jesus being the son of God Himself, was declared to be a teacher during His earthly ministry.

......of all that Jesus began both to do and teach, (Acts 1:1)

The Gospels record that Jesus always taught in the synagogues and that He did not teach like the scribes but taught with authority. But at the end of His teaching ministry, He tells the disciples that He still has a lot that He could tell them. However, for the fact that they were not able to bear, He said when the Holy Spirit comes, He will guard them into all truth. In other words, the Spirit will continue to teach them from where He ended. So, God proved in Jesus and by His Spirit to us that He is a faithful teacher of the truth.

But the Helper, the Holy Spirit, whom the Father will send in My name, He will teach you all things, and bring to your remembrance all things that I said to you. (John 14:26)

But the anointing which you have received from Him abides in you, and you do not need that anyone teach you; but as the same anointing teaches you concerning all things, and is true, and is not a lie, and just as it has taught you, you will abide in Him. (1John 2:27)

How sweet are Your words to my taste, Sweeter than honey to my mouth (Ps 119:103)

It is evident that the Holy Spirit is our teacher. We also see from these verses that the anointing is the spirit. These verses also make us know that the anointing is a person. So, until you are taught of that anointing, you can't abide in God. So, because God wants you to abide in Him, He puts His Spirit in you so you can be taught of Him and thereby abide in Him.

Someone said a teacher tells, a good teacher explains, a better teacher demonstrates while the best teacher inspires.

The Holy Spirit or the Anointing in you is a wonderful teacher. He will tell you what you need to know. *Your ears shall hear a word behind you, saying, "This is the way, walk in it," Whenever you turn to the right hand or whenever you turn to the left, (Isaiah 30:21).* He will explain what you don't understand *...He will teach you all things... (John 14:26).* He will demonstrate when you need to be led. *He will guide you into all truth; (John 16:13).* And lastly, when you need inspiration He will be there to give you the best inspiration. *But there is a spirit in man, and the breath of the Almighty gives him understanding, (Job 32:8).* Believe me, the Holy Spirit is the best teacher there is. You can never overemphasize the teaching work of the Anointing in your life. He will go beyond just spiritual knowledge to telling you things about your job, career, family, and parenting. *I understand more than the ancients, because I keep Your precepts. (Psalms 119:100)*

The Character of a Second Sanctifier

You might be asking a question after noticing that we are now talking of sanctification the second time. In the previous chapter, we talked about the sanctifier in the capacity of acceptability before God. Hence the first sanctification talks of God making you pure before His eyes. This is to enable Him to relate with you without barriers. However, in this section, we will see sanctification on another level.

There is an experience I usually have. I don't know if this is true for you too. I found out that after wearing a wristwatch for so long, some times when I do not have a watch on, I still have the tendency of feeling that I still have a watch on; until I'm forced to look at my hand. You

know this kind of feeling happens to us sometimes even in our spirit. So, it is possible to be free from something but retains the feeling that you are still bound by that thing. And this is very dangerous at the spiritual level because it will stop you from living the fullness of the salvation you have in your spirit. So, to keep a wrong sensation is very dangerous for you as a Christian. Why is that? You may ask.
That is why it is written, *"Keep your heart with all diligence, For out of it spring the issues of life" (Proverbs 4:23)*. So, if God did not make room for this type of sanctification as I call it; then it would have been dangerous for us. I want you therefore to reason this out with me. *How much more shall the blood of Christ, who through the eternal Spirit offered Himself without spot to God, cleanse your conscience from dead works to serve the living God? (Hebrews 9:14)*

Understand that it is one thing for God to approve you pure and it's another thing entirely for you to accept the purity for yourself. It is one thing for God to declare you free and it's another thing for you to walk in the light or understanding of your freedom. You might be wondering in your mind. What on earth is he trying to say? Listen. I am not trying anything. I am saying that when God removes your sin from His consciousness, it does not automatically mean that your sins (i.e. dead works) have left your own consciousness. So, it is paramount for you to know how important it is for you to get this clear before we proceed. We find situations where God is working with you as sinless, but you are still relating to him with the idea that you are a sinner. You will agree with me that there are times or there had been situations in your walk with God in the past when you found it hard accepting that God had forgiven you: just like that or that He had done something just like that. So, God has to cleanse you from your own doubt, weakness and sin consciousness so that you can serve Him conveniently as you should, with all the freedom He has given or made available for you.
The Spirit Himself bears witness with our spirit that we are children of God. (Romans 8:16)
Now if anyone does not have the Spirit of Christ, he is not His. (Romans 8:9b)

This is the difference between us and religious folks. For after all their self-righteousness there is no Spirit of God in them to assure them of salvation. This is no doubt because, the scriptures say clearly that if you have not His Spirit, you are none of His. So, the only proof that we belong to God is that we have His Spirit. Apart from God's ownership, another reason why we have the Holy Spirit is that He helps us by witnessing to us our acceptance by God. Hence, we can stand on that acceptance, and accept all the benefits that belong to us as children. However, many do not still accept fully their godly freedom because they still have mind-renewal problems.

Next, the scriptures say, *"And they overcame him by the blood of the lamb ..." (Revelations12:11)* The "him" here talks of the devil and all his demons. This is one of those scriptures that has brought a lot of misconception in the churches. Why is that? The reason is we have a tendency to look at overcome only as a word for war. But even if it is for war; why not understand the type of war God is talking about. Today we find a lot of church folks when praying, cover themselves with the blood. They even cover entire roads for protection from road accidents. Listen as an environmentalist, I saw the way we use the blood of Jesus and started imagining that God is already running short of blood for the next generation so He is considering to build a blood recycling industry. Just kidding! Christians must stop wasting their time and the blood of Jesus on the devil and demons. They will never be cleansed by the blood. I know you will bring the Passover experience to my attention.

'Now the blood shall be a sign for you on the houses where you are. And when I see the blood, I will pass over you; and the plague shall not be on you to destroy you when I strike the land of Egypt. (Exodus 12:13)

Wait a minute! When God told the people to put blood on their door post was it to protect them from God's wrath or the attacks of the devil? If you have been familiar with the scripture you will remember the famous statement made by God Himself. *"It shall come to pass that when I see the blood I will pass over you."* So, we see that it was God who was killing the first sons of the Egyptians and not the devil. If you read well the first sanctification, we said that God has already removed his wrath from your life.

Brethren, I announce to you if you did not know: God has already passed over you in Christ.

The scriptures tell us of the blood from Old to New Testament how it was used for cleansing. Child of God; know therefore that even if you cover yourself with the blood, it is to protect you from God's wrath, not the Devil's. There is no place in the Bible when God said the people should kill goats or sheep and take the blood to the battlefront to defeat

their enemies. Maybe you have seen that, but I haven't. The scripture we read before in (Hebrews 9:14) will appear this way if we remove the middle phrase. *"How much more shall the blood of Christ cleanse your conscience from dead works to serve the living God."*
But if we walk in the light as He is in the light, we have fellowship with one another, and the blood of Jesus Christ His Son cleanses us from all sin. (1John1:7)

So, we note that the blood was meant to cleanse our conscience from sin. It was to make us know of a truth that we have rights with God and are co-heirs with Him. So, I repeat: stop wasting the blood of Jesus on demons because they will never repent, they will never give their lives to Jesus. With all this, the question is how then do we overcome with the blood?
Elect according to the foreknowledge of God the Father, in sanctification of the Spirit, for obedience and sprinkling of the blood of Jesus Christ: Grace to you and peace be multiplied (1Peter1:2)
Listen to the above sentence says it all and I pray you to understand.

Remember we are talking of the sanctifying character of the spirit and here it states clearly the sanctification of the spirit for obedience and sprinkling of the blood.

Listen; when the spirit sanctifies, He purges your conscience from dead works and prepares you for godly obedience through the sprinkling of the blood. In response to that, you will accept God's grace and peace that is being multiplied towards you and stand against the wiles of the enemy. On the contrary, some Christians cover themselves with the blood. You try to destroy the enemy with the blood but sometimes when disaster hits, you quickly forget the blood, give away your rights in Christ and accept the sickness saying it ought to happen to me because I sinned or God is punishing me for what I did. Brethren, what then is forgiveness, if God has to punish you for your sins? So the devil will plow your back on the basis of your ignorance until the day you say, wait a minute God has forgiven me it is no punishment at all that I now feel sick. Then and only then will you be bold enough to stand with confidence knowing that God is on your side and do what James knows how to do best— resist the devil thereby making him flee.
With this understanding, Revelation12:11 will read thus, *"and they overcome him (by the Grace and peace they obtained through the*

cleansing of their conscience) by the blood........" The blood was made available for your conscience cleansing.

The blood frees you from self-condemnation and is not a weapon to fight the devil.

Instead through the confidence that you have been sanctified by the Spirit, you are courageous to resist the enemy; knowing that God is on your side. Thus, the blood equips you for war but is not a fighting weapon. I am glad if I made you understand this principle and if you have understood, make sure you tell others.

The Spirit Connection

To say that humans are spirits is no news really because we have grown in knowledge to know that man is a spirit, he has a soul and he lives in the body. Therefore, it is more important for us to make a difference between the two kinds of spiritual natures found in humans on Earth today.

Jesus said; *"That which is born of the flesh is flesh, and that which is born of the Spirit is spirit." (John3:6)* By this He made clear, the fact that; there are two kinds of human beings on Earth. There are those who are born of flesh and those who are born of the Spirit. What is the flesh? Flesh in this scripture is not the body as some may suppose. The flesh is also (some form of a) spirit. So, if the spirit is spirit and flesh is a spirit, then Jesus was talking about two different types of spirits. First, I want us to understand the meaning of flesh.

It is the Spirit who gives life; the flesh profits nothing. The words that I speak to you are spirit, and they are life. (John6:63)

"Be fruitful and multiply; fill the earth and subdue it; have dominion over the fish of the sea, over the birds of the air, and over every living thing that moves on the earth. (Genesis 1:28)

Jesus said, "the words that I speak to you are spirit and life...." It, therefore, means that for something to be able to multiply, it has to be alive. Hence flesh is alive and because it is alive, it means it is spirit. Therefore, when Jesus talked of the flesh He was talking of a type of spiritual life. What type of spiritual life is this that is different from the one God has given us? And how is it different?

"But of the tree of the knowledge of good and evil you shall not eat, for in

the day that you eat of it you shall surely die. (Genesis 2:17)

Please. I want to give a short and simple explanation to this as possible so just follow me step by step. First, we see Adam in the Garden eating the fruit of good and evil. From the day Adam ate the fruit; two types of spirits or seeds entered him and started growing inside him. So good and evil became part of man's personality and configuration. Hence, whenever a child is born, he/she is born with good and evil in their DNA.

Behold, I was brought forth in iniquity, and in sin my mother conceived me. (Psalm 51:5)

What do I mean by DNA? I mean the child's nature has health and sickness, poverty and wealth, life and death, etc. Just to name a few. We will take time to explore this further in another publication. What I am making clear to you is that God does not need to put good in any man because it is part of who we are. Also, the devil does not have to put evil in us because it is part of who we are. When the human immune-deficiency virus (HIV) is free out of the body of man, it is called HIV. However, when it finds itself in a man, the combined condition of the man and the virus is called Acquired Immune Deficiency Syndrome (AIDs). If we consider the fruit of good and evil like this virus, it will help us better understand. The man was innocent of good and evil in the garden. By this, it meant he was not conscious of judgments since he had no knowledge of good or evil. The only thing he knew about what God did not like him to do was the command He gave them not to eat from the tree of good and evil. However, this all changed when man ate the fruit.

So, when good and evil came alive in Adam in Eden, their combined condition with man changed man's nature. So good and evil being two different spiritual entities, have now become part of man's spiritual configuration. If you say that it is not possible for another spirit to become part of who you are, I will also ask you my own question. How has the Spirit of God now become part of your spiritual configuration? Better still let's come to physical things. How is it possible that a virus, a bacteria or cancerous cell can start growing in you and become part of your physical configuration? Worst still; there are some families that have a common sickness at a certain age from one generation to the other. This sickness is passing through their DNA from one generation to another. Though that was an aside I thought it necessary to clear any doubts.

THE DIVINE NATURE OF GOD

For we know that the law is spiritual, but I am carnal, sold under sin. (Romans 7: 14)

For the wages of sin is death… (Romans 6:23)

Now if the Bible says the wages of sin is death, it means that sin and carnality have something in common; Death.

For as he thinks in his heart, so is he. "Eat and drink!" he says to you, but his heart is not with you. (Proverbs 23:7)

If the thought of a man's heart, is directly proportional to who he is; then for a man to be carnally minded means that he is a carnal person. I said before that sin and carnality are related to death. Now I show you how they are related. Paul said, "I am carnal, sold under sin." What! So, to be carnally minded simply means to be sold under sin, or to be subject to the person of sin in you.

Knowing this, that our old man was crucified with Him, that the body of sin might be done away with, that we should no longer be slaves of sin. (Romans 6:6)

This scripture agrees with what I say. Before we became born-again, we were slaves to sin as Jesus said, "He that sins is a slave to sin." Hence, we were all slaves to sin or carnal before becoming born again. But now being in Christ, we are no more subject to sin.

So, when Jesus said, "He that is born of the flesh is flesh" he meant that he that is born by a slave to sin is also a slave to sin.

So, flesh is a spiritual nature that is subjected or married to sin and has become his slave. On the other hand, He that is born of the Spirit (i.e. subjected to righteousness) is a slave to righteousness. So, when the spirit of man is subject to sin and death, it is called flesh while when the human spirit is subject to righteousness and life it is called spirit.

E. E. WISEMAN

The Process of Man's Bondage

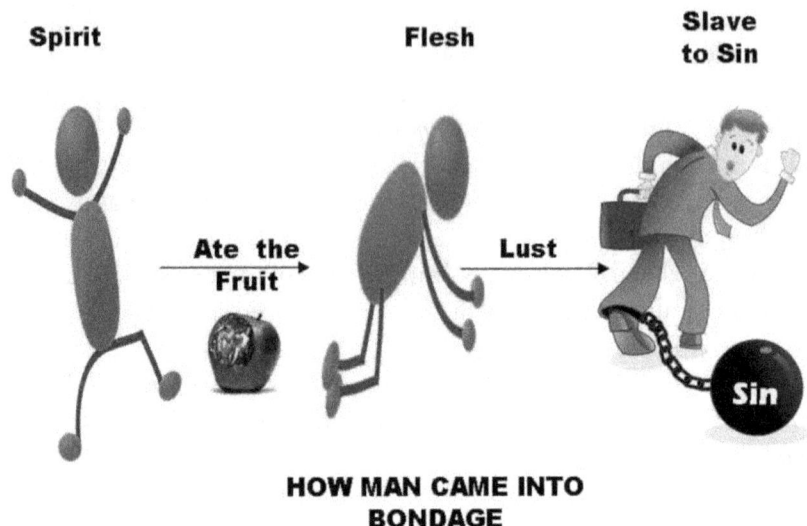

HOW MAN CAME INTO BONDAGE

And having been set free from sin, you became slaves of righteousness. (Romans 6: 18)

And just as it says to be carnally minded is death, it says to be spiritually minded is life. By this, we know that to be a slave to righteousness is life. Let's now proceed to talk about the life connection.
Looking at the life connection, it is so clear in the scriptures that we share the very life of God. The famous (John10:10) states *"The thief does not come except to steal, and to kill, and to destroy. I have come that they may have life and that they may have it abundantly."* Also (John20: 31) attests to this by saying *"...And that believing you may have life in his name."* These scriptures state clearly the reason d'être why Jesus came to earth. By saying I have come that they may have life, Jesus was saying He came to give us life. Then He added by saying that they should have it abundantly. The very next scripture declares that we who have believed already have that life. The question to ask now is simple. What kind of life did Jesus come to give us?
We know; that which is born of the Spirit is spirit. We also know from scripture that we were born of an incorruptible seed even the Word of God. It is important to get it clear at this point. Jesus also said, "the word

is spirit and life." Therefore, if He that is born of Spirit is spirit, it means that you have the same life as the person who gave birth to you. So being born of the Word it means that we are spirit and life. I want us to look at it deeper.

If He called them gods, to whom the word of God came (and the Scripture cannot be broken) (John 10:35)

This scripture makes the mystery clear; if the Word of God comes to you and you receive it, you become a god. Taking from the previous phrase, he that is born of the Spirit is spirit; the same will go for he that is born of God is a god. Still, Jesus said something profound that you might want to know.

For as the Father has life in Himself, so He has granted the Son to have life in Himself, (John5:26)

For you are all sons of God through faith in Christ Jesus. (Galatians 3:26).

Brethren we all have life in us and this life is called eternal life which is God's kind of life.

Thus, as the Father had life in Himself so has He granted us to have life in ourselves through faith in Christ Jesus and as children of God, we all have the same life with God. Talking of abundance, Jesus said that they may have it more abundantly. It means that we share in God's nature of growth and revitalization. Therefore He wants us to grow in the new life or the nature of God; until we have abundance in all life's attributes of freedom, wealth, health, incorruptibility, just to name of few.

Brethren, I do not think its great news to announce to you that you or we all share in the teaching ministry and ability of the Spirit. Yet for the purpose of reminder, it is important that we talk about this again lest we forget our responsibilities as partakers of His very life.

Jesus said to him, "Feed My sheep. (John21:17b)

This is a command that Jesus gave to Peter three times after asking him if he loved Him. For me, I will say that feeding the sheep of Christ could be directly proportional to your love for Him. Or better still this was what Jesus required from Peter. Not to take you out of focus, it is clear to say that God cannot ask you to do something He has not given you the ability to do. Jesus told Peter to feed the sheep with the Word of God. Thus, He wanted Peter to teach the sheep (Church) the Word of

God. I know that some will quickly deny this because they do not think of teaching as nature but as a gift. As it is written; he gave some apostles, prophet, teachers, pastors, and Evangelist. Listen, the teaching ability I am talking about is not the gift type, but the nature type. Hence having the nature of the Spirit, you are a teacher. The Bible says, "let your light so shine that men may see your good works and glorify your father in heaven." What does this mean? It means through your good works; you will teach men to glorify God. In case you forgot; does not your Bible say we all have to do the work of an evangelist? Please all of us cannot teach in the same capacity, but all of us are teachers at different levels as the scriptures rightly put it: be ye examples of the believers, so whether you know about it or not you are teaching someone indirectly because you are a teacher.

And a servant of the Lord must not quarrel but be gentle to all, able to teach, patient, (2Timothy 2:24)

This, therefore, is the question. Are you a servant of the Lord? Then you can teach; though some times, ought to be teachers still need someone to still teach them. Yet we are charged to grow up to the teacher that is buried within us.

Last but not the list is the connection of a sanctifier as the nature of the spirit. From what was discussed earlier, we noted that this sanctification was based on the ability of the spirit to bear witness within us; so, we can accept our forgiveness and thereby be able to serve God with a pure conscience. In line with this, I want us to see what God has made us and the expectations that He has for us who have this nature.

We then who are strong ought to bear with the scruples of the weak, and not to please ourselves. (Romans 15: 1)

Receive one who is weak in the faith, but not to disputes over doubtful things. (Romans 14: 1)

Please listen to me because sometimes we are sincerely mistaken in the way we treat one another. This is so because we sometimes use our physical senses and in so doing spend time pleasing ourselves, rather than serving others. I say so because sometimes there is no difference to the eye between a weak Christian and an unbeliever, hence if we do not grow in the ability of our spirits as sanctifiers; we will continue to do harm to babies in the house because we are babies ourselves (though sometimes decorated with titles). It, therefore, states clearly that we who are strong ought to bear with the scruples of the weak and not for passing judgments the way we feel or better still pleasing ourselves.

Who are you to judge another's servant? To his own master he stands or falls. Indeed, he will be made to stand, for God is able to make him stand. (Romans 14:4)

God has given to us the ministry of reconciliation so that we can together with Him learn to forgive, to bear one another and love to the extent that we show to the beloved as a witness to the fact that God loves them, and that He has shown mercy to them. By so doing we will build the self-esteem of the believers so they can stand with full assurance of their salvation.

Brethren, if a man is overtaken in any trespass, you who are spiritual restore such a one in a spirit of gentleness, considering yourself lest you also be tempted. (Galatians 6:1)

Brothers and sisters, God did not say; those that are spiritual should mock, laugh, judge or boast. Of course, you know that if you have been behaving in the similitude of the above character, it is merely a sign of immaturity, expressing its self in diverse forms. However, I bring good news to the weak. God does not condemn us when we fall into sin; He forgives us. God was in Christ reconciling the world to Himself; not counting their sin against them. Jesus did not come to condemn us: He came to save us. Yet some have ordained themselves as judges to the brethren instead of forbearers, making themselves contrary to the essence of their very lives.

Come to think of it. If a brother or sister falls into immorality or fornication, who did he or she sin against the pastor himself or the Lord? Now if the Lord forgives the brother or sister, why then does the pastor judge? I do not deny the fact that some have to be rebuked openly for an example, but still, the Word of God says if someone is overtaken by a trespass we should restore such a one with the spirit of gentleness. It says we should do it while considering ourselves lest we are tempted to feel self-righteous.

But for me, I will say clearly that whatever I did not do; by the grace of God I did not do it. Not because I was strong but because His grace was with me. Therefore the Lord has given us the nature of sanctifiers that with meekness we should bear one another's burdens, and so fulfill the law of Christ. Therefore, I charge you to be a sanctifier and not a judge to the brethren because that is what you are in your spiritual nature in Christ Jesus. For in so doing, you help to encourage the children in the process of their day to day sanctification and transformation with God.

The Spirit Connection

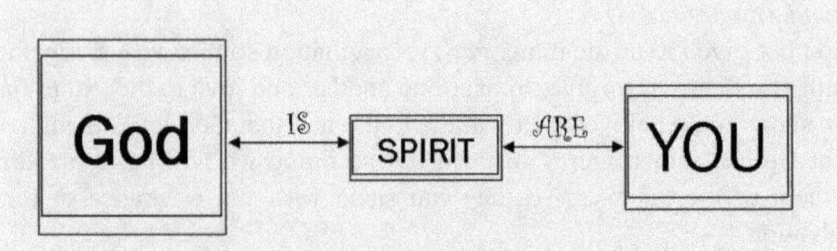

CHAPTER FIVE

GOD THE JUDGE

When a man thinks he has been wronged by another man, he will take him to the court and he that is on the high chair will hear the matter as it happened. The lawyer will defend their clients as far as they can. At the end of the session, the man on the high chair will give the final verdict. And it does not matter what anyone thinks, you can only pray that his verdict favors you. If not, there is nothing anybody can do about it; his verdict is final.

"Agree with your adversary quickly, while you are on the way with him, lest your adversary deliver you to the judge, the judge hand you over to the officer, and you be thrown into prison." (Matthew 5:25)

The end of that statement says you will be thrown into prison. Now no one loves to do things that will take them to prison. With great certainty the Word of God declares it. *What then shall we say to these things? If God is for us, who can be against us? (*Romans 8: 31)

In the declaration of the final verdict in a court session (for me) there is no better verse that matches the verdict of the judge, once it is out. If it is for you; no one can be against you. If it is against you; no one can be for you. Do your best to understand me. As I speak, judge for yourself if what I say is the truth. There might be people who still think that the judge is wrong. Their being against you is not a matter of feeling but a matter of ability to change the verdict. So even if they feel bad or good, there is nothing they can do about it.

.... He who opens and no one shuts, and shuts and no one opens (Revelation 3:7)

Wow! What a verdict. If God opens the door no one can shut, I am making you understand that only judges make such statements and to hear God speak like this will mean that He is acting as a judge Himself. Note that if the verdict has to be changed it will be done by the same judge or another on sit with reasons that are binding with the law. And until the verdict is changed the first verdict will stay in effect. To say that God is a judge is not bad yet this will not give us a clear understanding of His magistracy. Jesus told a parable of a landowner who planted his vineyard and sent servants to take care of it. When the time for harvest came, they will beat the people he sent to get his share of the harvest. Then finally he sent his son whom they killed. At the end of the parable, the scripture reads thus:

"Therefore, when the owner of the vineyard comes, what will he do to those vinedressers?" .... "He will destroy those wicked men miserably, and lease his vineyard to other vinedressers who will render to him the fruits in their seasons" (Matthew 21:33-41)

The Bible makes us understand that the Earth is the Lord's and the fullness thereof. It means that we all belong to God. Therefore, to understand God's magistracy, you must see Him as the owner of the universe for we are all the work of His hands. Listen, God owns this vineyard called Earth and so all of us are His servants. Even people who do not think they are serving God are serving him without knowledge of the agreement. From what I say, it means no man under the Earth can refuse to serve God; whether in evil or in good we are His servants. If you don't get it just read this.

'For by Him all things were created that are in heaven and that are on earth, visible and invisible, whether thrones or dominions or principalities or powers. All things were created through Him and for Him.' (Colosians1:16)

If this is true as the scriptures cannot be broken, it implies that we all were created by God; for God. If you were created by God, then know that you are working for Him like it or not, believe me. But some deny this allegation because they don't go to church or they serve idols. Even the brothers of Joseph thought like that when they sold Joseph to Egypt. The Pharisees and the Romans thought like that together with the devil when they crucified Jesus. But in the end, Joseph said they meant evil but God meant good. Also, on the third day, they declared celebration for the fact that they had killed Him only to see Him taking part in the same celebration. You can never deny serving God. At best you can only serve Him.

"Alexander the coppersmith did me much harm. May the Lord repay him according to his works." (2Timothy 4:14)

If God is coming to pay us for our work, it means we are all working for Him. Get it straight; you cannot work for MTN and receive pay from Spectrum just because they are both telephone network companies. So, you cannot work for someone else and then be paid by God therefore if God is the rewarder then He is the employer.

"And the King will answer and say to them, 'Assuredly, I say to you, inasmuch as you did it to one of the least of these my brethren, you did it to Me.' "Then He will answer them, saying, 'Assuredly, I say to you, inasmuch as you did not do it to one of the least of these, you did not do it to Me.'(Matthew 25:31-46)

Beloved, do not avenge yourselves, but rather give place to wrath; for it is written, "Vengeance is Mine, I will repay," says the Lord. (Romans12:19)

In the parable of the goats and the sheep, Jesus in His speech makes me know that the way we treat each other is counted as service to God because those who fed the hungry were given an inheritance; while those who did not give to the hungry were punished. So, by this, it is clear that God is a rewarder because He is our employer. That is why He says "vengeance is mine I will repay". God is a judge (since we all work for him as the universal employer) both in heaven and on earth because He will punish even the angels who disobeyed Him. With that made clear, we will now talk of the three characteristics that make God a judge.

The Character of Truth

'Of whom we have much to say, and hard to explain, since you have become dull of hearing." (Hebrews5:11)

Some things indeed are hard to utter. Though there are difficult explanations in the world none to my opinion is harder than certain revealed truths. So, I pray you not to be dull of hearing.

'Pilate therefore said to Him, "Are You a king then?" Jesus answered, "You say rightly that I am a king. For this cause I was born, and for this cause I have come into the world, that I should bear witness to the truth. Everyone who is of the truth hears My voice." Pilate said to Him, "What

is truth?" And when he had said this, he went out again to the Jews, and said to them, "I find no fault in Him at all. (John18:37-38)

Jesus has been arrested and He is before Pilate. Then Pilate says, "Are you a king then?" Jesus answered; "you say that I am." The question I ask is this: How on earth did Jesus hear you are a king from Pilate? Jesus did not say, 'yes I am a king' but said you say rightly. When and how did Jesus hear that? Pilate had heard that Jesus was the king of the Jew as a rumor. So, when he met Jesus he thought, I now have the opportunity to clear my doubts. However, in expressing his doubt, he declared Jesus to be king. Why is that? It is so because Jesus is truth and truth doesn't have the ability to hear or receive doubt. Then in the very next verse, Pilate asked a direct question "what is truth?" If Jesus had time to explain truth to Pilate then it would have been easy for me now. And this is the only place in scripture where a direct question was asked on the subject of truth. What then is truth? I think that we will answer that big question from the very next sentence. I said earlier that Jesus is truth.

"Jesus said to him, "I am the way, the truth, and the life..." (John 14:6)

From this statement, it is clear that Jesus is the truth. Follow me stepwise. "*Is*" is a conjugated form of the verb "to be." According to this verb, if you are something, it means that thing is also you. From my own definition of 'to be' which is "Not different from" that phrase will read thus: Jesus is not different from the truth. Therefore, if you see Jesus, you have seen truth and if you see truth knows that you have seen Jesus. I leave you with an example. When they say a man is a madman, it means if you want to see madness go and see the man. Do not be scared. That will never be said of you in Jesus name. Thus, in that same light the scriptures declare:

"...And it is the Spirit who bears witness, because the Spirit is truth." (1John5:6)

Therefore, if the Holy Spirit is truth it means the same explanation, I gave earlier also goes for the Spirit of God. Let's do a bit of mathematics. If the Holy Spirit is truth and truth is Jesus it means the Holy Spirit is Jesus; isn't He? No. Not so right. If we take that to be right, then it will strip them of personality difference. However, I will tell you shortly the context in which that analysis is right. Look at this scripture.

"But when the Helper comes, whom I shall send to you from the Father, the Spirit of truth who proceeds from the Father, He will testify of Me.

(John 15:26)
I come forth from the Father and have come into the world..."
(John 16:28)
These verses are so clear on the origin of both Jesus (the Son (Word) of God) and the Holy Spirit, declaring that both of them came from the Father.

Hence, from the law of production or origin, if both Jesus and the Spirit are truth, it means that the Father is truth Himself.

For there are three that bear witness in heaven: the Father, the Word, and the Holy Spirit; and these three are one. (I John 5:7)
What are these three bearing witness to? They all bear witness to the truth. All these bring us to the first meaning of truth which states that

❖ *Truth is the law of God's oneness.*

The Oneness of God

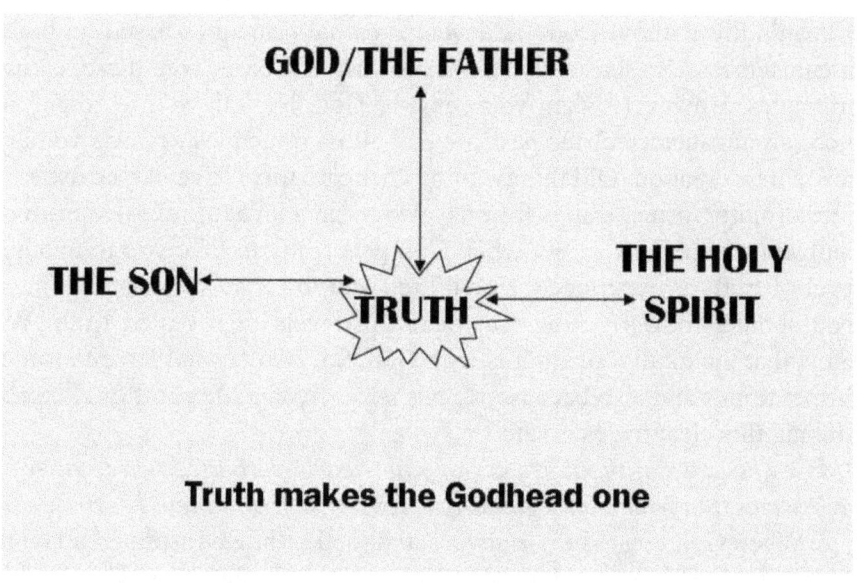

So, because of the law of truth, Jesus could say frankly that "I and my Father are one." They all have one operating law. So, it is impossible for the Son to do differently from the Father and likewise the Holy Spirit since they are all bound by the same law called Truth. Remember the first meaning of truth: the law of God's oneness or the principle of God's oneness.

"………. *who among them can declare this and show us former things? Let them bring forth their witness, that they may be justified or let them hear, and say it is truth. (Isaiah43:9)*

Secondly, if we chose the *"or"* part of this verse, we see that *'former things'* and *'it is truth'* fall to mean the same thing. So, it says, *'declare this and show us former things!'* let them hear and say, *"it is truth."'* Better still let them hear and agree that it is truth. Therefore the 'it' in that sentence stands for the truth. Then replacing 'it' with 'former things' the statement will read thus: "The former things are truth."
Now I will explain quickly before you misunderstand me. You must note that there is a difference between this "former things" and the one in the scripture below which says;

"Do not remember the former things. Nor consider the thing of old" (Isaiah43:18)

The former things of God and the former things of man are two different things. Firstly, the former things of man talk of experiences of man that he had or suffered, being far from God. Throughout the period of man's life without God, he develops carnal principles based on those circumstances. So basically, he lives his life based on these carnal principles. However, when you come to God, He tells you to forget all those circumstances of the past life and all its principles because you are now a new creation. Old things (of brother carnality) have passed away.
Furthermore, former things for men also mean a level of revealed truth or unpleasant experiences. So, when God gets ready to take you to another level of truth or experience, He will tell you to forget the former things. You should know by now that there are levels of revealed truth. We know that the totality of truth is with God. So, He does not have to forget former things and also because He has never lived a life short of Himself. Making this clearer, Jesus said,

"Moses because of the hardness of your hearts permitted you to divorce your wives, but from the beginning it was not so" (Matthew 19: 8)

When God created the Heavens and the Earth, He instituted a law to govern both Heaven and Earth. When Satan disobeyed God with his pride, the man also being deceived disobeyed God; by eating the fruit in the garden. So, the laws of both Heaven and Earth were altered so God instituted another law through Moses so that after a period of time, He will bring back the law that was from the beginning. So, when Jesus

THE DIVINE NATURE OF GOD

came, He said, "I did not come to break the law but to fulfill it." Therefore, the fulfillment of the law was the reestablishment of what He called the law of the beginning or the law of the former things.

❖ *Therefore, the law that existed before things went wrong is called Truth.*

Next, I give you the last but not the least meaning of truth.
"All things were made through Him, and without Him nothing was made that was made." (John1:3)
"Then God said "Let there be light" and there was light. (Genesis1:3)
By faith we understand that the worlds were framed by the word of God, so that the things which are seen were not made of things which are visible. (Hebrews11:3)

As the Bible rightly says, '*nothing was made without the word*' of God and the Word is truth as well as the Spirit is truth. It means God could not create the things that we now see without truth. So, truth is the law that governs creation. So, God said, "let there be light" and there was light. But like I said before, if we take it at that, it will give us a wrong impression of creation. If the light just appeared, then it means God was resting and did nothing for a whole day. Yet on the seventh day, He rested from all the work that He had done. It means He was working hard through all those days.

Therefore, whenever, God wants to create something He releases two truths from Himself (the Father).

We understand this in His partnership in the new creation life. When God spoke the Word, the Word went out of God it prepared the grounds or set the stage for the Spirit to act upon and then comes creation. If God wants to light a fire He will release the truth of the word and the truth of the Spirit. The truth of the Word will go first to the place, pour petrol on the place until it gets to the level that will produce the kind of fire that is needed, then He will allow the truth of the Spirit to strike the match and control the flames. Note that this process takes time just as it took God the whole day to create light on the Earth. This, therefore, introduces the principle of faith and patience which works with the truth.

.... God, who gives life to the dead and calls those things which do not

exist as though they did.' (Romans 4:17)
If God calls things that do not exist like they do; it means even when there was no light on the Earth, He called light as though it was. Until finally it paid off through patience. Then He saw it and said it was good. Maybe He even said that it was good before He even saw it. So according to this law of creation, God cannot lie.
That by two immutable things, in which it was impossible for God to lie, we might have a strong consolation... (Hebrews6:18)

- ❖ Thus, even if God says a lie, it will finally become true after some time.

For after a time of faith and patient waiting, that truth will create that thing. By this understanding 'true' and 'truth' have two different meanings. Sometimes 'true' agrees with 'truth' but most times they do not agree. This is because, 'truth' is the reality of what is in Heaven and is to come on Earth, while 'true' is the reality of what appears presently on Earth. Therefore, note that without faith and patience the creative ability of truth will be hindered.
That they all may be condemned who did not believe the truth but had pleasure in unrighteousness. (2Thessalonians2:12)
For this people's heart is waxed gross, and their ears are dull of hearing, and their eyes they have closed; lest at any time they should see with their eyes, and hear with their ears, and should understand with their heart, and should be converted, and I should heal them. (Matthew 13:15)
Since they did not believe or accept the word, they could not be recreated or converted. So, when God says a truth to a man; if the man believes it, that truth will create the purpose of that word in the man. Jesus said; *"and I will heal them."* What this really means is that 'He will have no option but to heal them,' because He honors His Word more than His name. To say it straight, the only thing in God's Word that makes Him honor it more than His name is the "law of truth" that's in it. It is impossible to have truth in you and not command God's attention. And the level of truth you have in you, determines the amount of God's attention you will command.

Finally, we see Angel Gabriel talking to the father of John the Baptist.
"But behold, you will be mute and not able to speak until the day these things take place, because you did not believe my words which will be

fulfilled in their own time." (Luke1:20)
Note that God never sent Angel Gabriel with punishment for Zechariah's unbelief. It was the Angel who said that by himself. However, as the bearer of truth to Zachariah, the truth that he spoke defended itself by making the word of Gabriel come to pass. So, anyone, be it an angel or a man who bears the truth, has authority and confidence in the truth in that any command they give personally based on that truth will never fall to the ground. Truth always defends itself wherever 'it' is spoken (note that truth is God). We, therefore, do not have to doubt why God was confirming the Word with signs following because truth always defends itself.

Quick note: after the truth which is the foundation of all divine judgments, then come the other two characters of God as a judge. At this point, I want you to know that the nature of God as a judge makes Him the sole rewarder of every work done or not done by us through our time on earth. However, this reward character is divided into two different distinct Characters called forgiver born out of mercy and "convictor" accuser born out of wrath or judgment.

The Character of the Forgiver

This character is flooded in the scriptures. It is therefore assumed that everyone will know but unfortunately some church folks still don't know about it. It is therefore important for me to remind you again about this special character of God that we all need. When God created the world He finished it with the satisfaction that all that He had made was good. In the end, He gave man a command not to eat the fruit of good and evil that was at the center of the garden. Many times, we have the tendency of asking questions which are not stupid, though they sound so.

This is the question. Why did God put the fruit in the garden in the first place? Or must there be a commandment? He could have just left Adam free to himself. After this, you will ask that question no more as I bring you to understanding. God had just created man with great responsibilities for him. As any father will do with his children God had to train him to maturity; before trusting great responsibilities into his hands. After he has learned obedience, he will put the responsibility of judging even Angels into his hand. For the record, God did not put the fruit in the garden as a trap but as an element of training. Since man did not obey but failed from the start, God thought of what He will do to remedy the situation. Also, He was in a twist in Himself between mercy and judgment.

For judgment is without mercy to the one who has shown no mercy. Mercy triumphs over judgment. (James 2:13)

After a long struggle within Himself, mercy finally overcame judgment. He then decided a merciful plan for man in order to reconcile man to Himself. Note that the issue of forgiveness with God has been a long process coming down for generations. First, He started out by killing all the people except for Noah and his household. After that, he said, "no this option is not good," so He vowed never to do that again. Then God came up with a great idea which is: if any man believes in me, I will count it to him as righteousness. He demonstrated this in Abraham but later instituted the law as a schoolmaster to preserve the people until the time of the fulfillment of this His great idea. During this period, God caused them to sprinkle blood for forgiveness. The blood indeed cleaned the people's flesh to the point that God forgave them.

For if the blood of bulls and goats and the ashes of a heifer, sprinkling the unclean, sanctifies for the purifying of the flesh, (Hebrews 9:13)

Later they will need to repeat the same things every year because it did not cleanse their conscience from dead works. In the dispensation of the fullness of time, the Bible says;

But God demonstrates His own love toward us, in that while we were still sinners, Christ died for us. (Romans 5:8)

One reason why people think that they qualify for God is that they don't know why He came. Listen, He came to save sinners, the lost and the poor. If you ever find yourself in God, know indeed that you were either poor, lost, a sinner or all three. Believe me! And He did so because He came with forgiveness in His heart for all of us.

"That is, that God was in Christ reconciling the world to Himself, not imputing their trespasses to them…" (2 Corinthians 5:19)

I don't know why some of us have not learned to take advantage of this privilege. Instead, some mock it. However, we know that if Jesus ever counted one of our sins against us, we could never become righteous. Thank God He didn't. However, some people come to places in their Christian walk that they feel condemned and refuse to accept God's forgiveness. So, I ask a question to such who err not knowing the scriptures or the power of God. When have you been most sinful in your life? They usually say before they were born again.

If Jesus could die for you while you were yet a sinner; is it now that you have become His child that He will not forgive you?

Only proud people, in my opinion, do not easily accept God's forgiveness. He has said sorrow for sin is acceptable. So, if you feel sorry simply renounce it. God will not change His mind. But not a proud person because he or she might have been pointing fingers on those that are weak not knowing that if he/she did not sin it was because of grace; for by strength no man shall prevail (1Samuel 2:9). Take note: with God, after the death and resurrection of Christ, every sin in the world was made atonement for. It means in the atonement of Jesus Christ before God; every sin or human wrong was dealt with. Hence forgiveness is no longer something God does. It is something He did a long time ago and kept in the heavenly places. As a matter of fact, God is done with the issue of forgiveness because in Christ He has already given it. So, as it stands, your forgiveness has been given in Christ Jesus for all eternity.

So, I say God will not forgive you, he has forgiven you; all you need do now is take it when or if you need it.

However, before I leave this subject, I want you to understand something crucial about God's forgiving attitude. Jesus told a parable of the unmerciful servant and concluded with these words:
"So My heavenly Father also will do to you if each of you from his heart does not forgive his brother his trespasses" (Matthew18:35)
Also in another place, *"Blessed are the merciful for they shall obtain mercy." (Matthew 5:7)*
We were all like the servant Jesus talked about in the parable. We were all guilty before God so much such that if He wanted to judge us accordingly, we will lose our lives, all that we have and all we call family. After all, it will not be enough. So, for God to be this merciful toward us in the way He forgave us, there is nothing greater we could ever ask for.
For this is like the waters of Noah to Me; For as I have sworn that the waters of Noah would no longer cover the earth, So have I sworn that I would not be angry with you, nor rebuke you. (Isaiah 54:9)
Now in Christ, God had compassion on you and forgave you all your sins. Brother, this is what the mercy of God has done for you and I. If the waters of Noah have not covered the earth know also that He

cannot be angry with you. Wow! So even when you are angry with yourself for doing wrong or sinning He is not even angry with you. God will never be angry with you for a mistaken sin. He is only angry when you decide to crucify Jesus the second time by readopting a sinful lifestyle. So, this is God's mind about the matter. If you have understood what He has done for you; you should also do the same to those who hurt you, so you can command more of His mercy. Why will God want us to be merciful to obtain mercy? Is it trade by Bata? No. No. No, a very big NO. Though it sounds like if we don't show mercy He will not show us mercy, the real sense is that He has shown us mercy and wants us to do the same to others; as a sign of gratitude to Him. Then He will through our gratitude and exemplary conduct, show us more and more of His mercy. God says; if you have tasted the privilege of forgiveness give your neighbor that same privilege when they wrong you. If not, God will consider that you have rejected His forgiveness or forgotten how He forgave you.

But I say unto you, Love your enemies, bless them that curse you, do good to them that hate you, and pray for them which despitefully use you, and persecute you; That ye may be the children of your Father which is in heaven: for he maketh his sun to rise on the evil and on the good, and sendeth rain on the just and on the unjust. (Matthew 5:44-45)

Next, God wants you to be merciful as proof that you are His son or daughter. If you are His son or daughter, God expects you to prove that through your act of mercy. Thirdly, He wants you to be an extension of His love to your enemies. By so doing you give them a chance to also want to know Him. In a case where we refuse to show mercy for whatever reason; God will also not show us mercy in the following ways:

a) God can bring back punishment for things that He had forgiven you for upon you again. Do not say hay! Did you not read from the parable how the Lord called back the unmerciful and re-punished him?

b) God would withdraw His grace from you to a certain measure just as it is said that our prayer can be hindered.

c) He can allow you to fall into a temptation He was supposed to save you from in the future. Brother, that is God for you as far as mercy is concerned you have been given so much so you need to act like you know that. Hope you understand.

The Character of the Convictor

Previously we talked about God's nature of truth. One of the characteristics of truth we talked about is the creative character of truth. We said from above that truth could appear wrong from the very beginning but through faith and patience truth will finally become true. Now because God is love, His love for us is always bigger than His wrath. Therefore, God always starts by introducing the truth of His kindness to us. When the truth of love fails before the truth of wrath can now come in.

Or do you despise the riches of His goodness, forbearance, and longsuffering, not knowing that the goodness of God leads you to repentance? (Romans 2:4)

And even as they did not like to retain God in their knowledge, God gave them over to a debased mind, to do those things which are not fitting; (Romans 1:28)

Therefore, God expects us to never despise His goodness as it says in another place;

"Today, if you will hear His voice, do not harden your hearts." (Hebrews 4:7)

Why is that? It is so because God sends the truth of kindness first to you so that it will prepare you. Then when judgment or reward meets you, forgiveness and grace will reign over punishment. When it comes to conviction there are two major levels. Before we get to that; what is conviction to start with? Conviction is the ability to show clearly to someone that he/she has done something right or wrong before you reward (punish or award) them. By this, you recognize that conviction is in both positive and negative levels. The reason is they have to be convicted to accept that your judgment is fair or just. Looking at the two types of conviction, we have:

a) **Conviction unto Repentance:** The reason for this first level of conviction is that; if people do not know what they have done wrong, they cannot ask for forgiveness. Now if a man does not ask for forgiveness God cannot give it to him. For this reason, God is very patient with people because he wants them to repent.

The LORD is merciful and gracious, Slow to anger, and abounding in mercy. (Psalm103:8)

God has abundant kindness. Only God can be God because sometimes you see evil and are fed up to death with your friends, parents, children, politicians, etc. Then you ask the question; what in heaven is God doing? Is He blind? The above scripture says that He is as different from men (not us because we are like Him now) as heaven is from the earth in every greatness. Also, know that God loved and valued the world such that he even gave up his only son to save them. So, is it not logical that you will be patient with someone you already paid a great price for? Then how great will God's sluggishness be from the world's? God is sluggish to get angry because at the point where God is fed up He still gives one more chance. Jesus told a parable to this effect saying

...A certain man had a fig tree planted in his vineyard; and he came and sought fruit thereon, and found none. Then said he unto the dresser of his vineyard, Behold, these three years I come seeking fruit on this fig tree, and find none: cut it down; why cumbereth it the ground? And he answering said unto him, Lord, let it alone this year also, till I shall dig about it, and dung it: And if it bear fruit, well: and if not, then after that thou shalt cut it down. (Luke13:6-9)

Understand God. If a day to Him is like a thousand to us and vice versa then He stays for three years to get angry. Then in that His anger, part of Him (the keeper) tells Him to give another year and He accepts. Note that at this level, God convicts both unbelievers and believers alike.

Now, because this conviction is not the final judgment conviction; it is made by God to prepare people for change before the final judgment.

Therefore, it is in two phases. First, He will convict an unbeliever. If the unbeliever repents; he becomes born again. Hence this is the conviction that makes a man born again. If you refuse this conviction then God allows you for the second conviction. Secondly, after you become born again, because of His pruning work in your life He will convict you at different stages of your Christian walk so you can repent from carnal practices and dead works as you grow to become a mature and perfect Christian. So, Christians who submit to this conviction accept God's chastisement; while those who refuse become bastard children of God and are taken away as Jesus puts it.

Every branch in Me that does not bear fruit He takes away; and every

branch that bears fruit He prunes, that it may bear more fruit. (John15:2)

Note that this conviction happens only when you are still alive on Earth. A good example of this is when God sent Jonah to Nineveh. When he told them of God's judgment, they became convicted and repented; turning away the wrath of God. However, you know Jonah was angry with God for being so (stupidly) merciful.

    b) **Conviction unto Final Judgement:** This conviction could happen in this lifetime but most of it is at the final judgment. This is different from the first in that God does not give you the option to repent any longer. At this level, whatever you are convicted with will be your reward; be it good or bad. *...did it not to one of the least of these, ye did it not to me. (Matthew 25:45)* It is very clear from the scriptures above that God took time to explain to them both good and bad. However, He did not give them any chance to repent again. That is why this conviction is called final judgment conviction.

And as it is appointed for men to die once, but after this the judgment, (Hebrews 9: 27). For the wages of sin is death but the gift of God is eternal life in Christ Jesus our Lord. (Romans6:23)

You have to understand that God's final judgment will come at the end of this present world. So, God's kindness prevails over a man for a limited time. We understand that there will be a final judgment after the second coming of Jesus. But sometimes God could pass a final judgment on a man's life even before his death. At this stage, it will be difficult for those concerned to see the truth anymore since God hardens or blinds their eye forever not to see the truth.

This happened to Saul the king. When Samuel had prayed for him after a long time God told Samuel to stop praying seeing He will not change His mind and Saul died in the curse. Judas is also a good example, for after God had closed the door of repentance toward him an evil spirit entered him and he sold Jesus. So, the wages of all sin is death just as the gift of God or righteousness is eternal life in Christ. However, in all that you suffer due to your sins, there is still the possibility of forgiveness, transformation, change, and blessing as long as God's final verdict has not yet been passed on you.

Now, this final verdict is pronounced by the wrath of God as it is written, 'give place for wrath.' Now even though mercy always overcomes judgment, the wrath of God is the level of God's judgment that overcomes mercy. This is so because when God is fed up waiting on you to change, to no avail, His wrath or anger will be aroused against you. At which point mercy cannot help you anymore.

To conclude; conviction unto repentance is very vital for you and me today. For it is the expression of or the announcement of God's punishment to come. It is like the signpost that says danger is ahead of you, use the deviation. It can come from your conscience or heart as the Bible says, *"for if our heart condemns us, God is greater than our hearts and knows, all things" (1John3:20)* or it could come from another person with the Word of God rebuking you, as it says, *"when you hear the word of God do well not to harden your hearts" (Hebrews 3:8)*. After the death and resurrection of Jesus as the scriptures says, everyone who is of the world is guilty. *"And when He has come, he will convict the world of sin, and of righteousness, and of Judgment. (John16:18)*

Therefore, if you are not in Christ you are of the world and are guilty on all fronts. If you do well; the Holy Spirit will convict you. If you do badly He will convict you. If you judge He will convict you. So being in the world or loving the world is real enmity to God. Hence the Holy Spirit came to announce to the world that trouble is coming, run, no place is safe anymore except in Christ. Yet under God's rewards or judgment program, there is both good and bad conviction as well as good and bad rewards. So, if you have done well, He will judge or reward you with good. But if you did evil you will also get an evil reward or punishment; first in this life and the one to come. So be warned you who stand with God making sure you are doing everything to stand firm to the end.

THE DIVINE NATURE OF GOD

The Judgment system of God

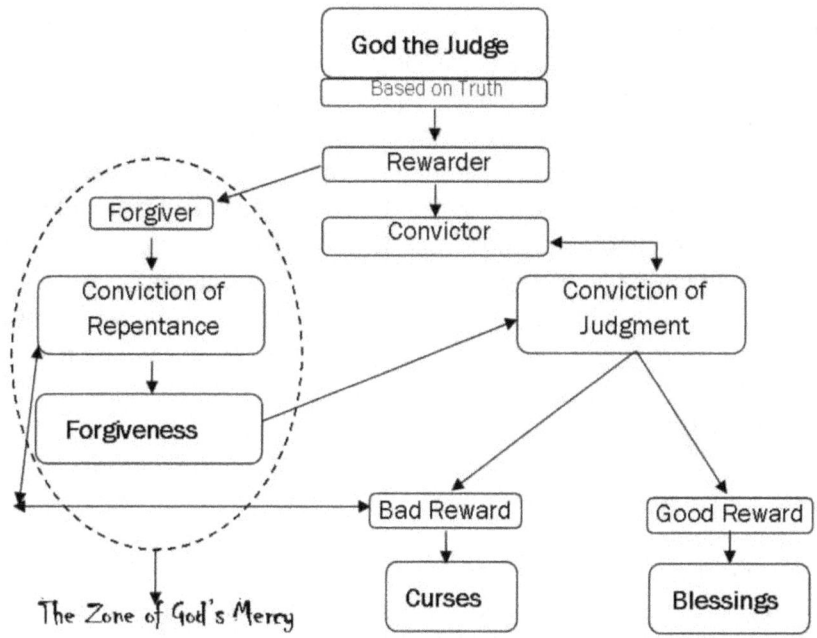

The Judge Connection

If we have believed from the beginning that we share in God's divine nature, then it is important to believe also that you are a judge even as He is a judge. After all, there are judges of men in every country in the world. Hence this section is not just to announce to us that we are also judges but to tell us how, where and when our nature as judges should operate. To begin with, we should know that the is a time and a place where we are and will be full judges.
Now I say that the heir, as long as he is a child, does not differ at all from a slave, though he is master of all, (Galatians 4: 1)
But as many as received him, to them gave he power to become the sons of God, (John1:12) For as many as are led by the Spirit of God, these are sons of God. (Romans 8:14)
"But if you are led by the Spirit, you are not under the law" (Galatians 5:18)

Thus, scriptures tell us clearly that though you are an heir to the judgment seat of God if you are a child you cannot exercise real judgment because you do not differ from a servant. The next scripture tells us that we were given the power to become sons. Hence God expects us to grow. Then if those that are led by the Spirit of God are sons of God; it means they have come of age to take their judgment responsibilities. Remarkably, the next scripture says being led we are not under the law. So, you can be a child of God and still be under the law because you are not led by the Spirit of God. I give you an example. If a state judge is convicted for fraud and is given a six months prison term, for all the time that he is in prison. Though he is a state judge, he cannot act like it because he is under the law. From the fact that we grow by faith, the level of faith you have will determine the level of judgment you can exercise.

Secondly talking of where it is written:

Who hath delivered us from the power of darkness, and hath translated us into the kingdom of his dear Son: (Colossians1:13)

We ought to know that we are now in a new kingdom (i.e. the kingdom of light and of His dear son). This is the only kingdom in which we can exercise our authority as Judges. So long as we stay in the light, we have rights to judge. This kingdom of His dear son is what is called heavenly places or Zion.

...raised us up together, and made us sit together in the heavenly places in Christ Jesus. (Ephesians2:6)

To get the place without its nature will not leave us with a clear understanding.

For we do not wrestle against flesh and blood, but against principalities, against powers, against the rulers of the darkness of this age, against spiritual hosts of wickedness in the heavenly places. (Ephesians 6:12)

So, this kingdom is spiritual and our magistracy cannot be different. So, we do not judge against flesh and blood. Although our judgment influences flesh and blood; it is not at the level of flesh and blood that we judge. Therefore, we ought to be spiritual in our judgment and not carnal for if we exercise carnality in judgment, our judgment will not stand. A Cameroonian judge cannot just go to Ghana and enter any court of his choice and start judging cases. He will be arrested for madness, wouldn't he? Now talking of the how we just have to know one thing

"But the just shall live by his faith" (Hebrews2:4)

If sound judgment is part of your livelihood, it means your

judgment can never be true, real or effective without faith. So, if you ask me how? I will say by faith. As simple as that! However, as we discuss the other characters you will understand more about the how of our judgment personality and rights.

Starting with the nature of truth we find out that we were born of an incorruptible seed even the Word of God. Also, in the gospel of John, Jesus said he that is born of the Spirit is spirit. Thus, if the Word of God and the Spirit of God which gave birth to us are both truth, it means that by birth we also are truth. This is true because he that is born of truth is truth.

Our Oneness with God

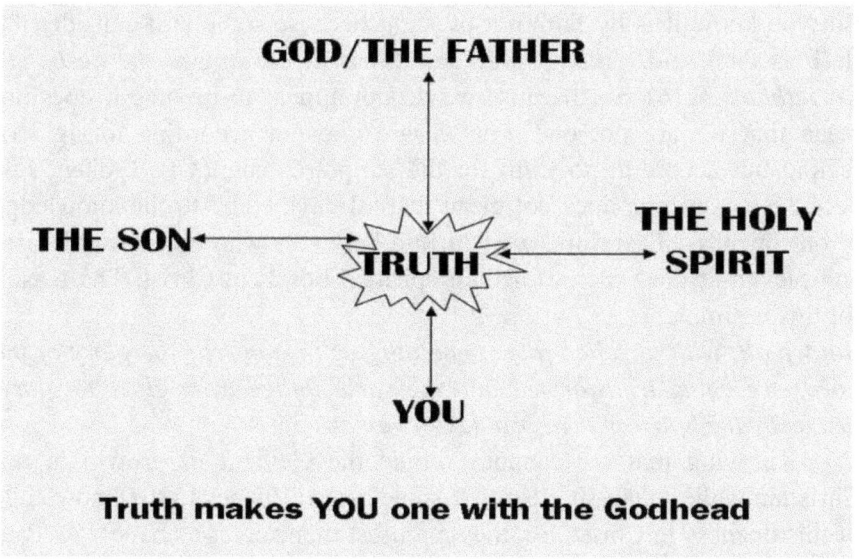

So, if we all agree to this, then we can start analyzing the nature of the truth that is in us and its functionality. If you remember well, we started by talking on the fact that truth is the law or element of God's oneness. So, it is possible that if we also are truth, then there should be a way that this oneness also applies to us. How?
That they all may be one, as You, Father, are in Me, and I in You; that they also may be one in Us, that the world may believe that You sent Me. And the glory which You gave Me I have given them, that they may be one just as We are one: (John 17: 21-22)
Jesus is praying to the Father for us who are going to believe His words

after He has gone, saying; "that they also may be one in us." Then He says, "I in them and you in me that they may be made perfect in one. Wow! *So we, being many, are one body in Christ, and individually members of one another. (Romans 12:5)*
There is neither Jew nor Greek, there is neither slave nor free, there is neither male nor female; for you are all one in Christ Jesus. (Galatians 3:28)

    The scripture says it expressly, that we are members one to another. Also, it states that we are one in Christ Jesus. This oneness as it is stated breaks across traditional, language, sexual, professional, national, cultural, financial, political and all other socio-cultural and spiritual barriers that separate people in this world. Hence when we are all born of God and of truth, we are from that point not different from each other. But you know it is by faith not by sight because some still consider the flesh as Paul said, *"though we knew Christ according to the flesh," (2 Corinthians 5:16)*. So, because we do not appear to be one, it does not mean that we are not one. For we are one not according to sight or feeling but according to truth for the scriptures cannot be broken. Just because we are one does not mean that all have come to the knowledge of our oneness. Therefore, we still find believers who promote tribalism and racism at the expense of their spiritual bonds in Christ. The reason for this is simple.

But we all, with unveiled face, beholding as in a mirror the glory of the Lord, are being transformed into the same image from glory to glory, just as by the Spirit of the Lord. (2Corinthians 3:18)

    Knowing that we cannot exclude the element of growth in our Christian walk, makes it clear that some are still babes to the knowledge of this oneness in Christ. So, they manifest themselves as babes. As Paul rightly puts it, "When I was a child" I acted like a child." In attesting to this, the scripture talks of the ministries that are meant to build the saints in this wise.

For the equipping of the saints for the work of ministry, for the edifying of the body of Christ till we all come to the unity of the faith..." (Ephesians 4:12 & 13a)

    Thus, we have to grow to become united in the faith. Until we can come to the place where we can stand for the saints; even at the expense of our blood relationships, we have not yet known the true meaning of the body of Christ. Is that too hard to say? Jesus said in the hearing of His mother that it is those who hear the Word of God and obey it that are

His real relations. Are you now greater than Jesus?

So let us grow up to know that: *Now, therefore, you are no longer strangers and foreigners, but fellow citizens with the saints and members of the household of God, (Ephesians 2:19)*

The next thing to note about truth is the fact that it is the law and nature of things from the very beginning. I want us to understand this mystery that has already been revealed

For we who have believed do enter that rest, as He has said: "So I swore in My wrath, 'They shall not enter My rest,'" although the works were finished from the foundation of the world (Hebrews 4:3)

...I will open my mouth in parables, I will utter things kept secret from the foundation of the world. (Matthew 13:35)

All who dwell on the earth will worship him, whose names have not been written in the Book of life of the lamb slain from the foundation of the world. (Revelation 13:8)

The works of God or all the happenings in the world today were finished from the foundations of the world. The Bible makes us know that even the kingdom of God we are waiting for had been prepared from the foundations of the world. So, what then? Just because it has been a secret, does not mean it is new. Everything was prepared and kept secret from the beginning and when the time for the manifestation of any comes; God then reveals it to us.

For we are His workmanship, created in Christ Jesus for good works... (Ephesians 2:10)

Thus, if we died with Him and it is true that He died from the foundations of the world, it, therefore, implies that we died from the foundations of the world. So, our recreation was before the world began. How do you know, you may ask? It is impossible to know something that does not exist. But God says, "For whom I foreknew, I also predestined to be conformed to the image of my son, that he might be the firstborn among many brethren"

Therefore, God had foreknowledge or an idea of who we were to be before He laid the foundation of the world. So He planned correctly the kind of life you will live through predestination. Thus, you are the revelation of that which had been kept secret from the beginning. So, brethren when God said in Genesis let us make man, you are the man that He saw. You are the man He made. However, He chose to start with Adam and kept you as a secret to be revealed in such a time as this.

Hence if truth is the law of the beginning, then you are the life of the beginning, praise God.

Furthermore, we talked of the creative power of truth, and how the power cannot function without faith and patience. Looking at the way truth manifest in us we see two main areas of its manifestation
1) The place of prayer and
2) Our declarations.

The Place of Prayer

First, I want us to understand here that prayer was instituted for communication between man and God. This I say communication of all kinds. Note that communication to God means in simple terms "involvement." So if you are doing something for which you want God's involvement, the means by which you get God involved is called prayer. With this understanding, we see that prayer is both verbal and nonverbal, visible and invisible, spiritual and physical. There is much we can talk about prayer but for the sake of this write up we will limit ourselves to what is relevant. The place of prayer also is in two parts:

a) **The fellowship ground:**
And to make all see what is the fellowship of the mystery, which from the beginning of the ages has been hidden in God who created all things through Jesus Christ; (Ephesians 3:9)

Prayer was instituted to make us have fellowship with the mystery that was hidden from the beginning. Why is that? It is because we are now in God and need to see the relationship that we have with Him. I have a great interest in the word "see." You too might have this same interest though you might not know. God said to Abraham, "as far as you can see, I have given to you." So, God was indeed saying I can only give you what you can see (with which eyes?) with your spiritual eyes.

Therefore, the word 'to see' at the level of the spirit is what we call experience at the level of the physical. So, through prayers, we are having an experience of fellowship with the mysteries that are hidden in God. Note that God did not remove the mysteries from within Him. He just took us to where the mysteries were hidden (that is in Him). So, by prayer, we enter into the storeroom of mysteries in God to have or experience the mysteries.

Therefore, we ourselves are becoming a mystery because we are being transformed into the image of the mysteries.

The mysteries were made mysteries because they were hidden in God.
... the fellowship of the Holy spirit be with you all Amen" (2Corinthians 13:14)

From this, we see that God wants us to fellowship with His Spirit. Hence He wants us to have a day and night relationship with the Holy Spirit. Prayer is one of the means by which we build our relationship with the Holy Spirit. Communion with the Holy Spirit means we should come to unity with the Holy Spirit. Then by that unity, we will understand and work together with Him.

Can two walk together, unless they are agreed? (Amos3:3)

If the Holy Spirit must work with us, we must come to the place of agreement (communion) with Him. Prayer, therefore, is the place where this agreement is worked out.

b) The giving ground:

The law of prayer is controlled by the law of love (according to me) which states that: "you can never take from something or someone you love; you can only give". So, the giving ground which is the place of asking and receiving is controlled by the law of love. When we are in church, sometimes we say I catch it, I take it by force. Mind you that when Jesus said the violent shall take it by force; He was saying that if we become violent, we will take by force from the place of the violence. But you know that the kingdom of God cannot suffer violence from God Himself. So, don't get it wrong. You cannot take it by force from God.

Jesus said: *"Therefore I say unto you, what things soever ye desire, when ye pray, believe that ye receive them, and ye shall have them" (Mark 11:24).*

Please follow me discreetly. A man can only receive from God when he has given something. Likewise, God can only receive from man after He has given him something. So, the law of love bounds, even God. If you hold God in the law of love you cannot miss, *'For God so loved the world that He gave His only begotten Son, that whoever believes in Him should not perish but have everlasting life' (John3:16).* "*Most assuredly, I say to you, unless a grain of wheat falls into the ground and dies, it remains alone; but if it dies, it produces much grain. (John12:24)*

So, for God to receive us as sons in glory, He gave His only son. While the son, in turn, gave His life to receive glory and become the Head of the Church. So, if a man gives according to love, he cannot go without receiving. When you ask something from God, be sure you go with something to give. Before you misunderstand me, let me explain.

.... for he who comes to God must believe that he is and that he is a rewarder of those who diligently seek Him. (Hebrews11:6)

When we go, therefore, to God we must know Him. Why? Because there is something special you can only give to someone when you know them. That thing is called Trust. So, if you ever ask God something without giving Him trust, believe me, you will never receive it. According to the law of love, if you do not give, you can't receive.

Hence you must give God your trust to get or receive anything from God. and trust can only come from knowledge. So, you can only receive from God according to the level of knowledge you have of him.

That said let's move to the second one.

Our Declarations:

Mind you that our declarations are a form of prayer themselves. They also show proof of the level of trust we have in the word of God.

Your words have been stout against me, saith the LORD. Yet ye say, What have we spoken so much against thee? Ye have said, It is vain to serve God: and what profit is it that we have kept his ordinance, and that we have walked mournfully before the LORD of hosts? And now we call the proud happy; yea, they that work wickedness are set up; yea, they that tempt God are even delivered. Then they that feared the LORD spake often one to another: and the LORD hearkened, and heard it, and a book of remembrance was written before him for them that feared the LORD, and that thought upon his name. (Malachi3:13-16) What is this scripture talking about?

Scripture is just making us know that we pray all the time.

Know that God hears what we say to one another, to ourselves and even what we think. The good part about it is not just the fact that He hears, but the fact that He reacts to it. If not He will not say a book of remembrance was opened in line with what they said. Remember, they were not praying. They were just talking one to another.

Now to Him who is able to do exceedingly abundantly above all that we ask or think, according to the power that works in us (Ephesians 3:20)
Therefore, God considers our imaginations and thoughts when answering our prayer. Mind you, we are talking about declarations, not thoughts.
Death and life are in the power of the tongue ... (Proverbs 18:21)

Brethren as big as death may be, and as bigger and greater life may be, the Word of God says they are all subjected to the power of the tongue. In other words, they cannot function without the permission of your tongue. This is great. So, if you speak death it will come alive for you and you will eat its fruit, but if you speak life it will come alive in you and you will eat its fruits. The Word of God makes it clear that we shall be judged for every word that comes out of our mouth (Matthew 12:36). For this, some only think it will happen on the last day. But that could be very misleading.

"For with what judgment you judge, you will be judged; and with the measure you use, it will be measured back to you. (Matthew 7:2)

Therefore, if we look or consider judgment from the above scripture as measurement, we recognize that the level or quality of life we live on earth is based on the weight of our words or the measure of our words.

For example, if a believer speaks or declares 10% life and 90% death, that is what he/she will experience on Earth.

You will also declare a thing, and it will be established for you, so light will shine on your ways. (Job 22:28)

The Word of God is clear on this, 'you will declare and I will establish.' Therefore, if you declare the wrong thing God will not establish the right one. The wrong that you declare, you will get. Jesus said to Peter, "whatever you bind on earth shall be bound in heaven," did He mean bind as with a rope? No. No. No. With your words or mouth!
But what does it say? "The word is near you, in your mouth and in your heart" (that is, the word of faith which we preach) (Romans 10:8)
If we confess with our mouths and believe in our hearts, the mountain will be buried in the sea. And we know without faith it is impossible to please God. So, what is faith in this context?

Faith is keeping your declaration consistent with the word of truth until you see it come to pass. This is different from casting out demons in that it is making sure all your daily conversations are based on God's word.

That you do not become sluggish, but imitate those who through faith and patience inherit the promises. (Hebrews 6:12). For you have need of endurance so that after you have done the will of God you may receive the promise. (Hebrews 10: 36)

The scriptures warn that we do not become sluggish in our spiritual responsibility but that by endurance we should imitate those who through faith and patience inherit the promises after doing the will of God. So, while we keep our confession, we must be engaged in a spiritual search for His will because it is after doing His will that we can obtain the promises. Talking of consistency, the Bible says, "*but let your yes, be yes and your "No" "No" lest you fall into judgment.* If you are asked or do declare something let your word about that issue be the same for all time do not say yes today and no tomorrow lest you fall into temptation.

Where the word of a king is, there is power, and who may say to him what are you doing? (Ecclesiastes 8: 4)

We have been made judges unto God. Therefore, anywhere our word is, power is there to perform that for which the word is released. Yet some have not learned to say or maintain their yes until they see the promised miracle.

Do not let your mouth cause your flesh to sin, nor say before the messenger of God that it was an error. Why should God be angry at your excuse and destroy the work of your hands? (Ecclesiastes 5:6)

Let your confession or declaration be yes, yes or no, no all the time. Do not confess according to what you see or feel because you will have to say to the angels; it was an error. Without faith, we cannot please God because our doubtfulness will mar us and make Him angry all the time.

The heart of the righteous studies how to answer, but the mouth of the wicked pours forth evil. (Proverbs 15:28)

Hence, we need to learn and train ourselves to know what to say or what to declare in every circumstance and/or conversation. By so doing, through studies and practice; we will come to the place of understanding, knowing what to say at every situation and circumstance. Then you will align yourself to His word, "Let the weak say, 'I am strong." Are you weak? Then you must learn to say that you are strong. Are you sick? Then you have to learn to say I am healed. Are you poor? Then you must learn to say I am rich. When we all learn this faith principle, then the Word of God that says the mouth of the upright will deliver them will come true for us. Then God will be pleased because His desire is that we all prosper in Him and have answers to all our prayers.

That said we now have to talk about the nature of our connection with God as forgivers. Jesus said to someone "may your sins be forgiven you." The Pharisees were angry with Him for saying that. Then He said to them; "which one is easy to say: your sin is forgiven or rise up and walk?" Before we conclude that analysis, we need to see the reason behind the anger of the Pharisees. In the days of the law, only the priests were given or had the right to cleans people from sin. The priests were from the tribe of Aaron, but we all know that Jesus came from the Tribe of Judah according to the flesh. So how did Jesus start forgiving the sins of people when He was not a priest and He was not using blood as the priests did in the temple?

It came to pass in those days that Jesus came from Nazareth of Galilee, and was baptized by John in the Jordan. (Mark 1:9)

The LORD has sworn and will not relent, "You are a priest forever according to the order of Melchizedek. (Psalm110: 4)

Jesus therefore became a priest by an oath; He did not have to come through the lineage of Aaron. However, to confirm the oath of God over His life, John being a priest conferred on him the priesthood on the day of baptism. Therefore, Jesus became a priest according to the order of Melchizedek (no father no mother).

But that you may know that the Son of Man has power on earth to forgive sins (Luke 5:24) For as the Father has life in Himself, so He has granted the Son to have life in Himself, and has given Him authority to execute judgment also, because He is the Son of Man. (John5:26-27)

We know God has willed the Earth to the sons of men and cannot come into the Earth to deal directly without passing through a man. Hence Jesus being the son of man said I have the power to forgive sins on the Earth because I am the son of man.

And has made us kings and priests to His God and Father, to Him be glory and dominion forever and ever. Amen. (Revelation1: 6)

So, we see that through Jesus we have received the ordination into the priesthood.

Therefore, as priests unto God, He has given us authority to judge in the Earth. The scriptures make us understand; we are now sons of God like Jesus was. Also, we are sons of men: so, we have the ability to forgive sins for people here on Earth. This is not forgiveness for someone who wrongs you. Note that this is not what I mean.

It means that we have the ability to forgive people in the place of God.

*If you forgive the sins of any, they are forgiven them......" (John20:23)
Now whom you forgive anything, I also forgive. For if indeed I have forgiven anything, I have forgiven that one for your sakes in the presence of Christ, (2Corinthians2:10)*

Thus, God will forgive any man we forgive here on Earth; in heaven. Therefore He commands us to forgive, like Him. This we will do; by learning to do good to those who hate us and not to reward evil for evil anymore. In so doing, we will be the children of our heavenly Father. Even as we know the principle of mercy, we, therefore, have to forgive more according to this statement of Jesus which says,
Then his lord, after that he had called him, said unto him, O thou wicked servant, I forgave thee all that debt, because thou desiredst me: Shouldest not thou also have had compassion on thy fellowservant, even as I had pity on thee? And his lord was wroth, and delivered him to the tormentors, till he should pay all that was due unto him. So likewise shall my heavenly Father do also unto you, if ye from your hearts forgive not everyone his brother their trespasses. (Matthew18:32-35)

Again, Jesus said another parable that concluded on the principle that if you do not forgive, God also will not forgive you. Therefore, we must learn to forgive from the heart as God also has forgiven us from our own sins and wrongs against Him. So, let us extend that forgiveness to our brothers and sisters.

To conclude; this is the logic: forgive as long as you remember how much He has forgiven you.

If there are any people that will not forgive it will be the proud. That is why pride goes before a fall. A proud man feels that he merits God's grace and boasts a lot of things on his strength and abilities. Therefore, he expects everybody around him to be responsible for everything they do wrong. So, a proud man does not easily receive the mercy of God because of his philosophy of unforgiveness. Hence, because most proud people are unmerciful, they also scarcely receive mercy. Therefore, God is forced to resist them. Please learn to forgive, I know it does not feel good sometimes but once you give yourself to that new man of forgiveness in you, you will grow to feel better about it for whenever you forgive you are being a forgiver just as God is manifest towards you. By this I mean forgive them because you love them and not so God will forgive you for in that there is no benefit since you did it for yourself.

There are some Christians today in the world who wish a lot of things and some time they wish ill luck or misfortune for some people. Some even go as far as praying for the death of their enemies. What a shame? Though you might be doing that sincerely, you might just find out later or after reading that you have been sincerely wrong. When conviction comes to us, we should know that there is conviction unto repentance and conviction unto punishment. Note that God has committed to us the conviction of repentance and of punishment. Yet He did not commit it to us in the way that some are using it now. This I say because He said:

Beloved, do not avenge yourselves, but rather give place to wrath; for it is written, "vengeance is mine, I will repay," says the Lord. (Romans12:19)

Therefore, I will like to explain the conviction of judgment to us. God starts by calling us beloved. Those who are Christ's are called Beloved because they have taken the form of Gods' first son. Therefore, they ought to as the scripture says, depart from iniquity. One of these iniquities in the church is what I make clear to you today. The very next phrase says: "do not avenge yourselves but rather give place to wrath." Wrath is the anger of God. If God was telling this person not to avenge themselves; it means they were avenging themselves. By this they were making free, people who were convicted for God's anger. Why is that?

Since it is a righteous thing with God to repay with tribulation those who trouble you, (2Thessalonians1:6)

If it is righteous for God to repay; it means He has not given us the right to repay anyone without Him. Even though God knew that people will trouble you on Earth, yet He reserved the power to avenge you with Him. This might be difficult for those who do not have the love of God in them. Know that this law is based on God's choosing ability.

For He says to Moses, "I will have mercy on whomever I will have mercy, and I will have compassion on whomever I will have compassion." (Romans 9:15)

What then is the meaning of this? You should understand that you are with God now because He revealed Himself to you. Thus, you ought to have some compassion for those who don't know Him. Now you must stop acting as if it was because you had something more than they that He chose you. As a matter of fact, you should understand that if it were based only on qualification, God will never choose you. Thank God that you were one of the base things in the world of whom the scriptures speak in this wise: out of the mouth of babes you have perfected praise (Psalm 8:2). Don't you feel sorry for them that will be punished for the same mistakes for which you have been forgiven? You were not different from them, but for the Grace of God, that is now on you. You must now learn to rejoice with those who rejoice and weep with those who weep.

Rejoice with those who rejoice, and weep with those who weep. (Romans12:15)

And if one member suffers, all the members suffer with it; or if one member is honored, all the members rejoice with it. (1Corinthians12:26):

I find this even more carnal and sorrowful when we are happy in the misfortune of a fellow brother in the Lord. But we are not all grown yet: so, some are still so childish that they rejoice when one of their members suffers. May God forgive you if you have been in that boat. Please save yourself from the company of such, for it is reasonable for you to be angry with someone. However, to be happy that something bad happened to them is proof that if that person was in your power you would have rewarded them with evil. Make no mistake I understand that there are some evil people who must be destroyed for our course to prosper. Those who have set themselves to destroy the legacy of God do not truly deserve our mercy since God is against them already. But I speak concerning brethren who make mistakes or ordinary people who out of ignorance despise or hurt you. God said do not let the sun go down on your anger. By this, He was saying do not let your anger turn to hate. What does it say concerning them that are out of the house? Jesus said, *"but I say to you, love your enemies, bless those who curse you, do good to those who hate you, and pray for those who spitefully use you and persecute you"* (Matthew5:43-45).

Therefore "if your enemy is hungry, feed him if he is thirsty, give him a drink; For in so doing you will heap coals of fire on his head." (Romans 12:20)

Jesus is in this scripture explaining the meaning of giving place to wrath. Saying we should not treat others based on the way they treat us, but should be perfect even as God is perfect. By this, He said if we love only those who love us it is no news at all in the world because that is what the unbelievers do. Then Paul tells us to give food to our enemies, showing them that we are not like them. By doing so, we will prepare them for God's judgment: either unto repentance or condemnation. Since it is righteous for God to repay; we should not repay evil for evil to anyone. Again, talking of conviction unto judgment, Jesus says

And whosoever shall not receive you, nor hear your words, when ye depart out of that house or city, shake off the dust of your feet. Verily I say unto you, It shall be more tolerable for the land of Sodom and Gomorrha in the day of judgment, than for that city. (Matthew 10:14-15)

Therefore, if you preach to people and they do not accept your word, do not take it personally. Note that you are not alone doing what you are doing. So, because you did not preach for yourselves; allow the one who sent you to be angry with them. Is He not the one who said that anyone who receives you receives Him? Stop behaving like you had hidden agendas and allow God to punish them if He must. Instead, you have to feel sorry for them because they will perish if they do not come to the saving knowledge of Christ.

When you go out with His Word and you are rejected, dust your feet and leave them with God.

Concerning the conviction of love; the Bible says
Now I rejoice, not that you were made sorry, but that your sorrow led to repentance. For you were made sorry in a godly manner, that you might suffer loss from us in nothing. For godly sorrow produces repentance leading to salvation, not to be regretted; but the sorrow of the world produces death. (2Corinthians 7:9-10)

We know that God was in Christ reconciling the world to Himself not counting their sins against them. So, the good news in the gospel is the fact that it convicts us with the forgiveness clause. Therefore, God is in the gospel making us recognize our sin and see the need for us to come to Him. So, Paul said, "I rejoice not for the fact that you cried when you heard the truth of the gospel, but I rejoice for the fact that it made you have the kind of sorrow that makes a man reconcile himself with God." This conviction of love is what makes a man, see his emptiness and receives God's forgiveness through Christ in his life. God never wants us to feel sorry for nothing. He always makes us sorry so that we can see how bad we have been doing. And that at the end we will come to Him, obtain mercy for the wrong and be able to find grace not to leave like that anymore.

...and if in anything you think otherwise, God will reveal even this to you.' (Philippians3:15)

If God sees you in wrong (like the Roman centurion to whom God sent Peter was), He will send someone to reveal Him to you. That Word will convict you and make you ask the famous question that people often ask: what then shall I do? The conviction of love has two sorrows; the Godly part and the Worldly part. The Godly part is the one we just talked about. In which God said; "if I say I will destroy a man and you warn him: if he repents, he will be free from destruction." However, the worldly part works death.

Do not cover your lips and do not eat man's bread of sorrow. (Ezekiel 24:17b)

He said this to exclude us from the death that always follows worldly sorrow. But there is something more to worldly sorrow than this.

But whoever causes one of these little ones who believe in Me to sin, it would be better for him if a millstone were hung around his neck, and he were drowned in the depth of the sea. (Matthew18:6)

In this part of the story, Jesus is telling us that God's best punishment for those who wrong you is that the man is drowned in the sea. For God that is the best punishment, He can give for such a crime. Still, I want you to understand me in this:

Let the high praises of God be in their mouth, and a two-edged sword in their hand, to execute vengeance on the nations, and punishments on the peoples; to bind their kings with chains, and their nobles with fetters of iron; to execute on them the written judgment-This honor have all His saints. Praise the LORD! (Psalm149:6-9)

We first heard that vengeance is mine, says the Lord, now the scriptures make us know that God has given us the responsibility to execute the written judgment on the peoples. Is God confused? No, He is not. We need to understand what the Word of God says and also understand where it applies and where it does not.

So, Jesus had compassion and touched their eyes. And immediately their eyes received sight, and they followed Him. (Matthew20:34)

This and many other scriptural accounts of Jesus' miracles make us understand the power that His compassion had in all the miracles He did. So as powerful as He was, He could not heal them without compassion.

Knowing that compassion comes from love, it takes us back to the law of Giving.

You cannot give spiritually without love.

And compassion is one of the giving abilities of love. By this God has given us the power of compassion to judge by love. By this compassion, you can pass judgment on the spiritual or physical circumstances troubling the one for whom you have compassion. In this light, we should come back to the better punishment issue Jesus talked about. If that be the better, it means that if God comes it will be worst. Hence if you have compassion for someone, you can punish the person responsible for the trouble of that person; be it spiritually or physically. It is in this context that God said we will bind kings and the nations with the two-edged sword. We will understand this through the actions of Paul on two different occasions where he was wronged.

In the first case, we read: *But Elymas the sorcerer (for so is his name by interpretation) withstood them, seeking to turn away the deputy from the faith. Then Saul, (who also is called Paul,) filled with the Holy Ghost, set his eyes on him, And said, O full of all subtilty and all mischief, thou child of the devil, thou enemy of all righteousness, wilt thou not cease to pervert the right ways of the Lord? And now, behold, the hand of the Lord is upon thee, and thou shalt be blind, not seeing the sun for a season. And immediately there fell on him a mist and a darkness; and he went about seeking some to lead him by the hand. Then the deputy, when he saw what was done, believed, being astonished at the doctrine of the Lord. (Acts 13:8-12)*

The Bible makes it clear that this man was trying to stop the deputy from believing the truth when Paul full of the Holy Spirit rebuked him. Note that he did not do it out of the flesh but out of the spirit. It was the compassion he had for the deputy that caused him to punish the sorcerer. Also, if you can take it, it was also the compassion he had for Elymas that made Paul give him temporal blindness. You may say how? I will explain. If you know that the least God will do is drown the person into the sea; then by compassion, you will give the person a lesser punishment so as to turn away the wrath of God from him. Remember that when God in his wrath wanted to kill Moses, his wife circumcised their son and threw the piece on him. Circumcision is painful but it is less painful than the wrath of God.

In the second he says, *"Alexander the coppersmith did me much harm. May the lord repay him according to this work"* (2Timothy4:14) Then in another place he says, *"of whom are Hymeneals and Alexander whom I delivered to Satan that they may learn not to blaspheme (1Timothy1:20).*

This is Paul; the same Paul who punished someone in the scripture we just read. Could he not have punished Alexander? Not Paul because he knew how to give place to wrath. So, for another man's sake, Paul's compassion made him punish another. Yet when he was wronged, he did not call fire down. Rather he said let God repay. Listen, brothers and sisters, if a man wrongs you, by love you ought to forgive that person or let God repay. But on another person by the Holy Ghost, you can punish disobedience when yours is complete.

To conclude, note that when Paul was handing someone to the devil; he did it out of love so that the person might learn not to blaspheme again. Why do you pray evil for people? Is it because of your love for them or because of your hatred for them? Jesus said, *"owe no man anything except love" (Romans13:8).* You can never completely pay the debt of love. Therefore, stop killing or wishing people dead. Know this; that even if God wants to punish someone, if He starts it and He finds you happy He will even stop. Child of God, I charge you to grow because if you remain in the flesh, you will surely be happy when others are in pain. But the Spirit does not judge like that.

The Judge Connection

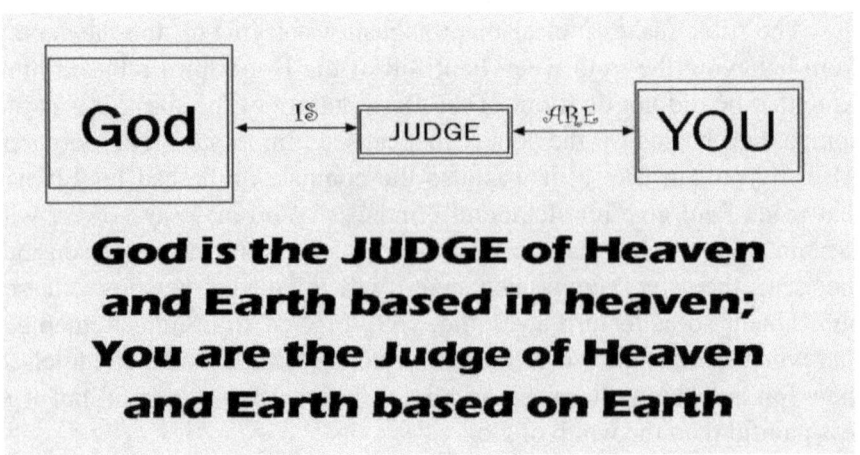

God is the JUDGE of Heaven and Earth based in heaven; You are the Judge of Heaven and Earth based on Earth

CHAPTER SIX

GOD THE KING

One thing we find today in the World is the fact that Democracy is gaining grounds and instead of kingdoms, we now have many countries in the world with the power of sovereignty. Though we still have kingdoms like that of the UK; the position of the king or Queen is mostly ceremonial. However, in the days of old, there was nothing like countries. What existed mostly in those days where territories ruled by kings. Nevertheless, according to scriptures, the name king was given to heads of towns and adjacent villages, it is noted that Moses was king in Jeshurun when the leaders of the people gathered.

Moses commanded a law for us, a heritage of the congregation of Jacob. And He was King in Jeshurun, When the leaders of the people were gathered, All the tribes of Israel together. (Deuteronomy 33:5).

In many cases, the kings in those days were no doubt like the sheiks of Arab tribes of this present day. Now let's not forget that we are talking about God. The Bible makes us know that from the day that God took the children of Israel out of Egypt He led them by the hand of Moses in a pillar of cloud by day and that of fire by night. Therefore, I want us to look at the characteristics of a king.

1. A king was never voted into power. He just grew into power. So, he was never voted out no matter what; he can only leave the thrown at death. Yet even when he dies, the thrown can be given to another lineage only in the case where he has no heir.
2. The king was the lawgiver, he was the one who gave the social

law, by which the people lived. He was the one who gave decrees to turn the course of affairs in the kingdom.
3. The king was the warrior. He was the leader of the army. And any time they are at war, it is the king that calls it and leads it. So, kings were noted in those days to be great warriors.
4. The king selects the rulers of the people. We should, however, note that kings always had advisers. In the case of Israel, kings were ordained by the high priest and received directions from the prophets. The king's reign was essentially a theocratic kind of government. Come to think of this, the Bible makes us know many things of God that tie with the four main characteristics of a king.

Firstly, we find out that God rules on the Earth, not because He was voted. And since He will never die, it means He will never leave His throne.

This decision is by the decree of the watchers, And the sentence by the word of the holy ones, In order that the living may know That the Most High rules in the kingdom of men, Gives it to whomever He will, And sets over it the lowest of men. (Daniel 4:17).

God was showing the king of Babylon that even though he had taken captive the children of Judah he should understand that they are only under him because He (God) decided it to be so. Hence, if he, in any case, will doubt His kingship over the Earth, then He will do something to make him know that He is the Most High and He rules in the kingdom of men. It goes further in this same verse to tell us that He sets over it whomever He wills. Taking from the fact that it was the king that appointed rulers over the people, even so, God also appoints rulers or kings over the Earth as He wills.

Secondly, when Moses took the children of Israel out of Egypt, he came to Mount Sinai and there he left the people and went up to the mountain for over a month. (40 days and 40 nights) when he came back, he had two tablets of the law that were given to him by God; for the people. Thus, God was the lawgiver in the land of Israel. He told them how everything was to be done. And as he told them, that was what they did. Just as every law is for good to those who obey it and punishment to those who disobey, even so, the law of God had benefits and punishment or blessings and curses.

We see clearly the declaration of blessings according to the Word of God that comes to those who obey the laws of God. However, there is something else that I want us to see in this scripture. Moses said clearly that the people were to "observe carefully all His (God) laws or commandments which He commands them in those days." In other words, the commandments were not Moses' but he was given the mandate to give the laws to the people. As they had told him in another place in scripture that whatever God will speak through him to them, they will obey.

The LORD of hosts is with us; the God of Jacob is our refuge. Selah. (Psalm46:7)

Thirdly, the scripture describes God as Lord of hosts. The Host is what we know today as the army. But there it is used in the plural form. Therefore, God is the Lord or the Commander of Armies (that is many groups of soldiers). In the days of Jehoshaphat; when he was about going for war, the Word of God came to him saying,

"Listen, all you of Judah and you inhabitants of Jerusalem, and you, King Jehoshaphat! Thus says the LORD to you: 'Do not be afraid nor dismayed because of this great multitude, for the battle is not yours, but God's. (2Chronicles20:15).

The LORD shall fight for you, and ye shall hold your peace. (Exodus14:14)

It is clear therefore that God was the one leading the battle of the Israelites as their King. And just because He was not seen physically does not cancel the fact that He was there. You will agree that whenever the Lord of hosts was with the Israelites, they were on the winning side. Therefore, all the four characteristics of a king are all attributed to God. This makes clear to us that He is a King.

These shall make war with the Lamb, and the Lamb shall overcome them: for he is Lord of lords, and King of kings: and they that are with him are called, and chosen, and faithful. (Revelation17:14)

And he hath on his vesture and on his thigh a name written, KING OF KINGS, AND LORD OF LORDS. (Revelation19:16)

The lord said to Samuel, "Heed the voice of the people in all that they say to you; for they have not rejected you, but they have rejected Me, that I should not reign over them. (1Samuel 8:7)

If you still doubt, it is no reason to beat around the bush. The scriptures state already that He is the King of kings and the Lord of lords. Please the Word of God declares Him to be king already if you cannot understand from what we have explained. It is the Word of a king; a decree from the Most High. Do you not read how God said the people rejected that He should not reign over them by asking another king when He was already their king?

The character of Lordship

This is God speaking and He says, *"The Lord of Hosts is with us…"* *(Psalm 46:7a)* God describes Himself as the Lord of hosts. However, if you are Lord; it has to be over something or somebody. If we consider Lordship as being a commander today then, that same verse will read thus, "The Commander of Armies is with us." It, therefore, means that you can become a Lord of money, health, people, wealth, etc., by my understanding. We might not get to the details of showing how God is Lord over many things but we will show you His character when it comes to his lordship. In doing this, I want you to understand something from Genesis. After Joseph had been in prison, he was called by Pharaoh to tell him the meaning of his dream. After he did, Pharaoh said to him:
You shall be over my house, and all my people shall be ruled according to your word; only in regard to the throne will I be greater than you." (Genesis 41:40)
Pharaoh also said to Joseph, "I am Pharaoh, and without your consent no man may lift his hand or foot in all the land of Egypt." (Genesis 41:44)

History holds that Joseph became Lord of Egypt according to the word of the King from that day. This Joseph's position in the Old Testament was a shadow of what was to take place in the New Testament as the scriptures declare of Jesus. Note that Joseph gave every command that was given and no word from Joseph fell to the ground from that time in Egypt. Pharaoh also said to Joseph, "I am Pharaoh, and without your consent, no man may lift his hand or foot in all the land of Egypt." So Joseph became the number one; all in all, of Egypt from that day. Talking of Jesus who is also in the image of God it says in the similitude of Joseph in the old.
For "He has put all things under His feet." But when He says "all things are put under Him," it is evident that He who put all things under Him is excepted. (1Corinthians 15:27)
You have made him to have dominion over the works of Your hands; You have put all things under his feet, (Psalm 8:6)

THE DIVINE NATURE OF GOD

Therefore, we see that Papa God has put all His authority under Jesus. He gave Him all dominion as Jesus Himself said; *"that all authority has been given to me in heaven and on Earth" (Matthew28:18).*

Jesus received authority from His Father. Thus the Fathers' authority is the authority of the Son since He gave it all to Him. Thus, the Lordship of Jesus is the Lordship of the entire Godhead. It pleased the Father that all fullness should dwell in Him bodily. What fullness? The fullness of His authority. So as Joseph had command over Egypt so Jesus now has power over all of Heaven and Earth. Therefore, it is written; *"Kiss the son, lest He be angry, and you perish in the way..." (Psalm 2:12)* why now? Because the Son now has all authority; if you do not kiss Him you will be in trouble. Hence God is Lord by His authority. But what is the authority and how did God get this authority that He now has given to Jesus? Did His Father give it to Him as the kings of the Earth do? Let's find out.

In the Bible, there is a good story that led to one of the miracles that Jesus did. This story I think will give us an understanding of what God calls authority.

"For I also am a man under authority, having soldiers under me. And I say to this one, 'Go,' and he goes; and to another, 'Come,' and he comes; and to my servant, 'Do this,' and he does it." (Matthew8:9)

Before the above verse, the centurion had said; "just say a word and my servant will be healed," then he went further to explain why he said that. Then Jesus said he had not seen such great faith.

So, to have authority means to have physical or spiritual control.

So, when Jesus said the world was under His authority He meant that the world was under His control. And with this control, anything you desire will be as the scripture puts it.

Where the word of a king is, there is power; and who may say to him, "What are you doing?"(Ecclesiastes8:4)
For who has known the mind of the Lord that he may instruct him ..." (1Corinthians2:16a)
For who has known the mind of the Lord? Or who has become His counsellor? (Romans11:34)

The word authority is spelled out in this phrase: And who may say to him, what are you doing? Therefore, when someone has authority over something no one can ask him or judge whether he is right or wrong. When the command is given by someone with authority no one can alter it. You might think otherwise, but you will do as you have been told because where the word of a king is there is power. Then it says no one has known his mind to instruct him. So, you cannot command God on what to do. So, the authority of God is in His Word as it is said: "just say a word". Listen to me according to God's authority He has made everything and everything is under Him such that you cannot ask Him what He is doing because He is Lord of all. Please do not misunderstand me. You have a right as His child to ask God questions about the kingdom and His leading in your life. What you should not do is question or doubt His authority. Like the children of Israel did saying, *"can God furnish a table in the wilderness?"* (Psalms78:19). That is wrong. How did God get this authority?

First, I will like us to know or see how men get authority. There are basically three main ways by which men get authority.

i) **By Will:**

This method of gaining authority is called willed authority. By this the king, before he dies give his authority as king to one of his sons that will be heir to his throne. Or as in our world today the father will confer the family authority to one of his sons. From that day all the control or authority of the father or king is bestowed on his son who now takes charge and everybody will now answer to the new king.

ii) **By Vote:**

This method is familiar to us who are living in the era of Democracy. Basically, I want you to understand that this method of gaining authority has a hidden philosophy called creation. When a country needs a future president, politicians will come up with new ideas. Note that creation starts with an idea. When they create a new idea on how the future will be in their hands, they will communicate it to people. As they do so, people will start believing in them. The more people believe in them, the more their authority increases. You see this in the fact that for a man to be president in a country he must not be voted by everybody. If what he created was more realistic or convincing, he will have more believers and the more his followers, the more his votes. The person with the highest number of believers will

THE DIVINE NATURE OF GOD

rule the nation (that is if it was free and fair) in the ideal case.

iii) By force:
This method of claiming authority is the most dangerous and unwanted method. Yet it still exists today. In those days when a king wants to increase the territory of his authority, he will match with his army into other kingdoms and any king he defeats, the people that were under that king will now be forced to be and pay allegiance to him as their new king. Today when a man is not pleased with the way his country is ruled and no one is giving him the opportunity to bring change; he might take arms as the last option. He will then take upon himself the appellation of a rebel leader. If he fights against the existing president and succeeds, he will declare himself as the new president of that country.

Now I want to inform you that all these methods of usurping authority have been used by God. First, we saw how Jesus was given authority by His Father so that all authority of the Heavens and the Earth now belong to Him. It is recorded in scriptures how Jesus took Peter, James, and John to a mountain and was transfigured before them in the presence of Moses and Elijah. And Peter being so mouthy, started talking even when he did not know what to say. However, before he could finish talking, something strange happened.

And a cloud came and overshadowed them; and a voice came out of the cloud, saying, "This is My beloved Son. Hear Him (Mark 9:7)

So, God gave authority to Jesus and told the whole world to hear Him: Peter, James, and John being the world's representatives in this case. So, Jesus obtained authority by the will of His Father. Secondly, the method of usurping authority by vote or creation will make it clear to us how the Father had the authority that He now gave to His Son.

In the beginning God created the heavens and the earth. (Genesis1:1)
I am the Alpha and the Omega, the Beginning and the End," says the Lord, "who is and who was and who is to come, the Almighty (Revelation1:8)

If God created the Heavens and the Earth, then all of it is under His authority. You know sometimes people are angry just like the devil was angry, why they have to be under God's authority. But I will explain something to you. Another word for creation that is commonly used today is the word to manufacture. From childhood, I grew up to see a lot of things manufactured by man. In all, I noticed that there was something common to all of them: The element of control. For example, when cars are made, the creator puts a steering wheel to control the direction of the car. He puts pedals to control the speed of the car as well as when and where it should stop. Closely looking at your TV set; you see a channel button, a volume button, and an ON/OF button to help the owner gain control of the TV set. Imagine you had a TV set in your house that comes on when it wants and chooses the channel that it wants you to watch. Then one night it comes on by itself at 1:00 am with its maximum volume. Honestly, tell me; will you be happy with such a TV? Come to think of it, when we say that electronics are bad, are we not merely saying that we lost control of the equipment because the buttons no longer give us the expected results?

The question I ask is; why don't you give the TV set a chance to express itself the way it wants. If it shows nothing, be happy. Don't throw it away it is just freely expressing itself. Why then do you take it for repair or get a new one? Listen when God created the Earth and everything that is in it, He also put control buttons in them; even you. Hence only God has the ability to say something He created is bad because He knows the reason for which he created it. A dog cannot tell when a TV set is bad or good because it did not create it. But even if it does there is nothing it can do about it.

We just talked on the issue of creation: based on ideas and philosophies. Yet there is an addition to God's authority of creation that is different from the voting type. Looking at the life of a couple, two people come together and decide that they want to have children. When they have these children, they have to answer for them in everything. The couple will raise their children the way they deem fit. Even if they are wrong, at a certain level, no man can ask them what they are doing. They were never voted to be parents. That new baby, because it came out of them, he/she is like their created baby. The baby did not vote for his /her parents. You know, if we were all given the opportunity to choose our parents then some will never have children. However, we find a class of people having more children than they can take care of. Since we are not talking about childbearing or control, I want us to see the clear picture.

God created you, though He is higher than what you can imagine, yet He is similar to your earthly parents. You know how the Word of God tells us; our parents had authority over us for a season and brought us up the way they wanted and we could not escape from their hands when we did something wrong.

Furthermore we have had fathers of our flesh which corrected us, and we gave them reverence: shall we not much rather be in subjection unto the Father of spirits, and live? For they verily for a few days chastened us after their own pleasure; but he for our profit, that we might be partakers of his holiness. (Hebrews 12:9-10)

See this, our parents did that without knowing who we were, where we are coming from, what we will be in life and where we are going. Yet they had such authority over us. But God who created all of us is greater than our parents in that He knows who we are because He designed us to be that way. He knows where we are from and where we are going because He carved our path. The scriptures declare that our ways are always before Him. To sum it up, while our parents lose their control on us as we grow, God is supposed to gain control as we grow. Thus, as you grow and begin making your own decisions, God starts holding you responsible for your actions. So, it is impossible to escape from God as the scriptures declare in the book of Daniel. Do not make God write on the wall on your behalf else you will be finished and no one will save you from Him.

When God said to the rich fool, "today your soul will be required from you." He could have thought otherwise but there was nothing He could do to change it. Also, if God is for you, no one can be against you. It also speaks the same that if He is against you, no one can be for you. If one with God is the majority, you should judge for yourself so that you can be wise. For the day He will say "be not," that day we will cry and yet you will still be not because He who holds all things by the Word of His power has spoken. If we must fear before anyone it should be before God. Even as it is said; *do not fear him that can kill the body and do nothing to the soul. But fear him who can kill the body and cast your soul in hell (Luke12:4-5).*

Though there are areas that God has given us to choose, we cannot choose who our creator is. Also, we cannot choose our God. No matter what you do the scripture says they that fall on the rock shall be broken but upon whom that rock will fall it will grind him to dust. Therefore, it is either now or later. So, one day we will all meet face to face with our maker where there will be no hiding place. So, God has authority over you; like it or not. Like in some countries they did not vote for their presidents. In fact, some grow up knowing only one president for all their lifetime. Yet their rule is affecting them every day even when they do not like them at all. Until that authority is changed you are not expected to speak contrary without checking your audience, even if you are right.

However, God is very different because even though we cannot vote Him, as God He gives us the will to choose what we want Him to be or do for us. And it is also written of Him in this way: taste and see that the Lord is good. For if the longevity of some president's term of office was characterized by glory and prosperity of their land, their people would have been happy to have them as president. So, Jesus said of God. There is none that is good safe, God. So, this God even though He is sovereign, I am glad to have Him as God because He is the epitome of goodness. Just imagine having the devil as your God for one day without the intervention of God. Wow! To say, you will be finished in a split second is an understatement.

Furthermore, we saw the last method of usurping authority which is by force. In the days when God told Abraham that his children will go to Egypt and be there for 400 years, He also told him that it had to be so for the sins of the people of that land to be full. Even though God wanted to wipe them from the face of the earth, and give their land to the Israelites. He still will not do it without a reason good enough. I have found out that God never destroys without warning. Before the master of the talents in Jesus' parable could take by force from the lazy servant, he, first of all, gave him an equal chance to do something with it. Listen, I want you to know that God can never be judged when He takes from you by force. Come to think of it, is He not the owner of all things? Yet He being God will not take by force without a reason or fault.

And he said unto Abram, Know of a surety that thy seed shall be a stranger in a land that is not theirs, and shall serve them; and they shall afflict them four hundred years; And also that nation, whom they shall serve, will I judge: and afterward shall they come out with great substance. And thou shalt go to thy fathers in peace; thou shalt be buried in a good old age. But in the fourth generation they shall come hither again: for the iniquity of the Amorites is not yet full. (Genesis 15:13-16)

Even so, the sins of the people had to be full for Him to take the land from them and give it to the Israelites. When the Israelites came out of Egypt, God brought them out with a strong hand. He also drove out the inhabitants of the land from before the Israelites by force. Looking at the Old Testament as a shadow of things to come, God sent Jesus to Earth so He can deal with the problem of man once and for all. He did this because He could no longer bear the sufferings of man in the world without hope. Jesus gave a parable that explains clearly what He came to do, saying;

"Or how can one enter a strong man's house and plunder his goods, unless he first binds the strong man? And then he will plunder his house. (Matthew 12:29)
For You will not leave my soul in Sheol, Nor will You allow Your Holy One to see corruption. (Psalm16:10)
Inasmuch then as the children have partaken of flesh and blood, He Himself likewise shared in the same, that through death He might destroy him who had the power of death, that is, the devil, (Hebrews 2:14)
Having disarmed principalities and powers, He made a public spectacle of them, triumphing over them in it. (Colossians 2:15)

Here these scriptures tell us clearly that Jesus came to make war with the Devil, to take full authority over the Earth. Hence the scriptures make us understand that Jesus did not just resurrect as many may think. When scriptures talk of the power of His resurrection we should see beyond the silence of the soldiers at the door of His tomb. The Bible says that He went down and made war in Hell. As it is said in Psalms, "thou did not leave my soul in Sheol." Jesus had to take the keys of life and death from the devil. As it is rightly said, He was made manifest to destroy him that had the power of death even the devil. In another place, it says, *"as he ascended on high he led captivity captive and gave gifts to men"* (Ephesians 4:18). Thus, Jesus destroyed the Devil's power, took ownership of the world from the devil before He could ever resurrect. What am I saying? If Jesus resurrected, then it is a sign that He won the battle against the devil. Note that before that time, Jesus had been tempted by the Devil at the beginning of His ministry. That if He (Jesus) would bow down to him, he (devil) will give Him the world. Of a truth the Devil was not wrong to say this because of truth; he had control of the world.

And Jesus came and spoke to them, saying, "All authority has been given to Me in heaven and on earth. (Matthew 28:18)

However, when Jesus resurrected, He told the disciples all power in Heaven and on Earth has been given to Him. Know that God had willed the ownership of the Earth to man. Thus, as a man lost it, only a man could get it back. Hence God was with Jesus as He went to the grave and gave Him the power to take back the ownership of the world from the Devil as a man.

The Authority of Jesus

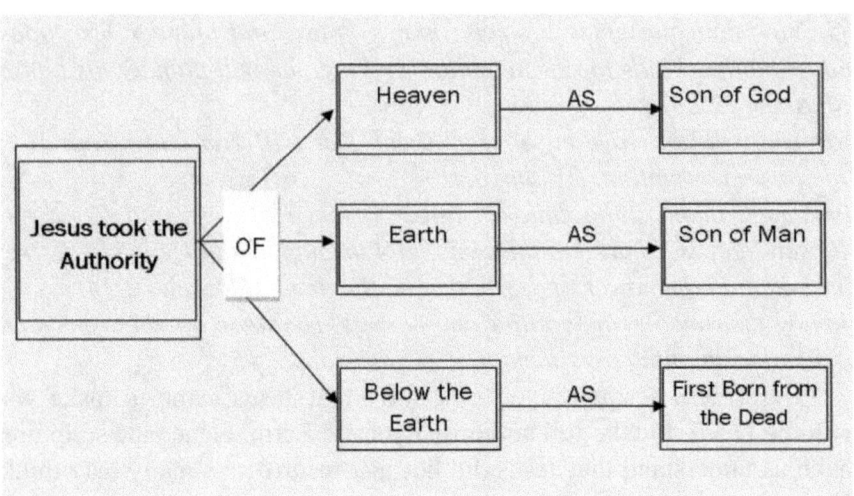

When He said all powers in Heaven and Earth, it is better if you understand it this way. He took the authority of Heaven as the Son of God. He took that on Earth as the son of man and that under the Earth as the firstborn from the dead. Therefore, Jesus did not get this authority without a fight because the devil could not just let go like that. When Jesus said on the cross it is finished, He simply meant that the war was won. Thank God that Jesus by the authority of God defeated the Devil, delivering us from all his works. Yet there remains a controversy that I must explain to you.

For you were bought at a price; therefore glorify God in your body and in your spirit, which are God's. (1Corinthians 6:20)

The scriptures tell of the fact that we were bought with a price. These talks of the blood and life of Jesus shed or sacrificed on the cross. Listen, when God said this; He did not say that He was buying us from someone or the Devil. By the way, do you think the devil would have sold us to God if God actually wanted to buy us?

God bought us for Himself from ourselves and not from the Devil as some may think.

The scriptures say that all have sinned and come short of the glory of God. It was possible for God to make war with the devil without the shedding of His Son's blood. It is not the blood that defeated the devil but the power of God as Ephesians rightly puts it.

And what is the exceeding greatness of his power to us-ward who believe, according to the working of his mighty power, Which he wrought in Christ, when he raised him from the dead, and set him at his own right hand in the heavenly places, (Ephesians 1:19-20)

Thus, without the blood, God could have still taken the authority or the world from the Devil. Hence to complete His work, He used His blood to bring us to Himself. By His blood, therefore, He bought our conscience so we can relate with Him at the level He always wanted. Because we were afar off, He used His blood to fill the gap that was between Him and us.

So, we see that Jesus being God's Son had His authority by inheritance, vote or creation and also by force. By this, it is clear why Jesus said all authority in Heaven, on Earth and under the Earth has been given to me. Do not wonder why I have used all this time to explain the event of Jesus' authority. Note that it is seemingly impossible to explain the nature of God without considering His relationship with people who walked with Him especially Jesus who was His first Son. And all those who have ever had victory with God from Moses over Pharaoh, David over Goliath to Jesus over the Devil and the world, they only could do so first because God gave them right of ownership to what He owns as creator and then used His power to back them up victoriously to the end.

For example, when God was threatened by the Devil for His throne in Heaven, what did He do? Sit and say, "I don't like war?" No, He said to the entire Heaven, "you have all known Me as creator but now, you will know Me as the Mighty Man in battle." And so He commanded and the Devil was thrown out of Heaven by force. God has shown that as a king, He can both act as reasonable with people as well as use brute force when it's necessary, so do not take His patience for granted

The Character of the Seal

We know that most of what men do is at a certain level similar to God. For it is written; even the people who do not have the law, He shows Himself to them even in nature. What then is a seal? For me, simply put; a seal is a symbol of identity. It could be for the purpose of authority, authenticity, marketing, etc. There are many seals in the world today and they range from physical to spiritual based on a few used examples from scriptures.

Spiritual Seals

By knowledge, we understand that the Word of God is the most valuable resource for spiritual things. Hence, we will see the spiritual seals that were used by men in their lifetime and relationship with God as stated in the Bible.

- **The rainbow:** In the days of Noah, after the flood, God made a covenant with Noah never to destroy the Earth with flood and the seal that He used to represent that promise was the rainbow
- **The Blood:** *In whom we have redemption through His blood, the forgiveness of sins. (Colossians 1:14)* In the days of Moses, the blood of lambs was used as a seal on the doorposts of the Israelites to save them from the wrath of God. Also, the blood of Jesus Christ is a spiritual seal of redemption for every Christian.
- **The Word:** *Out of the ground the LORD God formed every beast of the field and every bird of the air, and brought them to Adam to see what he would call them. And whatever Adam called each living creature that was its name. (Genesis 2:19)* The Bible records that in the beginning when God made man, He brought the animals He had created to the man in order to see what He will call them. Then it says whatever he called them they became. Listen, the word 'became' here is used to describe the character of the animals. Hence the word of Adam defined the character of the animals as he named them. Therefore, by his word he sealed the character of the animals. The physical composition or appearance of the animals could not have changed, but the spiritual characteristics of the animals were defined by the names he gave them. So, the characters you see today in animals were given to them by Adam. Note here, that Adam was speaking to the Animals as a prophet with spiritual understanding
- **The Sacrifice:** Note that in the Old Testament, goats and sheep were not sacrificed only to clean people from sins. It was also used as a method of giving to God and also to seal relationships with Him. The Bible says that when God took Abraham to the land of Canaan and told him, "this is the land I will give to you and your descendants." Abraham built an altar of sacrifice in that place and made an offering unto God to seal the word God had spoken to him. *Then the LORD appeared to Abram and said, "To your descendants I will give this land." And there he built an*

THE DIVINE NATURE OF GOD

altar to the LORD, who had appeared to him. (Genesis12:7)
- **The Staff:** We see in the scriptures that when Moses was called by God, He told him to throw his staff on the ground. We know the story of how it turned into a serpent. Then He told him to pick it by the tail because he was afraid. That said; the stick or rod was a seal in Moses' hand to prove to the Israelites and the Egyptians that it was God who had sent him. Also, Judah's staff was used to identify him concerning the pregnancy of Tamar. *Then he said, "What pledge shall I give you?" So she said, "Your signet and cord, and your staff that is in your hand." Then he gave them to her, and went in to her, and she conceived by him. (Genesis38:18) "And you shall take this rod in your hand, with which you shall do the signs." (Exodus 4:17)*
- **Handkerchiefs and aprons:** *So that from his body were brought unto the sick handkerchiefs or aprons, and the diseases departed from them, and the evil spirits went out of them. (Acts 19:12)* We read from the above scripture that aprons were taken from Paul and Peter, to serve spiritual purposes like healing and deliverance for sick and possessed folks respectively. These also were used in this case to seal spiritual power by faith. It is clear from this that you can now use anything to seal spiritual power by faith.

Physical Seals
Talking of physical seals, we have the following.
- **The Ring:** When a woman is engaged to be married to a man, she will most often nowadays, receive a ring from the man as a symbol of their engagement. Next, when they finally get married, they both wear rings in their fingers to identify them with their new status. Also, there are other organizations or posts of responsibilities that are symbolized with rings.
- **A Trade Mark:** When a company or someone creates a new product, they develop what we call a trademark to identify that product in the market. That trademark acts as a seal for every product manufactured by that company or person.
- **A Logo:** Today we see all sorts of logos, ranging from international organizations to national emblems, then local organizations and industries, etc. All these organizations have a symbol for quick identification. This logo is unique to that

particular organization or country.
- **The anthem:** Every country in the world now has what is known as a national anthem which is a special song, specific to that country. No two countries can have the same anthem. Hence this also is a seal of identification for that country. Note that some organizations also have anthems.
- **Stamps:** It is a common phenomenon to see at the end of any official document, stamps of various kinds. Ranging from ink to dry stamps in different sizes and shapes. These stamps carry the logo and sometimes the names of the organization or company so as to officially identify the document wherever it goes. Note that in the days of old stamps were inscribed at the back of men's rings. Especially kings.
- **Signatures:** Signatures are always used as personal seals. No two people have the same signature. The essence is that each seal should be unique to a particular person or group of persons. So, therefore, a signature is unique for each individual.
- **Finger Print:** The fingerprint also, as they say, is unique for every person. It means no two persons can have the same fingerprint in the world. So, fingerprints are used as seals to identify individuals.

However, a seal with God is different in certain ways. As God is always higher than men as the Heavens is from the Earth. What then is the character of seals with God? The scriptures rightly put it when it talks of God as a covenant keeping God. The word 'covenant keeping' defines God's character of seals. Hence you can by this say that Jehovah is a God of seals. We said earlier that seals were used as a symbol of identification for anything and also for binding agreements. God as the author of seals has two main reasons why He made seals.

God made seals for identity representation and for relationships that are binding with Him.

Identity Representation: After God had created the Earth with all that was in it, He then decided to create man. Why did He create man? He did create man simply to establish a representative of His authority in the world. That is why the man had to be separate from Him but identical to Him. To be responsible for whatever God had to be responsible for if He was on the Earth. Therefore, the man in the Garden of Eden was a seal

THE DIVINE NATURE OF GOD

that God was the one who created the Earth and owned it. Hence He left His first son to control everything on Earth, by His directions. And even after the fall, God has never left the Earth without people representing Him and so it will always be. The day God sees the risk of no one being on the Earth to represent Him, the world would come to an end. But that will never come because it is written 'world without end, amen.'

Then God blessed them, and God said to them, "Be fruitful and multiply; fill the earth and subdue it; have dominion over the fish of the sea, over the birds of the air, and over every living thing that moves on the earth." (Genesis1:28)

God's idea of man was that whatever I am in Heaven, man should be on Earth. Thus, when God saw that the children of God could not represent Him to the full, He sent Jesus to come and create a new order by which He will have a real representative in the world. Hence, Christians are the fulfillment of that new order of representatives in the world: as the Bible says, "ye are the light of the world." And just as seals are always used in relationships, it has a part that is binding for both parties.

In whom ye also trusted, after that ye heard the word of truth, the gospel of your salvation: in whom also after that ye believed, ye were sealed with that Holy Spirit of promise, (Ephesians1:13)

The scriptures tell us that the Holy Spirit is the seal that God has put on us to mark us as His own, separating us from the rest of the world and making us the light of the world. However, in any written agreement, the two persons involved must put their signatures in it. Therefore, the scriptures say that if anyone has not the son, he has not the life in him. So, we had to hear God's report or agreement with His Son and sign with our belief, so He also can sign with His Spirit. Hence the Spirit of God in you is the signature that He has put in you to show you that you belong to Him and also that He belongs to you. Do not think that this is too big *to say.* The Bible says, "the Lord is my portion." Also, it says, "the Lord is my inheritance," and again it says, "the spirit of the prophet is subject to the prophet."

Relationship: God in the old and new testament has shown us that He is a covenant keeping God. In the old, after God had destroyed the whole earth with a flood, He smelled the sacrifice of Noah after he came out of the ark. Then He felt sorry for destroying the Earth with water and made an agreement with Noah that He will never destroy the Earth again with water. There He made the rainbow to represent or be the seal for the agreement He made with man. And said whenever He sees the rainbow, He will remember the agreement. Also, whenever man sees the rainbow, he remembers the agreement he made with God on this matter.

I do set my bow in the cloud, and it shall be for a token of a covenant between me and the earth. (Genesis 9:13)

I hereby remind you of a story in the Bible that will make us understand the nature of God's seals.

Then the king Ahasuerus said unto Esther the queen and to Mordecai the Jew, Behold, I have given Esther the house of Haman, and him they have hanged upon the gallows, because he laid his hand upon the Jews. Write ye also for the Jews, as it liketh you, in the king's name, and seal it with the king's ring: for the writing which is written in the king's name, and sealed with the king's ring, may no man reverse.
(Esther 8:7-8)

    This is the covenant nature of God. In the book of Esther, the Bible talks of the fact that a decree had been signed with the seal of the king by Haman. Later, when Esther came and declared the matter to the king and he realized how bad that decree was, he could not change it. Even in the kingdom of men they could have just said the decree has been canceled. The king has changed his mind. The Jews should no longer be killed. Yet he could not change it. So instead they signed another decree to add to the one that had been sent out already.

Then the king, when he heard these words, was sore displeased with himself, and set his heart on Daniel to deliver him: and he laboured till the going down of the sun to deliver him. Then these men assembled unto the king, and said unto the king, Know, O king, that the law of the Medes and Persians is, That no decree nor statute which the king establisheth may be changed. (Daniel 6:14-15)

    Also, the Bible speaks of the laws of the Medes and Persians, by which Daniel was ordered into the lion's den. It is said as we read that even when the king realized that what he did was wrong, he could not change it. Even though he did not sleep the whole night for Daniel's sake, he still could not change his own decree. Nobody likes to see his friend being thrown into the lion's den. Again, nobody likes to spend a sleepless night. Thus, we see that by every feeling and good reason, the king wanted to change that decree but he could not. Likewise, when God talks of His seal it cannot be revoked. That is why the gifts and callings of God are without repentance because He gave them to us by the seal of the Holy Spirit. In scriptures, we find how Paul explained the shortcomings of the old covenant. How it brought the people into bondage. Yet Jesus in His speech said; I did not come to destroy the law but I came to fulfill it. Hence just as Esther could not cancel the decree, even so, Jesus could not cancel the law; but add only to it. Again, Jesus said Heaven and Earth will pass away, but not one of these written words shall go unfulfilled. If you must know, therefore, every time you call God faithful, you are saying that He is a covenant keeping God. Jesus said the scriptures cannot be broken: even by God. The reason we trust God's faithfulness is based on the fact that if He said something, you can go and come back after a million years and He will still stand on that word. Because He Himself has sealed it, He cannot repent from it. That is why it is said of God in the Word that *"he is not man that he should lie neither is he the son of man that he should repent has he said it and will he not do it (Numbers23:19).*

So, Jesus likened a man that is taught in the scriptures as one that brings out of his treasure things new and old. Therefore, the new cannot stand without the old and the old is not complete without the new. So, with God, the Old Testament gets its completion, fulfillment, and perfection in the new covenant. While the new covenant gets its foundation from the old covenant, we cannot separate them because God is faithful and He is the God of seals. Once it is written, it cannot be annulled. It can only be fulfilled. Therefore, the first covenant (The Law) puts the people in bondage; it gives them a death sentence. However, the second covenant (Grace) gives them the right to fight for their lives.

Therefore, the psalmist said, "wait I say upon the lord." Why should we? He is faithful. He has given a decree that even He himself cannot alter. Even if He feels differently about it He cannot change it. So, if God gave you a new name, believe it. If He promised you something, believe because He is not a man that He should lie. What He has written, He cannot change because He is the God of seals. Even when He feels like bringing rain He cannot; because the rainbow is there to remind Him. That is God for you and you can count on Him because of that.

The Character of the Oath

We all are used to elections in this generation. Whether it is a presidential or municipal election, we all know that when new elections are conducted it always ends with a winner. After that, a date is set for his or her official swearing into the office. On the set date amongst others, the winner makes an oath before his people promising to serve them according to the stipulated constitution of the nation. Apart from this, there are other professions that require an oath on graduation day. Therefore, what is an oath? An oath according to me is a public verbal declaration made by a man that binds him to the regulations laid down concerning his relationship to an office, responsibility, things or person. It is also a formal promise to do something. This is done to ensure faithfulness from that person towards the law. In this we see that oaths have been with us, going from one generation to the other. Yet we must note that oaths are different from seals though they both have the same power of none revocation. Listen, the day a man or woman violates the oath of his profession, he or she is asked to resign because they lost the trust that was conferred on them.

So also, is our God in His relationship with us. He did not force us to trust Him. Instead, He took time to write out a constitution for His kingdom (i.e. the Bible). Note that the constitution is binding for everyone in the state even the president. It is the constitution that gives power to the president. So, God took time to write a constitution that is binding for both Him and us. This constitution is what we call the Word of God. Note that a man does not take an oath without something being read out loud to him in public. As the president is bound to the constitution, so also God is bound to His Word. Therefore, God said He has exalted His Word more than His name. Hence the constitution He has written between us and Him is even bigger than Him. In that case, even if His name requires something, He can only get it within the limits of the constitution of Heaven and Earth. Thus, God, Himself took authority with an oath.

(For they have become priests without an oath, but He with an oath by Him who said to Him: "The LORD has sworn and will not relent, 'You are a priest forever according to the order of Melchizedek'"), by so much more Jesus has become a surety of a better covenant. (Hebrews 7:21-22) For when God made a promise to Abraham, because He could swear by no one greater, He swore by Himself, (Hebrews 6:13).

Thus, Jesus was made a High Priest in the order of Melchizedek by God's oath. It also says that because oaths are made before someone higher, He did not see anyone higher so He swore by Himself. Can you imagine God swearing by Himself? He did not make an oath because someone forced Him. He did it by Himself. I think God could just barge into our lives any time, anyhow because He is the one who created all of us. If God had done that, He will not be judged by any one of us because He made us. Instead, He made Himself His own judge and swore never to bypass our will. Then He negotiates with man through a laid down constitution. Then He made an oath to follow it to the letter. That is why He says no man can ever find Him guilty.

"But in the fourth generation they shall return here, for the iniquity of the Amorites is not yet complete." (Genesis 15:16)

In the promise that God gave Abraham, He told him that his children will go down to Egypt and be there for four hundred years until the sins of the people of that land are full. Abraham had pleased God so well that he would have wanted to give him Canaan at once. But, how could He? When the constitution states that you cannot punish a man beyond his crime. So, God had to wait for four hundred years until those people finally committed sins enough to be guilty of total annihilation.

But when the king heard thereof, he was wroth: and he sent forth his armies, and destroyed those murderers, and burned up their city. Then saith he to his servants, The wedding is ready, but they which were bidden were not worthy. Go ye therefore into the highways, and as many as ye shall find, bid to the marriage. So those servants went out into the highways, and gathered together all as many as they found, both bad and good: and the wedding was furnished with guests. (Matthew 22:7-10)

Also, we see this (in the oath controlling God) in the extension of the gospel to us who were called Gentiles. God had made a covenant to bless the whole earth with salvation through Abraham, yet He had a covenant with the lineage of Abraham. He too could not just stand and change without enough reason in the constitution to do so. In so doing He will destroy the oath. Therefore, on account of this Jesus gave us a parable how the master of the banquette sent word to invite those for whom the banquette was made. But when they all rejected his invitation; he was now left with no choice but to give an open invitation to everyone else who could come for the banquette.

These twelve Jesus sent out and commanded them, saying: "Do not go into the way of the Gentiles, and do not enter a city of the Samaritans. But go rather to the lost sheep of the house of Israel. (Matthew 10:5)

But he answered and said, I am not sent but unto the lost sheep of the house of Israel. (Matthew 15:24)

Then Paul and Barnabas waxed bold, and said, It was necessary that the word of God should first have been spoken to you: but seeing ye put it from you, and judge yourselves unworthy of everlasting life, lo, we turn

to the Gentiles. For so hath the Lord commanded us, saying, I have set thee to be a light of the Gentiles, that thou shouldest be for salvation unto the ends of the earth. And when the Gentiles heard this, they were glad, and glorified the word of the Lord: and as many as were ordained to eternal life believed.
(Acts 13:46-48)

This was seen in the ministry of Jesus such that even when He sent out the disciples, He did not send them to the Gentiles but to the lost Jews. He also said He was sent to the lost sheep of Israel. However, Paul later concluded due to the rejection of the gospel of Jesus Christ by the Jews saying, "From this, I know that God has rejected you as Jesus said that many will come from far and sit with Abraham while the Jews will be cast away." Then in concluding Paul said, "I will now go to the Gentiles because you have rejected the gospel which is the invitation of God." If the Jews did not reject Jesus as they did, it would have been difficult but not impossible for God to include us in the plan of salvation.

Thus, He would have been forced to use another clause in the constitution that will make us have a chance. But as you see they broke their own part of the deal, giving Him reason enough to break His. I am humbled to know this of God that He will swear by Himself in the relationship He has with man to do justice even when He does not feel pleased with them. He does this to show us how far He would go to win our trust and confidence rather than make us submit by force. Therefore He says anyone that comes to Him must know that He is and that He is a rewarder of them that diligently seek Him. It also says; *Every good gift and every perfect gift is from above, and comes down from the Father of lights, with whom there is no variation or shadow of turning. (James 1:17)*

So, God makes oaths in the relationship He has with us, so as to win our trust as a king. When a presidential candidate knows that He has the love of his people, he is confident at the poles. However, when he does not trust himself, he will try to seize power by force. Why? This is so because in life we lead the obedient and rule the disobedient. So, kings take oaths to win the trust and love of their people. This will cause people to trust their leadership.

To the woman He said: "I will greatly multiply your sorrow and your conception; In pain you shall bring forth children; Your desire shall be for your husband, And he shall rule over you." Then to Adam He said, "Because you have heeded the voice of your wife, and have eaten from the tree of which I commanded you, saying, 'You shall not eat of it': "Cursed is the ground for your sake; In toil you shall eat of it all the days of your life. (Genesis 3:16-17)

Therefore, oaths are basically made to win trust and love which will then develop obedience. And obedience removes ruler-ship from relationships. With this in mind, I will explain the crime of Eve in the garden so you can better understand. One school of thought says that Adam did not take time to explain the law of God to Eve as he should. But as we read the story, we find Eve discussing with the serpent. We do not know how long their conversation took. It could have been for months according to whatever timing system they were using then. So as the story tells Eve finally ate the fruit and succeeded in convincing Adam to also eat. Note the punishment they received. Eve never heard God give the command but she was arguing with the serpent about the fact that they should not eat the fruit. This means Adam had shown her that tree and the implications of eating from it.

Hence when God spoke to Adam He did not say, "I punish you because you did not tell your wife about the tree and its commands." Instead, he said, "because you have listened to the words of Eve and disobeyed my command; this and that will be your punishment." So from the explanation of the crime, we understand that Adam told Eve everything she had to know about that tree and even went further to tell her not to even go near or touch it. So, when God came to Eve He said to her, "because you have convinced your husband to eat from the tree that I bid him not to eat …." Then He pronounced a curse on Eve that brought the aspect of ruler-ship into the world of man. He said, "your heart will be to your husband and he shall rule over you." In this, we see that God originally never wanted man to rule over his wife.

This is because where there is trust there is obedience and where there is obedience there is submission and where there is submission, ruler-ship is unnecessary.

But love gives birth to trust just like the oath of God. He came to us with the oath of love so that we will trust and obey Him. Then He will not have to rule us anymore. It is good for us therefore, to take time to know Him so we can grow to love, trust and obey him. For when we obey there will be no room for ruler-ship as there was none from the beginning. This too is a law of the beginning. If you know the constitution, you will never doubt what the just king will do. The just king (God) will never do anything contrary to the word He has given to us. Hence, He says, "I am not variable in my character. My yes is yes and My no is no and I have sworn never to turn away from the constitution of My kingdom; i.e. My Word."

The king connection

Notice: when God called and said He had made us kings and priests; it is not a strange thing for Him to say so because from the very beginning He made man to have dominion over the works of His hands. He also commanded man from the beginning to subdue the earth. It is important therefore for us not to take lightly the kingship responsibilities that we have of God. However, in order for us to take our position as kings, we have to start by understanding how we were made kings. Also, we need to understand the functionality of our kingship.

He who comes from above is above all; he who is of the earth is earthly and speaks of the earth. He who comes from heaven is above all. (John3:31)

Herein is our love made perfect, that we may have boldness in the day of judgment: because as he is, so are we in this world. (1John4:17)

First, we know that Jesus came to this Earth as a king by the declaration that He was from above. Because we know that he that is from above is above all. Then the holy scriptures inform us that as he is so are, we on this Earth. Therefore as He sent Jesus king of the Earth so has he sent us kings upon the Earth. The scripture further declares Him as the King of kings, indicating that we are the kings He is reigning over. However, we will better understand our kingship by analyzing the three major characteristics of a king during the Bible days.

1. **Kings are not voted**: *You did not choose Me, but I chose you and appointed you that you should go and bear fruit, and that your fruit should remain ... (John 15:16)* Knowing that a king is never voted (by man), we find out that Jesus said we did not choose Him but He chose us. The same way David and Saul were elected kings by God, so has He chosen us to be kings. We were not voted into power and looking critically we did not even vote ourselves. This is because we did not feel qualified to contest for election; if there were any. Yes, there was an election.

THE DIVINE NATURE OF GOD

However, the election was God's choice. That is why we are all exhorted to make our election sure. Yet God handpicked us and made us kings and priests. Noting the difference, you will see something very remarkable. In human democracy, men declare their own qualification by themselves while with kings their qualification is declared by another person, and in our case God.

2. **Lawgivers:** From the fact that kings were the lawgivers, God has given us the mandate to give His law to the Earth. By both the proclamation of the gospel and the establishment of doctrine. Talking of doctrine, doctrines are the law of God or better still the rules and regulations governing the body of Christ. So, the church is given the mandate to give these laws. We find in this that according to the revelation of God given to us, we are by it given the mandate to develop and create laws for our lives and ministry. Yet these doctrines are subject to change as the revelations change or increase. Hence laws are expected to differ from one person to the other or one group to the other, depending on the revelation on which that law was made. Note that not all revelation is current enough to be correct. *Verily I say unto you, Whatsoever ye shall bind on earth shall be bound in heaven: and whatsoever ye shall loose on earth shall be loosed in heaven. (Matthew 18:18)*

3. **Warriors:** *For we wrestle not against flesh and blood, but against principalities, against powers, against the rulers of the darkness of this world, against spiritual wickedness in high places. (Ephesians 6:12)* Talking on the fact that kings in those days were warriors, the scriptures clearly tell us that we do not wrestle against flesh and blood but against principalities and powers. Again, in another place, it says,' fight the good fight of faith." Listen, brothers and sisters, the earlier we all recognize the war we are already in the better for all of us. This is a battle and the Bible clearly tells us that there is a fight to fight and a war to win. *"And from the days of John the Baptist until now the kingdom of heaven suffers violence, and the violent take it by force. (Matthew 11:12)* Jesus declared our war when He said the kingdom of God suffers violence and the violent take it by force. Only in a war do we gather spoils. So, if you do not fight, your honor as a king will be taken away from you. Every child of God is a king unto God. Hence life will require kingship

characteristics from you; if you have to enter your reigning position in life. Then the Bible says we shall reign upon the Earth not in heaven. So, if you are a child of God, know today that you are a king upon the Earth. If you knew this before now, just take it as a reminder, for kings sometimes forget that they are kings. So, stretch yourself and resist anything that wants to stop you from reigning on the Earth for if you do not reign on the Earth, you will never reign. Please, the president of Cameroon cannot directly command the soldiers of the USA. So, the earlier we all come to accept this; the better for all of us. This will stop this false consolation ministry that says we should suffer for all the while we are on Earth hoping that we will reign in Heaven. For your information, Heaven is God's throne, not yours. Your own throne is here on the Earth. So, exercise your reigning here or never.

That said, we will now look at the different characters of the kings that we are.
As You sent Me into the world, I also have sent them into the world. (John17:18)
For David himself said by the Holy Spirit: 'The LORD said to my Lord, "Sit at My right hand, Till I make Your enemies Your footstool. (Mark 12:36)
Scriptures declare that Jesus sent us into this world the same way the Father sent Him. Considering the statement of Jesus about His lordship on which He said, "David said the Lord said unto my Lord sit you down …" so Jesus said that David called Him Lord. And as Jesus was sent as Lord so also did He send us as lords upon the Earth. For if He is Lord of lords, then we are the lords He is lording over. So according to this, Jesus Himself said, *"I give you authority to trample upon serpents and scorpions and over all the power of the enemy and nothing shall by any means hurt you"* (Luke 10:19). Why is that? Only lords have powers as such. Jesus was actually saying, "I make you lords over all the powers of the enemy." Jesus made us lords over the entire kingdom of darkness. But how did we obtain this authority by which it is said; whatever you bind on Earth is bound in Heaven.

First, our authority was willed to us by the Word of God which says, *if children, then heirs of God and joint heirs with Christ… (Romans 8:17)*

So, Jesus was given up by God as the only begotten of the Father and received again as the firstborn from the dead. Hence Jesus is now made the first Son of God by which He is not ashamed to call us His brothers. Therefore, it is our inheritance from God as His sons to partake in His lordship as Jesus also is Lord. So as God is Lord in Himself, so has He given His sons to be lords in themselves. Now we have inherited lordship from God as He calls us sons of the highest. And says again; "he that is from above is above all."

Secondly, when we talked about authority by vote, we took time to explain the hidden or silent power of usurping authority by-election: which is the power of creation. So, God has given us His nature of creativity so that we can also create our world; thus, exercising our own lordship. Note that it is the law of creation that brings specificity in our lordship. At the level of inherited lordship, all of us could be on the same plane or advantage. But creation and election make our lordship to differ in specificity as we are not called to create the same things. Since we somehow understand in part as it is written. How then does this manifest? Paul said, "we are all members of one body." *So we, being many, are one body in Christ, and individually members of one another. (Romans 12:5)*

We are all part of the Christ body. So, a man called to be a businessman will create a company by the grace of God and then become the chief executive officer. When God leads you to write a book you automatically become the lord of that book as the author. Therefore, to become a lord by-election, we are all called to create something big or small. Child of God, be a creator and do not spare lengthening your cords. Last but not least, we are all called to exercise our lordship over the devil and the entire kingdom of darkness by force. The kingdom of God suffers violence and the violent take it by force. It also says, *"submit yourself to God, resist the devil and he will flee from you" (James 4:7).*

By this God makes us understand that He has reduced the devil to nothing before us. So, God will not come to resist the devil for you. If you would assume your position as lord, then you must resist the devil until he flees. Then and only then will you experience the joy of your victory. With all the authority you have, to keep praying and asking God to take the devil out of your life is futile. With that you will only make yourself the loser because it is written, *"Greater is he that is in you than he that is in the world"* (1John4:4).

The scriptures did not say, 'greater is he that is in heaven than he that is in the world. This is simply because God cannot bypass your own lordship. If God were to bypass your authority, He would have said, "greater is he that is in heaven than he that is in the earth." Again He could say, "greater is he that is in heaven than he that is in you." For it is written that if your conscience judges you in that which you allow, know that God is greater. So instead he says unto him who is able to do according to the power that is in you. Not the power in heaven.

So, God is Lord of lords because it is your lordship that establishes His lordship here on Earth.

He has given you authority to show the world and the kingdom of darkness His power.
To the intent that now the manifold wisdom of God might be made known by the church to the principalities and powers in the heavenly places, (Ephesians 3:10)
Therefore, by us, the manifold wisdom of God is made known to the principalities and powers. It is clearly stated in the Word of God that we are kings and lords. If there is no doubt about that it means we too have the power of seals. We talked earlier that seals were both for identity representation and covenant relationship. In line with identity representation, God made the first man Adam in his image and likeness.

Also, it is written that Jesus came to restore the identity of man to the nature of God, by which we are all declared to be the very express image of God. Now Jesus said, "you shall receive power after that the Holy Ghost is come upon you and you shall be witnesses unto me...." What He meant was not that we would go about just telling His story. What He meant was that we will have the power to become everything He was on Earth and more. Listen, when a president cannot attend a meeting, he delegates his authority to someone else with the speech he was to present at the occasion. This person goes in the name of the president and does everything the president was to do on that occasion. As long as this person is in the witnessing area or occasion, he is the president. He sits on the seat reserved for the president and enjoys all the services kept for the president. We, therefore, are witnessing for God as acting kings until He comes. Jesus said, "as you have sent me, even so, do I send them." So we are sent with the same capacity with which Jesus was sent into the world. When Jesus was on Earth he said, "as long as I am on the Earth I am the light of the world." Then He said again that we are the light of the world.

So now that Jesus is no longer in the world, He is in effect no longer the light of the world: *you are now the light of the World.* If Jesus is still the light of the world today He is or can only be in the capacity of our shinning. By which He said; *"And the glory which You gave Me I have given them, that they may be one just as We are one:" (John17:22)* Therefore you (child of God) are a symbol of identity to testify of the fact that Jesus is alive and that God is real.

Next, talking of our covenant relationship we know that according to the law of decrees, whenever a decree is signed it cannot be revoked. So, the scriptures warn us by this covenant relationship that we have with the Lord, saying we should be steadfast to the end. But Jesus said to him, *"No one, having put his hand to the plow, and looking back, is fit for the kingdom of God" (Luke 9:62).* God said all this to make us understand that we are now in Christ and have a deal of life with Him. So, come what may, it is a treaty we have signed with God in Christ Jesus which should not be revoked no matter what. God expects us to keep our own side of the agreement so as to maintain the treaties that exist between the kingdom of God and the kingdom of Heaven. As long as this treaty stands, the rights and privileges that go with it will remain ours.

You will also declare a thing, and it will be established for you; (Job 22:28)

Where the word of a king is, there is power; (Ecclesiastes 8:4)

By this treaty, it is said that ye shall declare a thing and it shall be established unto you. Again, it says whatever you bound on Earth shall be bound in Heaven and whatever you loose on Earth shall be loosed. Why this? You may ask. It is simply because we are kings and where the word of a king is there is power. By this power, angels are ministering spirits sent to serve the heirs of salvation. Therefore, every believer is in the company of innumerable angels who are at their command. The scriptures then warn us saying, "do not say to an angel it was a joke." It means angels respond to our every command. And just as the decree of the king cannot be changed, the scriptures say to let your yes be yes and your no be no. If you say yes today, you should not say no tomorrow. You should not confuse Heaven by binding and losing one thing over and over. For example, today you are for; tomorrow you are against. Do not be a hypocritical king, by being neither hot nor cold. Today you say I am healed, the next day you say I am sick. Hence the scriptures say to the kings; "let the weak say I am strong and let the poor say I am rich" for where the word of a king is there is power.

Concerning the oath, we see that the oath can talk of two things. Firstly, the king can make a verbal (that is unwritten) decree to do a particular thing. This type of verbal decree is bound by an oath that the king cannot change. For it to be binding it has to be done in the presence of an audience. A good example of this kind of oath led to the beheading of John the Baptist.

yet for his oath's sake, and for their sakes which sat with him, he would not reject her. And immediately the king sent an executioner, and commanded his head to be brought: and he went and beheaded him in the prison, (Mark 6:26-27)

Secondly, we see the oath as a decision and public declaration of the king to abide by the rules and regulations governing the state or nation also called the constitution. It is this type of oath that I want us to talk about because the other is just like an unwritten decree. But this one is called the oath of inauguration. Hence the keyword for the oath of God in our life is called integrity. We are expected to do all according to the integrity of our hearts. Just as an oath bounds a man to the ethics of his profession so also does integrity bound a man to the law of his God. Just as a man is required to take an oath to win the trust of people, so also a man is required to be integral to win the trust of God and man.

And Jesus increased in wisdom and stature, and in favour with God and men. (Luke 2:52)

Jesus as a child grew in favor with God and with man. Therefore He grew to win the trust of God and that of man. When you grow up to bind yourself to the laws of God or the revelation of the word of God, you will continually grow in integrity. As you grow in integrity you grow to win the trust of God and that of man. Note that even though God called, you still have a choice to decide to live by His Word or obey His commands.

"He who has My commandments and keeps them, it is he who loves Me... (John14:21) Nevertheless the solid foundation of God stands, having this seal: "The Lord knows those who are His," and, "Let everyone who names the name of Christ depart from iniquity. (2Timothy 2:19)

It is, therefore, possible to be in Christ and not grow in your ability to bind yourself to His Word or will. Looking at the above verse, it means you can name the name of the Lord in iniquity because you still have the responsibility to depart from it. So, the question is. Can God trust you? If God gives you the 'anointing' will He regret it or rejoice over you?

I say this because many are asking God for authority and mistaking it for the anointing; not knowing that as a Christian you have the anointing and the authority. But is it not because we did not believe when He said He has given us authority and that the anointing in you shall teach you; that we have gone back to ask him again that which we already have? Like I said it is your responsibility. God always wants you to increase in your authority, but it will only come by you growing in your integrity. You know that if a president refuses to take the presidential inauguration oath, come what may he will never be declared president even if he has won the election. If a man and a woman do not take the marriage vows, they will never be pronounced husband and wife.

Note that an oath's power comes from its public formal declaration. Therefore, Jesus said anyone that is ashamed of me before men; I also will be ashamed of him before the angels. So, you need to know that your integrity to God must be publicly declared to take effect. God is therefore mostly pleased with you at the level of your faith integrity. So, you must decide where you want to be; whether in the valley or on the mountain. According to the oath, people will trust you to obey the constitution.

Therefore, just as we know by the oath that God will never do anything contrary to His Word, so also God should be able to know by your integrity that you will never do anything contrary to His Word. Note that we all start Christianity at zero levels, but must all grow in integrity if we will win the favor of God and that of man. I will like to draw your attention to this; that integrity might not mean what you think. Some mistake integrity for Christian tradition, called religion today. It is common to see people in the church who are still faithful to an old command thinking that it makes them integral. No.

Obeying Christian tradition does not make you integral. Listen to me, integrity vows to obey the law. But the law itself is subject to change. Just as constitutions change in every nation to meet the demands of the era, so integrity says whatever the law says I will abide by it. Hence in Christ, we have taken an oath to live by the Word of God. However, we know that we are bound to the Word of God according to the current revelation. As revelation grows or changes, so also must we adjust to these changes.

Thus, I will define integrity by this understanding as the ability to adjust your lifestyle to every revelation you get from the Word of God and the leadership of the Holy Spirit.

In other words, integrity flows with new revelation. It does not resist change or new revelation; rather it seeks new knowledge and always changes with it. Thus, being adamant to change by clinging to an old doctrine is not integrity but sheer tradition and stiff-necked-ness. God, therefore, tests our integrity in our ability to change and adjust to every revelation He gives us. The more you seek and change with respect to the revelations the more you find favor before Him.

Who also made us sufficient as ministers of the new covenant, not of the letter but of the Spirit; for the letter kills, but the Spirit gives life. (2Corinthians 3:6)

"In your seed all the nations of the earth shall be blessed, because you have obeyed My voice. (Genesis22:18)

'Also I said to you, "I am the LORD your God; do not fear the gods of the Amorites, in whose land you dwell." But you have not obeyed My voice. (Judges 6:10)

To lay more emphasis, I want to say that Christians whose Christianity is based solely on what is written in the (Letter) Bible can never win God's trust. Do you not know that the letter alone kills? Please understand how in the old, God had an interest in people with respect to their obedience to His voice and not just in the reading of the law. Come to think of it, the only reason we read our Bibles is to make sure we can hear and obey God's voice clearly. If this obedience to His voice relationship is not well established, it is impossible for you to be integral. This is not an overstatement. Do you think the Holy Spirit God gave you was in vain? But some have closed their ears to the voice of God being buried in traditions of men that make void the power in the Word of God.

Just imagine this: If Abraham was like some Christians today, he would have killed Isaac. If you have grieved the Holy One of God you must repent and rebuild fellowship.

On the aspect of our authority, you and I received authority the same way Jesus received His authority. We received authority from Heaven as sons of God, we received authority on Earth as sons of men and we received authority from below the earth as sons from the dead because it is considered that we all died with Him and resurrected together.

THE DIVINE NATURE OF GOD

Your Authority as a Christian

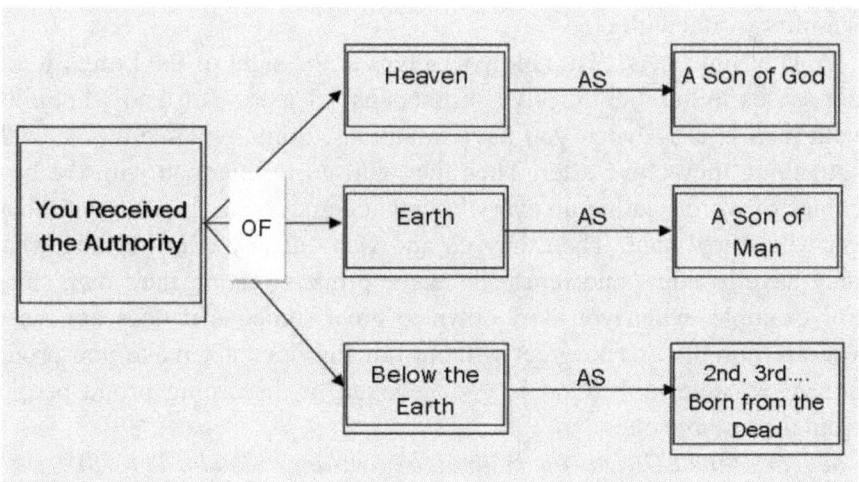

I think we can from this conclude that we have a complete comprehension of why we are kings and the functionality of our kingship. Note that the Bible says we are kings unto God not unto one another hence God did not call us kings to rule over our brothers and sisters. As it is said, *"be ye subject one to another."* Also *"he that is great among you shall be your servant."* (Ephesians 5:21; Matthew 23:11)

To complete this chapter, we will not do it successfully without talking about a very important ingredient of authority and ruler-ship called Humility. Humility in itself can be very confusing when you talk of it in men's perspective because you can never know a humble man from appearance.

Humble yourselves in the sight of the Lord, and He will lift you up. (James 4:10)

When God talked about humility, He commanded us to humble ourselves in His sight. Why should we humble ourselves in the sight of God and not in the sight of men? It is so because humility is a heart business and as we all know men are not good at diagnosing the state of the heart. Some, as a matter of fact, do not even understand their own hearts so how can they stand to discern the hearts of others.

Also, humility is not a hobby of some nowadays. Even in the church, this aspect to some has not really been taught in real sense. And you know until something is taught right people cannot be made free. I do not want to go in depth on this matter because I intend for us to limit ourselves to the purpose of this section; which is to show you how humility works with God.

The Bible says, "Humble yourselves in the sight of the Lord." It did not ask us to humble ourselves in the sight of men. You know humility with men is easy when you have intentions. Some will see a man with something they crave after. Then they will go to this man with the best choice of words, eating up everything that comes from the man until they get what they want. Then they go and wait for any man needing what they have to come and repeat the same process (eating their own shit). For example, when you bow down to greet someone it does not mean you are humble and to greet without bowing does not make you proud either. To note, only God is good enough at discerning proud people from the humble ones.

The fear of the LORD is the beginning of wisdom; (Psalm 111:10)

To better understand, the Bible says that the fear of the Lord is the beginning of wisdom. When talking of wisdom, know that wisdom never stands on its own. Wisdom is always given for something. For example, we have wisdom for success, wisdom for wealth, wisdom for health, etc.

So, in that light, we can say the fear of the Lord is the beginning of the wisdom for humility.

Hence you can never have the wisdom for humility when you do not fear God. But you know that nowadays there are some Christians who do not fear God. Some of those who try to fear Him still fall prey to thinking that fear means to be afraid. So, they go all the way being afraid of God rather than fear Him. You know when you fear people you please them increasingly (i.e. you grow to please them as time goes on) but when you are afraid of them, you always try not to cross the lines with them or avoid them thinking that it pleases them. Therefore, you can only know wisdom by learning to know God and change as you go towards Him. I want you to know that humility is not a gift at birth. You can learn to be humble. In fact, every Christian must learn to be humble and grow in humility all their lives. The truth about most of us is that because God has made us kings, it is but normal for us to desire honor. The problem comes when we get up and choose the wrong way of seeking honor. That is the way of pride and not the way of humility.

Before destruction the heart of a man is haughty, and before honour is humility. (Proverbs 18:12) You see clearly from above how God shows us the way to getting the honor He has given us like kings. Brethren, I, therefore, count it a privilege to declare to you that if you must attain the glory of your calling, then you must start working seriously on your humility quotient. This then is the apogee of the matter.

Let this mind be in you which was also in Christ Jesus, who, being in the form of God, did not consider it robbery to be equal with God, but made Himself of no reputation, taking the form of a bondservant, and coming in the likeness of men. And being found in appearance as a man, He humbled Himself and became obedient to the point of death, even the death of the cross. (Philippians 2:5-8)

For though I am free from all men, I have made myself a servant to all, that I might win the more; (1Corinthians 9:19)

From this, you see that humility is a mindset for people who know who they are. Hence a man with an inferiority complex and or low self-esteem can never know true humility. These are the class of people who lose all their humility at the feet of an event that builds their self-esteem. This even might be the possession of a car, sudden promotion, or increase in wealth. But not Jesus, because Jesus first knew that he was equal with God and that it was not a bad thing for Him to think that He was equal with God. Yet He made a choice after all that self-awareness to humble Himself until the death on the cross. Paul made a statement of his own humility when he said, "though I know I am free from all men, yet I have made myself a servant to all." Do you see that? Paul knew that he was not a servant to any man before he now chose to be the servant of all men.

Beloved, what you need to know is that true humility begins with a true knowledge of oneself. The question is why is that? It is so because right now you might be laying your life at the altar of God and other people because you think that it's the best a low life like you deserve. But how many of us will still put our lives at the altar of sacrifice after we have known that we are worth more than a million? When you have known who you are, that is when lesson one of humility actually begins. The reason why I took this time to talk or stress the need for you to be humble is that just as love is the only thing that can bind a man to perfection, only humility can bind you to your lordship or authority. If you think you are not humble then you are already one step into it. Do not be discouraged because it takes humility to realize that you are not humble or even not humble enough. So, make up your mind to learn it because humility can be learned.

The Kings Connection

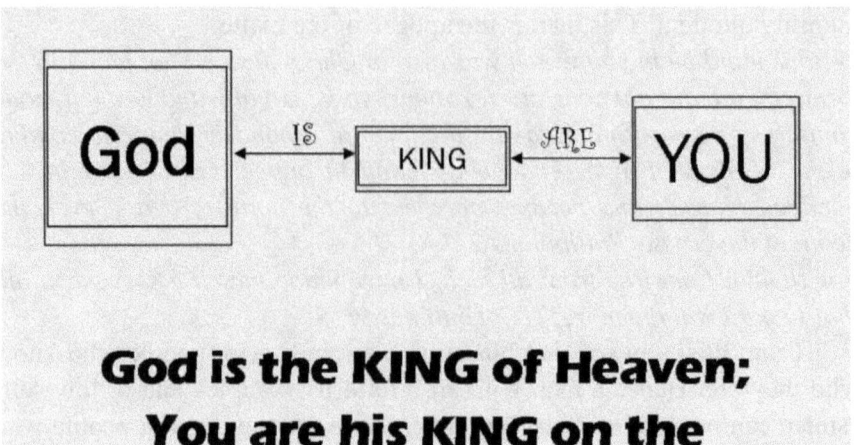

CHAPTER SEVEN

GOD THE FATHER

There are many things we might want to be in life. Of all these things, one of the most valuable is the aspect of parenting. For men, they want to enjoy being a father, while for women they want to enjoy being mothers. God has blessed my wife and me with a baby girl and I have been opportune to deal with baby Christians and so I have clues on matters of fatherhood. Also, today knowledge is everywhere so you can just imagine me stumbling on some. In my understanding, I came to know that the mother and the father have similar if not the same interest in what they want their children to be. But their interest level for this interest is antagonistic in the sense that what men or fathers' value most in children is different from what women value most. When we look at life from the most basic point, there are only two things that hold life and the world together. These things are Love and Responsibility.

So, when a child is growing up, the parents want them to grow in love and responsibility. But when the worst comes to the worst, fathers will moderate love to build responsibility in a child while mothers, on the other hand, will postpone responsibility to build love. So, in a normal home, while the father is working to build the child's ability to respond to life the mother is busy making lovers. This is why babies will normally follow their mother in most cases because they feel good just loving and feeling at that age when mummy is taking care of them. But sooner or later when mummy cannot take care any longer, they then see the mess mummy has put them into. That is why it is good for a mother and father to be involved in the upbringing of a child. Know that for every child, feelings develop before reason so love and emotions also come before responsibility. You might be asking yourself; why are we talking about God being a father but wasting time on natural parenting? Mind you that the things we see were made from things or beings we do not see. One of those beings we do not see is God. So, we can learn God from the things we see. Talking therefore about the relationship God has with us, as His children, He is all of what a father is and also all of what a mother is. We know that God is given a masculine address always in the Bible. I do not know if it's because most of the Bible was written by men.

However, I want to make you know that the word 'father'; as used for God can be likened to both the word parent as well as a father as we all know. I say so because you can have a female parent as well as a male parent. But looking at God, you will see that He exercises both the male and feminine characteristics of parenting. So, to me looking at God's way I know that every child has two fathers the male father and the female father. That is to call it the way we see it expressed in the Word of God. Please try to understand me as we move on.

So, while women want their children to be responsible in love, men, on the other hand, want their children to love responsibility.

Masculine and Feminine fatherhood of God

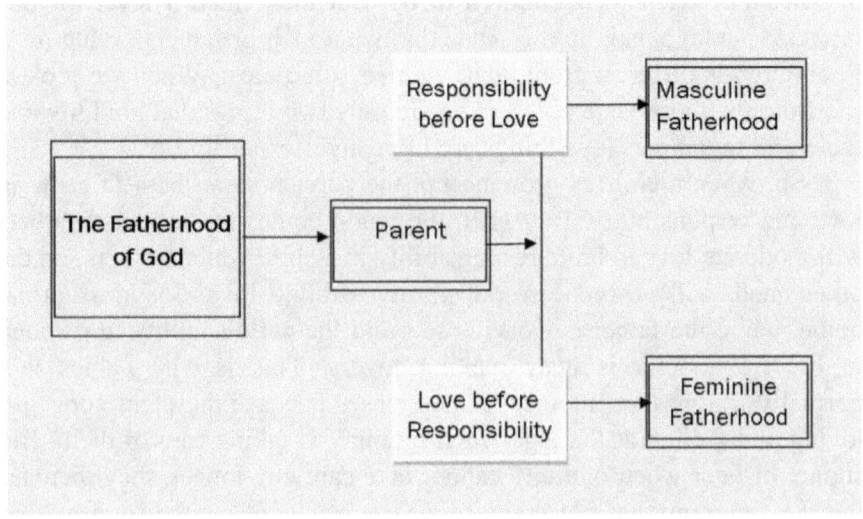

This is to strike a balance because if a child is woman-trained, they will love feeling too much to be able to help anyone. If they are men trained, they will be too responsible to really care for anyone. I do not say it is always like this but stating clearly that if they both will stay in their jurisdiction then that's what will result. Therefore, if you see God's character on this you will hear the voice of a father and that of a mother.
For even when we were with you, we commanded you this: If anyone will not work, neither shall he eat. (2Thessalonians 3:10)
Nevertheless I have this against you, that you have left your first love. (Revelation 2:4)

The same God who says if anyone will not work, neither shall he eat; will come again to rebuke you to return to your first love. This is so that he can strike the balance of the father and the mother. This makes me conclude that the fatherhood of God combines both the father and the mother. And from this you can remember, that was the nature of Adam before Eve was taken out of him. So, it truly takes a man and a woman to have a complete "man". With this in mind, I will like us to move to more important matters but before that, there is something I want to leave you with. Talking about fathers and mothers, fathers usually deal with their wives the same way they deal with their children while it is vice versa for mothers. In this light, fathers know that their wife is their responsibility. So, they take care of their wife. The same will go for the way a man will treat his child. For a woman, the man is her love or lover so she cares for him. So also, she will care for the children. Note the difference in their love-responsibility relationship. There is a difference therefore between taking care of someone and caring for someone. So, as we move ahead in this chapter you will see God manifesting himself in both attributes.

The Character of the Husband and Father

From the very beginning, after God finished making the Earth, on the sixth day He said, "let us make man in our likeness and image."
Then God said, "Let Us make man in Our image, according to Our likeness; let them have dominion over the fish of the sea, over the birds of the air, and over the cattle, over all the earth and over every creeping thing that creeps on the earth. (Genesis1:26)
the son of Enosh, the son of Seth, the son of Adam, the son of God. (Luke 3:38)

He made man to have dominion and Luke tells us in the genealogy of Jesus that Adam was the son of God. So simply put God from the very beginning wanted to have a son who was like Him. But since He was the king in Heaven He decided to create the domain of man which is Earth. So, the man could freely be like him on the earth as it is said, *but the earth He has given to the children of men. (Psalm 115:16)* Now, after Jesus was born, he became the only begotten Son of the Father. In other words; after the fall of Adam God had a plan to restore man so He can have sons again upon the Earth. The birth of Jesus fulfilled God's hope and once again after many years, there was now a son of God upon the Earth. That, however, was not the end of the plan. Jesus was given up by His Father through His death on the cross. *For God so loved the world that He gave His only begotten Son, that whoever believes in Him should not perish but have everlasting life. (John3:16)*

That said, Jesus died on the cross, He was buried and after that, He resurrected to be the firstborn (Son of God) from the dead. He is no longer the "only son" because he opened the door for us to be reborn by God and be filled again with the Holy Spirit of God. As it is said as many as are led by the spirit, they are sons of God. So, we see why Jesus is no longer the only son but the first because you and I are now sons of God too. That is if you are born again.

And Adam said: "This is now bone of my bones and flesh of my flesh; She shall be called Woman, because she was taken out of Man. (Genesis 2:23)

But he who is joined to the Lord is one spirit with Him. (1Corinthians 6:17)

So, we are the sons of God, meaning God is our Father. Next is the fact that when Adam saw Eve for the first time, he said of her this is flesh of my flesh and bone of my bones. Why, because Eve came out of him. Then God further explained saying, therefore, shall a man leave his father and mother and cleave to his wife and they two shall become one flesh. Then we know Jesus is the word (God) which became flesh and dwelled amongst us. It proceeds to clearly state that we are the bride of Christ just like Eve was the bride of Adam. Then it concludes it this way he that is joined with Christ is one spirit. So, it is clear that God the Father is our Father, and His Son has become our husband. Hence, we are the sons of the Father and the bride of the Son. To round this up it will not be complete if we do not talk about the part of the Holy Spirit.

Or do you not know that your body is the temple of the Holy Spirit who is in you, whom you have from God, and you are not your own? (1Corinthians 6:19)

Therefore, we are the sons of the Father, the brides of the Son and the dwelling place or temple of the Holy Spirit. The question you might want to ask is, why all this analysis? Remember we are talking about God's fatherhood and husband hood which brings His jealousy into play. Jealousy in this context is not sharing His temple with anyone.

'(for you shall worship no other god, for the LORD, whose name is Jealous, is a jealous God), (Exodus 34:14)

Then according to His jealousy, on a general note, He says, "The foundations of God's (jealousy) stands sure with this seal God knows them that are his." So, God requires commitment from everyone that is related to Him because He is jealous. But it is by jealousy that God requires us to respond to Him in a certain way. He expects that our relationship with Him be proven by a certain level of loyalty. So, when He says "I am a jealous God," He is simply saying that in relating with you I will require certain responses from you as I also respond to you. God does not do this for response sake only. Also, He wants to boast about you as He grows to trust you. However, the major reason for God's jealousy is found in the investment that He invested to get you. See; no one gave you to God. When Adam fell, he fell on his own accord. It was not God who sold him. He sold himself for nothing but after that, the kingdom of darkness had taken a hold of us until there was no way out. God also, did not receive you as a gift from the devil. The Bible says to this respect that *"you were bought at a price;"* ... (1Corinthians 7:23)

The price that was worth your value was Jesus Christ that was crucified on the cross. So, God did not just sit and wait. No, He had to buy you with a price from the sinful nature into the kingdom of His dear Son. And as you know a man will be more jealous of a shoe that he bought for $200 than for a shoe he bought for $14. So also, God is jealous of you because you were so expensive to get that He had to give the only Son He had to get you. So, if God is jealous of you, you should understand that it is because you were very expensive to buy. Note that even if you were the only person on the Earth Jesus would have still died. Therefore, God gives a command that we love Him with all our heart, mind and strength. Some will look at this with an evil eye asking: why demand too much from us?

You have not yet resisted to bloodshed, striving against sin. (Hebrews 12:4)

Brothers and sisters listen, the Bible says that we have not resisted unto bloodshed. But do you know that for your sake Jesus resisted until he had to shed His blood? In the Garden of Gethsemane, he cried blood just for you. So, by that cross, Jesus in God paid your bride price in full to become the husband of the church. Is that too much to ask seeing that He Himself loved you with his own very life until he went to the cross, crying out His love for you. So, it is because of this jealousy that God wants us to see or recognize what He has done for us and do the same.
For whom the LORD loves He chastens, and scourges every son whom He receives. (Hebrews12:6)

So, as a father he chastises you to make you grow up to be like Him. As a husband He wants you to be one with Him in every aspect and as His temple, He does not want to share you with anyone else.

So, by God's jealousy, you are His investment and He wants to take total responsibility and glory over you because He worked very hard to get you and wants to make sure that the reason why he bought you is fulfilled. No man wants his wife pregnant for his neighbor.

Brethren I have found out that it is because of God's jealousy that He says, "let anyone that name the name of the Lord depart from iniquity." God's jealousy commands us to honor Him as our Father, submit to Him as our Husband and purify or sanctify our vessels only for Him who is the owner and in-dweller of our vessels (body).

The Character of the Provider

Every responsible father knows that it is his responsibility to provide for his child. To provide for them according to his means everything that they need for life. God being our Father knows His responsibility towards us as His children.
As His divine power has given to us all things that pertain to life and godliness, through the knowledge of Him who called us by glory and virtue, (2Peter 1:3)
"If you then, being evil, know how to give good gifts to your children, how much more will your Father who is in heaven give good things to those who ask Him! (Matthew 7:11)

By which He said that He has given us everything that pertains to life and godliness. So, we find out that Jesus explaining the responsibility of the father to this respect says, "if you being wicked, know how to give good gifts to your children how much more shall God give to them that ask him." Now we see that our earthly fathers are sometimes limited by their means but as the Bible says God is rich toward all that call to Him. God can never be short of resources because all the cattle on a thousand hills belong to Him.

As you well know; *the earth is the LORD'S, and all its fullness, the world and those who dwell therein. (Psalm 24:1)*

He who did not spare His own Son, but delivered Him up for us all, how shall He not with Him also freely give us all things? (Romans 8:32)

The whole Earth belongs to Him. God can never be poor or short of resources to meet your needs. He has also given us all things freely through His Son who died for us. Then he that asks; receives, he that seeks; finds and to him who knocks; the door shall be opened. So, you cannot ask and not receive except you did not ask from God because the Bible again states that every good and perfect gift comes from Him. So, we can rest assured because He is faithful in that He will never turn from us.

Then as a husband, he that is joined with Christ is one spirit. So, as we have one spirit with Him as His bride He has blessed us with every spiritual blessing in heavenly places. And as a true Husband, He loved us so much that He laid down His life for us so we could have life.

For you know the grace of our Lord Jesus Christ, that though He was rich, yet for your sakes He became poor, that you through His poverty might become rich. (2Corinthians 8:9)

He has sanctified us with His presence and graced us with the beauty of His holiness. By this, He gave us the same glory that He had so we can also shine with His light upon the Earth.

Thus says the LORD: "Cursed is the man who trusts in man and makes flesh his strength, whose heart departs from the LORD. For he shall be like a shrub in the desert, And shall not see when good comes, But shall inhabit the parched places in the wilderness, In a salt land which is not inhabited. (Jeremiah 17:5-6)

That is why God wants us to trust Him because He is the only one that can really provide for us. When God says, "Cursed be the man that trusts in man" He is not saying that He is going to curse anyone that trusts in a man. No! Believe me, He is not going to curse you if you trust men. Who is man that you even trust him? Do you not know that the heart of man is desperately wicked? Sometimes until you are handled by men, you will think that God is over stressing their wickedness. The man again is very selfish in his nature, such that he only wants to help himself. In other words, if he does not see his interest, he will not help you. So, the scripture goes further saying; you will not see when good comes. Wow! Do you know why? This is the reason; if a man sees really good, he will think of himself first not you. Yet every good and perfect gift comes from God. Hence what can man or his father the devil give to you? Only bad and imperfect gifts of course! After all this, the part that I like is the story of Jesus concerning this issue.

Behold the fowls of the air: for they sow not, neither do they reap, nor gather into barns; yet your heavenly Father feedeth them. Are ye not much better than they? Which of you by taking thought can add one cubit unto his stature? And why take ye thought for raiment? Consider the lilies of the field, how they grow; they toil not, neither do they spin: And yet I say unto you, That even Solomon in all his glory was not arrayed like one of these. (Matthew 6:26,29)

Look at the birds; they are so lazy and unorganized in the sense that they never sow or reap, neither do they even gather into barns. Thus, they do not have a storehouse yet your heavenly Father feeds them. Then he goes further to say concerning the lilies in the valley which are up today and tomorrow are no more yet your heavenly Father decorates them to the point where even Solomon in all his beauty cannot meet up to them. What then would I say to you? Beloved Jesus then concludes, "oh ye of little faith (unable to believe)." Thus, even if God's children become as lazy as a sparrow, God will make sure He provides for them. If you become as limited in your life like the lilies, He will clothe you more than Solomon. Then He says, if you will hear all this and choose to seek first the kingdom of God and His righteousness, He will add you all these other things because as you all know He already knows the things that we need long before we even ask Him. So, God tries to show us from these verses that He is the only one that can and wants to provide for us.

Unless the LORD builds the house, they labor in vain who build it; Unless the LORD guards the city, The watchman stays awake in vain. (Psalm 127:1)

Our God is very responsible for us as even our promotion can only come from above. In other words, if he does not provide or promote you, any promotion you get is not going to meet your real needs. Then he goes further to say, *"Now to Him who is able to do exceedingly abundantly above all that we ask or think, according to the power that works in us,"*

(Ephesians 3:20). So, God is so rich towards us that he even wants to provide us with more than we can ever demand or require of Him.

Then Amaziah said to the man of God, "But what shall we do about the hundred talents which I have given to the troops of Israel?" And the man of God answered, "The LORD is able to give you much more than this." (2Chronicles 25:9)

In line with this, I remember the king who gave money to soldiers he wanted to help him in battle. God later told him not to go with the soldiers he had paid. So, he asked the man of God what to do concerning the money he had given them. Then God told him through the prophet to forget about the money and that He was able to give him much more than that. But you see to conclude this matter like this will leave you with yesterday's revelation. So, what does it say now? God has given to us all things that pertain to life and Godliness. I hereby declare to you that God will not give you much more; He has given you much more. Yet these things will become yours as you grow in the knowledge of God. Can you believe that about your God and provider?

The Character of the Caretaker

Sometimes many people see the person who gives them what they need as the person who takes care of them. Nothing can be farther from the truth. I want you to understand me on this. There is a difference between providing for someone and taking care of that person. In America, we have single mothers who receive provision for their children according to the law of child support. Money is taken from the father and sent to the mother for the child every month. The father, in this case, provides for the child while only the mother takes care of the child. But such children most of the time grow up very angry with their father; that is; if they do not hate them. Why do they hate a man who provides for them? The issue is, to provide for someone does not mean you really care. You know men being what they are. You can see a man provide for someone to get glory or something for himself. These days men give women things not out of care but because they want to lure them to bed. Then the women also accept to have sex not out of love but so that they can get more of the men's money. In such a case giving is not out of care but a mere scheme to please oneself. What am I saying? God is not like a divorced father who sends money to a faraway son He hardly knows while being ever angry why He has to be spending His money for nothing. On the part of God David said: *I have been young, and now am old; Yet I have not seen the righteous forsaken, Nor his descendants begging bread. (Psalm 37:25)*

Why did he say this? He said it because it is possible to forsakenly provide for someone. Now let me show you how God provides for people He really does not care about. It is written that God causes His rain to fall on both the just and the unjust; the ungodly and the godly; the good and the wicked. Does that mean He cares for the unjust, or ungodly? No. So for this ungodly people, God will not call them His sons as He calls us but He provides for them because He is a provider to all mankind. You might now be wondering why God is a provider for people whom He has reserved for destruction. If you doubt me on this one, ask wives who have everything they need from their husband but are very frustrated in their emotions because he doesn't care. Care is more implicating than just giving someone money or things.

Don't you know that if you truly care for your child there are some things you will not give them because of that care?

Hence our Father (God) takes this responsibility very seriously. So, we see God saying time and again that he will never leave nor forsake us. Listen the Bible says; let every man be a lie but let God be truthful.
...For He Himself has said, "I will never leave you nor forsake you." (Hebrews 13:5)
"I will not leave you orphans; I will come to you. (John 14:18)
So, believe me God will never forsake you. It has never crossed His mind, therefore, how can He accomplish something He never thinks about? I see caretaking as the feminine father's responsibility for love and dream. Remember the deep things of God are not far from us because it takes very simple things to see who God is. However, you know "big eyes" have a problem seeing very little things.

The Love of Care

Talking about love, God is not just the epitome of love, He is love. So He being love will never fall short of the demands of love. Looking at love, it is care for another person. Love wants to make you special; he wants to know and make sure everything is well with you. He wants to share the pain and joy. By this love of the father, Jesus said I will not leave you orphans. So, we see that God sent us a true comforter and

helper to come and be with us: not for five days but forever. So, God is now living in us by His Spirit and is with us helping our progress and taking care of us in the day and in the night. You must note that it's at this level where the feminine aspect of God's fatherhood truly stands out.
And shall not God avenge his own elect, which cry day and night unto him, though he bear long with them? I tell you that he will avenge them speedily. (Luke18:7&8)

God so loves us that he wants to deliver us speedily from any situation, so why will he have to bear with us very long. The reason is that it hurts Him to see us suffer from our ignorance and foolishness. Yet He has to wait for us to grow to maturity. That's why the Holy Spirit came to be our comforter; to comfort us as a mother will comfort a child when he fails an exam or hurt himself.
And when he hath found it, he layeth it on his shoulders, rejoicing. And when he cometh home, he calleth together his friends and neighbours, saying unto them, Rejoice with me; for I have found my sheep which was lost. (Luke15:5&6)

Also, God is a consuming fire, yet toward us His children, we see His tender mercy manifesting as He leaves His flock on the mountain to look for the one sheep that's gone astray to bring it back to the fold. This He does because He is not just out to make us do His will such that, He abandons us when we fail. No! As a mother "He" feels for us, He understands what you are going through and cares for you, even when you do not meet his standards. At such moments when it looks like life is caving in on you, you will hear that still voice saying let your heart not be troubled, be of good cheer. I love you with an everlasting love and will never forsake you; when you are feeling lonely. Though He wants you to do his will, he will not just abandon you because you made a mistake. He will become for you like the GPS after you miss your route, calculating a new way out, giving you a second change until you are able to find your way. Brethren Even though GPS is a machine you must understand that our God is living and very good. Hence, He is working on our behalf to make a way where there seems to be no way. Therefore, do not let the devil tell you a lie about God saying He does not care about you because you failed in something. God loved you and gave His son to die for you when you were a complete and utter failure. So, your mistake does not touch His love for you.

Hear this; God is pleased when you do His will but He loves you for who you are: His child.

The Dream of Caring

Talking about the dream part of caretaking, every man has a dream for his wife and children. It is on the dream part of caring that you will see clearly that provision and caretaking are two different things; even though they work together in the father (God).

For I know the thoughts that I think toward you, says the LORD, thoughts of peace and not of evil, to give you a future and a hope. (Jeremiah29:11)

Listen God has a dream for us all. There is a purposed life that He wants us to live. So, since we are His babies, He puts us on a growth or building plan as one aspect of his caretaking plan to ensure our growth. Therefore He says, "if the Lord does not build the house, they that build do so in vain." The reason He says so is that every father knows that he is the best person to take care of his child. No good father will let his child to be taken care of by another man when he can do it himself. And as you well know God has the means and He knows that with the dream He has for you, He only can take you there. He, therefore, says by this that He has thoughts of good and not of evil for you, to bring you to an expected end.

So, God being the only one with the ability to take you there, He knows that the labor of any other person even you alone will be in vain. Hence God will chastise everyone He loves and scourges every son whom He receives. So, you see that training a child is an aspect of love that is regarded more on the dream or the responsibility part as we talked at the beginning of this chapter. Now because God knows the dream He has for you, He cannot just provide you with anything in the name of love. To better understand this, we will take a simple example. If you are a parent you will better understand me. If you have ever given something to your neighbor's child you find out that you always provide for them as off the hook. However, when you provide for your child you want to find out if that provision will go to further the plan of growth and development you dream for your child. Sometimes you will go as far as delay provision of certain things to make sure that the child is mature enough to handle it.

"And shall God not avenge His own elect who cry out day and night to Him, though He bears long with them? (Luke 18:7)
You ask and do not receive, because you ask amiss, that you may spend it

on your pleasures. (James 4:3)

So also, because God really cares about you He monitors even the provision to see whether it serves the dream he has for you. Sometimes Christians ask and do not receive because they want things that do not have a part in God's plan for their lives. Instead, those things if granted, will serve as doors of real distraction or destruction. And you know a little leaven will cause the entire dough to rise. So, you can have one distraction and you are distracted forever and that is what God does not want for you. Thus, anyone who comes to the Lord shall be built or trained: like it or not. This is the reason why some don't like going nearer to God because they don't want His training. God, therefore, builds you in His training or caretaking program to make sure you grow up in the image of Christ. We know that if we ask anything according to His will; He hears us. You ought to know that God will easily hear you when you ask Him things that are in line with His will and dream for your life. Take for example your will is to train up your child to be like you (strong in the Lord and educated). If your ten-year-old child gets up and says to you "daddy or mummy I want you to drop me today at the night club and come back for me at about 4:00 a.m." I will no doubt say: the set child will receive a treatment that will make him/her never allow their mind to wonder that far again. If we do this for our kids, how much more will our heavenly Father do to us in His training process; seeing that He knows the end of all things?

Casting all your care upon Him, for He cares for you. (1Peter 5:7)

God takes care of us as He says to cast your cares upon me for I care. We need to learn to really cast those cares to Him because He truly cares for us just as He says without mincing words. But know that caretaking is both on love and responsibility or dream. Therefore because of the dream part of caretaking, God will delay provision until you become responsible enough. No man gives his inheritance to a son he is not sure of. But it is during the process of caretaking that he knows the son he can trust. So also, God will not just hand the proceeds of such a sacrifice on the cross to your hand without first chastening you to see if He can trust you. So, if you want your heavenly Father to trust you, you must submit yourself willingly to His chastisement. That is God for you; child of God.

The Father Connection

There are no reasons why I should go into very deep revelations on this because we all have fathers; be they masculine fathers or feminine fathers (mothers). However, I will like to explain a little further so we can understand our fatherhood in light of the reason for this section. First of all, I want us to know that we as the children of God are expected to be physical-spiritual fathers as well as spiritual fathers since we are to be part of what God is fathering here on Earth.

Physical-spiritual Fathers

Now looking at the aspect of physico-spiritual fatherhood, the bible says:
But did He not make them one, having a remnant of the Spirit? And why one? He seeks godly offspring. Therefore take heed to your spirit, And let none deal treacherously with the wife of his youth. (Malachi 2:15).
For the unbelieving husband is sanctified by the wife, and the unbelieving wife is sanctified by the husband; otherwise your children would be unclean, but now they are holy. (1Corinthians 7:14)
It is therefore clear that God makes them one because He seeks a godly seed or offspring. To ensure the continuity of Gods' plan here on Earth, He makes sure that godly children are born on Earth. How is this going on? We have been made to understand that when you give birth to a child as a believer that child is holy or sanctified from birth. Now in a case where both parents are not believers it says, the children are sanctified by the believer. How many believe this? Instead, some say when their children grow, they will choose to repent because they cannot become born again as babies.

But read what God said, "Levi paid tithes in the loins of Abraham." Notice that Levi was the third-generation son of Abraham. But what Abraham did was counted on his behalf. Listen, the day you gave your life to God; that day your child also who was in your loins also gave his or her life to God. That day was salvation day for all your generation after you. So now God has just left you with the responsibility to train them in the way they should go so they will not depart from who they are. If you fail to train them, they will go the other way but know God will hold you responsible for the good or the bad. Can God trust you in this? The child you have is physical but in the spirit of that child, he or she is not born with the nature of the first Adam but that of the second

Adam.

Spiritual Fathers

On the second aspect which is the aspect of strict spiritual fatherhood the Bible says.

And God hath set some in the church, first apostles, secondarily prophets, thirdly teachers, after that miracles, then gifts of healings, helps, governments, diversities of tongues. (ICorinthians12:28)

You realize that these people did not just become apostles and prophets etc. they were called and sent by God to lead His church because they are very important for the life-line of the church. This fatherhood or leadership plays a very important role in training the church in the way God wants it to be. Without it, there will be chaos in the house of God. See; because God could not come down to lead His flock, He, therefore, appointed pastors and prophets to help Him shepherd His sheep. So, all called leaders should know that there is no other profession in the world as noble as this profession. Being called of God as a co-laborer in His vineyard is the greatest honor ever. They have the responsibility to watch over the souls of the church until they become mature in Christ.

Is any one of you sick? He should call the elders of the church to pray over him and anoint him with oil in the name of the Lord. (James5:14)

That said I want you to know that there are two main ways by which people become leaders in the house of God. According to scriptures, we see the word Elders, and then we hear of apostles and prophets and pastors. When we read this, we might be tempted to think they mean the same thing but they are different. The first form of spiritual leadership talks of those called into spiritual leadership. So, God will call many pastors and apostles to lead His church in a generation.

The second way people become leaders in the house of God is by growing to become more and more spiritually mature. These are those called elders in the above scriptures. An elder is just a mature Christian. It has nothing to do with the fact that they were called to lead the church as pastors or not. They become leaders simply by becoming mature in the house of God. As a matter of fact, God always uses or works better with Elders than with those he called to lead. Let me explain. All Christians are called to elder-hood because we are all called to maturity. Be it a called pastor or a church entrepreneur or the usher, we are all called to grow and grow and grow until we all become spiritual giants in the house of God. The reason therefore why God works with elders more than with the called is that the level of relationship or service we can ever give to God is based more on our maturity and not our calling. By this I mean it is possible to have a called pastor who is more of a spiritual baby than a church cleaner. Who do you think God will elevate? The pastor: just because he is a pastor? No.

Maturity is the difference between a baby Christian and an elder in the house of God. By the way, you have to know everyone in the church is called by God; they might not just be called in the five-fold ministry as we all know. Now since God calls people very early in their Christian walk, we have to understand that he does so to ensure we all become spiritually mature bearing the responsibility of the calling in our hands to build experience. That is basically why many are called but few are chosen because many who are called never become mature enough for God to work with them. Therefore, if you are a baby with the calling of an apostle, God will not work with you just because He called you. Don't you know the first calling of every Christian is the call unto maturity?

So, no matter your calling, just keep growing spiritually in every aspect and God will start trusting you with people as it is written let them meet the elders. Immaturity also leads to the rejection of many and the changing of calling for some. If God calls you for something and you refuse to grow to maturity, He could reject you and give your calling to someone who probably never thought they could become like you, simply because they grew up. So, if you must be anything; be an elder and no matter where you are God will work with you to help His people. Being a pastor or an apostle is just like getting a job. But being an Elder is like becoming the big brother or big sister such that your Father (God) can trust you to take care of your siblings. Isn't that wonderful?

Don't you know the only reason God chose David and rejected Saul was because David was more mature in heart than Saul? What did David have at the time he was anointed? He didn't even have a say in his family but his relationship with God and his maturity in the faith made God to remove him from taking care of sheep to taking care of His people. There is no limit to what God can do with a man who has a truly mature relationship with Him.

Let the elders that rule well be counted worthy of double honour, especially they who labour in the word and doctrine (I Timothy5:17)
That is the reason why it is recommended that elders who do their work well, be treated with honor because to become spiritually mature is not an easy task talk less of having to take others with you.

I planted, Apollos watered, but God gave the increase. (1Corinthians 3:6)
Children, obey your parents in the Lord, for this is right. (Ephesians 6:1)

As Christians, though we boast in the increase that God brings, we cannot annul the planting and watering of great men and women who travail to see us through these moments. Therefore, as it is rightly said we need to obey our fathers in the Lord because it is the right thing to do.
Obey them that have the rule over you, and submit yourselves: for they watch for your souls, as they that must give account, that they may do it with joy, and not with grief: for that is unprofitable for you. (Hebrews13:17)

We should understand that submitting to men and women God has put over you is considered by God as submission to Him. You cannot just say I am submitting only to God because there are people whom God has placed over you. So, let people help you get to where God called you because that's their reason for being there. And if you disobey authority or refuse to submit to authority, it can lead to the destruction of God's plan for your life and land you in a curse instead; so, do the right thing before God and man.

Before we end, I will like to explain the mystery behind Christian leadership. You have to understand that though we have spiritual fatherhood on Earth, the only true spiritual father is God. Also, though we have spiritual leadership or authority, the only true Lord is Jesus. Therefore, we should lead God's people in a way as not to provoke His jealousy.

"Do not call anyone on earth your father; for One is your Father, He who is in heaven. (Matthew 23:9)
And Judah took a wife for Er his firstborn, whose name was Tamar. And Er, Judah's firstborn, was wicked in the sight of the LORD; and the LORD slew him. And Judah said unto Onan, Go in unto thy brother's wife, and marry her, and raise up seed to thy brother. And Onan knew that the seed should not be his; and it came to pass, when he went in unto his brother's wife, that he spilled it on the ground, lest that he should give seed to his brother. And the thing which he did displeased the LORD: wherefore he slew him also. (Genesis38:6-10)

God is so jealous in this that He says to us "call no man your father here on earth." Know that the one and the only true father of every Christian is God the Father in Heaven. I do not care if you agree or not for, we all are to be subject to the Word of God. Therefore, we as stewards should know that the essence of our spiritual fatherhood or guidance is to ensure that the people grow to be connected to their real father who is God and not to ourselves only. They might begin by us, but they must grow past us to relating with their real and true father who is God. As it is said, "my little children on whom I travail until Christ be formed in you." So, the real deal is to make sure that Christ is formed in those God has given you to shepherd, and not to keep them bound to a false yoke of leadership or mentorship. Do not expect Christians to pay you for what you have done for them. You made an agreement with their Father to take care of them so do not fall into the temptation of expecting them to pay you: let God pay you. Listen, babysitters do not ask the babies they are sitting for their pay. They ask their parents.

The reason why some ministers of God complain about the ungenerousness of Christians is that they are never learning the lesson of not expecting pay from the babies. I do not by this insinuate that Christians should be ungrateful or not share carnal things with their spiritual leaders which thing is their obligation. Yet only God can pay you because He employed you in the first place remember. Next very important about this is the fact that we are not living for ourselves being in Christ. We are all exalted to live our lives to please Him who died for us: Jesus. In the above verses, Er represents Jesus who died for our sins and left his wife Tamar (the church) in the hands of present church leaders in the person of Onan. Church pastors or leaders, therefore, have a huge responsibility to lead and relate with the church in a way that makes them relate with God and Jesus their true husband. So, we need to make sure we are doing everything according to the grace given to us to grow the church according to God's will. We, therefore, need not be like Onan who by wickedness had pleasure with Tamar (the church) but preventing her from ever getting pregnant for Er (Jesus our Lord).

If you are a leader or pastor in the house of God it is a wonderful opportunity given to you by God to serve His people. Do not let temptation overtake you because the time has come when God will wipe out this generation of "Onanic" leaders like he killed their father Onan. Please know this; if you are a father in the church you have a responsibility to feed the church as God commanded Peter by instruction, rebuke, and doctrine and to be as an example for others to follow. Know this you are not their lord because you did not die for them. We are not to lord it over our brothers and boast as though we did not receive what we now have in Christ. Fellow brethren and leaders in the house of God I encourage you to do the work of the ministry as one who knows he will give an account but more so, I encourage you to do it because there is nothing you will do to serve the will of God and His people that will go unrewarded. So, with all diligence, run this race as someone who knows he is running for the prize. I will like to leave this for the sake of context knowing by God's grace if He will permit me; we will talk more on this under another title. However, I will like us to continue with the connection we have with the jealousy of God.

While I was with them in the world, I kept them in thy name: those that thou gavest me I have kept, and none of them is lost, but the son of perdition; that the scripture might be fulfilled. (John17:12)

"Simon, Simon! Indeed, Satan has asked for you, that he may sift you as wheat. But I have prayed for you, that your faith should not fail; and when you have returned to Me, strengthen your brethren.". (Luke 22:31-32)

On this we see Jesus at the end of His ministry in prayer told God how all that He gave Him He did not lose any. Mind you that Jesus in His earthly ministry is very much likened to us, in every sense of the word. But what made that possible? The only thing that made it possible was the fact that He guarded them with His jealousy. So He was so jealous of them that like a mother hen He covered all of them. In the case of Peter, He could not just let the devil get rid of him so He prayed for him. I want to use this opportunity to say that our jealousy for the church should be expressed by the extent to which we are willing to go to lay down our lives for the strengthening of the church. I find again that Jesus has given us the mandate to help strengthen our brothers even as He has made us strong through the help of others.

I marvel that ye are so soon removed from him that called you into the grace of Christ unto another gospel: Which is not another; but there be some that trouble you, and would pervert the gospel of Christ. But though we, or an angel from heaven, preach any other gospel unto you than that which we have preached unto you, let him be accursed. As we said before, so say I now again, If any man preach any other gospel unto you than that ye have received, let him be accursed. For do I now persuade men, or God? or do I seek to please men? for if I yet pleased men, I should not be the servant of Christ. (Galatians1:6-10)

Paul demonstrated his jealousy for the gospel of Christ saying if even angels or he preaches another gospel they should all be accursed. Wow! Why take such a risk? It is because he was jealous of the Gospel of Christ. Paul wanted to make sure that the people he had taught stay and grow in the spirit as he had taught them. Then he ended by giving the reason why some are not jealous of the gospel. The desire to please men: either themselves or people they want approval from. Do you want to please people or yourself as you declare the Word of God? To some their belly is become their God. We must all grow to direct our passion and jealousy to make sure we are promoting the gospel of Christ in the Church of God. Let us become so passionate about it to a point where we are so consumed. Only then will we be able to ensure the growth of Christ-likeness in the church. So, if we commit ourselves to make sure Christ is formed in them, they will so grow until the anointing in them will teach them how to respect every man of God and to honor those who have been a blessing to their lives. But if as leaders you screw or crook them to respect you, they will snap because baby Christians always do. I see God in His own jealousy not to lose us. That though He does not trust us He will always leave us still with a remnant. Let us, therefore, be jealous of the Word of God that he has committed to us to see the body of Christ being built by it.

Next is the provider connection. On this note, the Word of God gives us an encouragement that we should give and it shall be given to us; in good measure shall men give to us. But I want to say here that God has called us as both spiritual and physical providers.

"Give, and it will be given to you: good measure, pressed down, shaken together, and running over will be put into your bosom. For with the same measure that you use, it will be measured back to you. (Luke 6:38)
"Heal the sick, cleanse the lepers, raise the dead, cast out demons. Freely you have received, freely give. (Matthew 10:8)
...He said to him again a second time, "Simon, son of Jonah, do you love Me?" He said to Him, "Yes, Lord; You know that I love You." He said to him, "Tend My sheep." (John 21:16)

On the spiritual aspects, Jesus sent the apostles and made a profound statement that they should give freely as they have also received freely. What was he talking about? He gave them spiritual ability to heal the sick freely so he wanted them to also heal the sick freely. In another place, Jesus asked Peter three times if he loved Him with the charge "feed my sheep." God has given us the mandate of spiritual leadership to feed the sheep of God with his word. That is to teach them the sound Word of God which is our act of providing them with spiritual food until they grow and become perfect in Christ. Before

Jesus fed five thousand people, the disciples had asked Him to send them away but He told them to feed the people. So, after He gave thanks to God He handed the bread to the disciples who then gave to the people.

By this Jesus was saying that in order for us to feed the church of God we must receive the Word from Him and give it to the people.

On the physical aspect, James is a little harsh saying "show me your faith and I will show you my works."
If a brother or sister be naked, and destitute of daily food, and one of you say unto them, Depart in peace, be ye warmed and filled; notwithstanding ye give them not those things which are needful to the body; what doth it profit? (James 2:15-16)
He went further to warn against the fact that you cannot see someone who is hungry and you pray for the person and say be warm without giving food to the person. It is not strange to still find very stingy Christians in the church today who only care about themselves and their little families. Literarily, they forget and are insensitive to the needs of the body of Christ or the church. But for this, the Word of God charges us not to mind only our own things but those of others also. It also makes us know through the exaltation of Paul that we should not be weary in well doing for in due time we shall receive our reward if we faint not.
And let us not grow weary while doing good, for in due season we shall reap if we do not lose heart. (Galatians 6:9)
Therefore, brothers and sisters, it is rather unfortunate that today we find some with the individualistic mindset in the church, such that some trust the Lord only for their own blessing. In all these Christians are tempted more and more to trust God only for their increase and not for the increase of another. Yet in "Acts of the Apostles", we are told how believers sold their stuff for the needs of the saints. One remarkable account is the one which says they were all together in one accord having all things common and they that had, were as though they did not have and they that did not have didn't lack. I trust the Lord that we will see a revival of church values such as sharing more than it has ever been in the past; when people will go out of their way to make way for others in giving. Please, you ought to know fellow saints that God is counting on us to take care of others especially them of the household of God.

The need for outright giving cannot be overemphasized in this 21st century; when disasters, wickedness and all forms of evil are creating humanitarian crisis every now and then. Let the church get up and respond to the needs of this world for God is indeed counting on us. For those who are doing this already, we do appreciate your efforts and encourage you in all your efforts knowing in so doing you are expressing yourself more and more as a giver like your Father God.

And God is able to make all grace abound toward you; that ye, always having all sufficiency in all things, may abound to every good work: Being enriched in every thing to all bountifulness, which causeth through us thanksgiving to God. (2Corinthians 9:8, 11)

Do you know that God expects thanks from people on account of our good works on the Earth? That is why He has made all grace available to us. Therefore, just as God so loved us that He gave. Let us also love both our brethren and the people of this world enough to oblige ourselves and be responsible for their needs in the name of Jesus Christ. I know that some have been taught heretically to give only to church leaders but I do want to say that our churches to this effect should develop help friendly systems that can reach the grassroots of the church. If we do this half of the problems of believers would have been solved. Let us, therefore, be fellow providers with the Lord to give and to do good to both friends and enemies alike whenever the need arises.

Last but not least is the aspect of care-taking. Talking of care-taking you will remember we talked of two aspects: the aspect of love and the aspect of responsibility installation. On the aspect of love, one of the ways we prove that we love God is demonstrated in the fact that we love the beloved.

If someone says, "I love God," and hates his brother, he is a liar; for he who does not love his brother whom he has seen, how can he love God whom he has not seen? (1John 4:20)

Also, as it is rightly put in the above scripture, stop deceiving yourself because you cannot love God when you hate people around you. God, Himself is in the business of ensuring that our love for Him is reflected in our love and care for the beloved. What is the point? We are exalted in scriptures to be perfect just as He is perfect. And only the care that comes out of love will make us come to grips with His perfection.

When Jesus spoke about the Holy Spirit, He said that God was sending us another comforter. God sent a comforter to come and live in us forever so we can grow to comfort others with the same comfort we have received. Now on the aspect of instilling responsibility, Paul expressed his deep desire for Christians to grow. We are therefore required to desire the sincere milk that we might grow thereby. See; Paul was not just marking time with the believers. He made sure they were growing into spiritual maturity and responsibility. The only reason why God would call special people and put them to lead the church is to ensure that the church grows to a level of responsibility. So do not exercise your ministry without really understanding the passion of your calling to train people to take spiritual responsibility. Let us, therefore, not become a manifestation of blind people leading the blind. How would they become responsible enough to know the reason for their calling when they have not been trained to take their own responsibilities? So, we are called as Paul said, to plant and water Christians to maturity.

So, whether you are called specially for this or not, you need to stand tall for God and help another Christian to grow and become responsible. Both in the aspect of praying for them, teaching them and counseling them on issues that concern their faith lives. For we are all co-laborers with the Lord building the house of God. Let us, therefore, hold in high esteem first our own growth responsibilities and then that of others.

Hypocrite! First remove the plank from your own eye, and then you will see clearly to remove the speck from your brother's eye. (Matthew 7:5)

As Jesus said we are to first remove the log in our own eyes so we can see clearly to remove the speck in another's eyes. For when someone has become spiritually responsible, it becomes easier to stir up responsibility in others. Let us not copy those who just keep themselves or those they lead as forever-babies; who will never grow to spiritual responsibility. Understand me. To train someone to strictly obey the do's and don'ts in the church can create a false sense of responsibility that makes people boast in themselves being under law rather than under grace.

Remember for everything we do; we want to make sure we do it with the right frame of mind and motive. People who are trained in responsibility have grown spiritually and have learned to take strong meat by reason of use; having been able to exercise their senses to know good from evil. So, when a man becomes responsible it is a physical response that comes through spiritual transformation.

When I was a child, I spoke as a child, I understood as a child, I thought as a child; but when I became a man, I put away childish things. (1Corinthians 13:11)

So, you see that he became a man, then by himself, he dropped childish things. He was not put under laws to do things that he hadn't enough transformation to know why he was doing them. If then you are a leader, you must go before the sheep like our master the good shepherd.

By this, brothers and sisters, we should understand that we have a deal with the Father as caretakers of His flock. So, let us do it with all our sincerity as it's the noblest of all professions to be co-laborers with the Father of Heaven and Earth.

The Fatherhood Connection

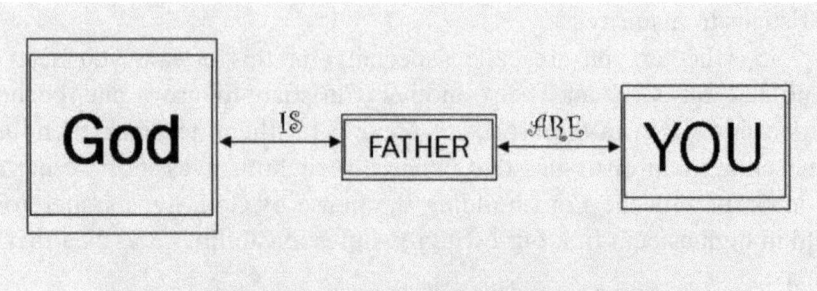

God is the FATHER of Heaven; You are (or should become)the Elder of the Church on Earth

CHAPTER EIGHT

DIVINITY AND THE PROMISE

Ladies and gentlemen, it is with great joy that I bring you this good news. As we talked before on this issue of God's divine nature and the privilege that He gave us to partake,

I want you to know that true Christianity is more about being or becoming than it is about doing.

I feel led to conclude this write up with a word of faith to make you understand the functionality of our own divine nature and how we can grow to fully partake in the very nature of God.

My Father, who has given them to Me, is greater than all; and no one is able to snatch them out of My Father's hand. I and My Father are one. Then the Jews took up stones again to stone Him. Jesus answered them, "Many good works I have shown you from My Father. For which of those works do you stone Me? The Jews answered Him, saying, "For a good work we do not stone You, but for blasphemy, and because You, being a Man, make Yourself God." Jesus answered them, "Is it not written in your law, 'I said, "You are gods"'? If He called them gods, to whom the word of God came (and the Scripture cannot be broken), do you say of Him whom the Father sanctified and sent into the world, 'You are blaspheming,' because I said, 'I am the Son of God'? (John10:29-36)

Above we see a clear picture of what being the son of God means. The Jews wanted to stone Jesus because He said: "I and my father are one." Then Jesus said why do you say I blaspheme just because I called myself the son of God? From this conversation I understand that to be one with your father and to be the son of your father meant the same thing. But being the son of man, he had a will of his own. He, therefore, could decide what he wanted to do. So, if He said He was one with the Father, He was talking in terms of their nature. Hence He by that statement said that though being in the flesh, He and the Father are one in nature in the spirit.

Those people received the word of God and they were called gods which were a shadow of things to come: "US." I say you and me because we are now the reality of the shadow gods that they were. How? You may ask. The Word of God states that we were born of an incorruptible seed even the Word of God. So, you did not just receive the Word of God you are the Word of God that has become flesh in the order of Christ Jesus. And that word was with God and was God.

Don't you know the same word that led to the Conception of Jesus also led to your Born-Again conception?

The only spiritual difference is the fact that after Mary heard the Word she conceived Jesus but you upon hearing the Word became pregnant with your new self or the born again you. When that Word became flesh it still remained one with the Father. So do not expect God to be different from you seeing that you have the same nature as Him. Who will believe me? A human of two months old is so little and filled with inabilities. However, the lad has the nature or potential to grow up and become like their parents; if they feed well over a period of time. Jesus even said that He has sent us in the same capacity that he was sent. So, we have been given the potential or power to become sons of God just like Jesus.

Know first of all that to be called the son of God means to be one with God.

Behold what manner of love the Father has bestowed on us, that we should be called children of God! Therefore the world does not know us, because it did not know Him. (1John 3:1)

This is truly an expression of love that came to us. God calling us His sons made us the same express image as the divine. Therefore, the world does not know us because it did not know Him. Then it continues with what you will say to a two-year-old. Now you are the son or daughter of your father but it does not yet appear what you will be but we know that when your father shall appear you shall be like him. Please understand; we are blending spiritual with physical so you might know and better understand. Not to make you see only the hope in this scripture which is the coming of Jesus in the clouds, I want to explain further.

But we all, with unveiled face, beholding as in a mirror the glory of the Lord, are being transformed into the same image from glory to glory, just as by the Spirit of the Lord. (2Corinthians 3:18)

As we look in the mirror we are being changed. Therefore, now as God or Christ appears or reveals Himself to you through the voice of the Holy Spirit or by revelation from the Word of God we also change continually to become like Him. So, therefore, if we all have this hope we should purify ourselves even as He is pure. And real purifying comes by the washing of water by the Word of God. Just as Jesus said they have been made clean through the words I have given them. For with the heart man believes and is made righteous before God. So, brothers and sisters let us quit looking ourselves as two-year-old lads all the time and start seeing the potential of us growing and becoming like God (our Father) Himself. However, we must now see that time and feeding investment is very necessary for that potential to grow. If we concentrate on watering ourselves, with time we will naturally grow to become spiritual men and women in terms of our nature as gods. And we will put iniquity out of our tents and reign on the Earth.

More so, God has planned our growth process. Hence the reason why God has given us great promises is so that we can grow up and become what He wants us to be (gods) here on earth.

As His divine power has given to us all things that pertain to life and godliness, through the knowledge of Him who called us by glory and virtue, by which have been given to us exceedingly great and precious promises, that through these you may be partakers of the divine nature (2Peter 1:3-4)

Looking unto Jesus, the author and finisher of our faith, who for the joy that was set before Him endured the cross, despising the shame, and has sat down at the right hand of the throne of God. (Hebrews 12:2)

If Jesus also went through this process then how much more us. Just as Jesus was able to endure the cross for the joy set before Him, God also has set promises of joy before us, so we can endure our own cross.

Therefore, by the time we get to our promise, we would have attained the nature of God. It is like a child learning how to walk and the father stands afar off and calls with a piece of cake in his hand. Thus, the cake which is a promise will cause the child to walk toward the father. But most at times what goes on in our minds is what also goes on in the mind of the child. Why can't daddy just give me the cake: must I walk, must I pray, must I study the Bible, must I give, must I obey? The answer is yes, you must walk. If physical lameness was caused by the decision of those who are victims themselves, then they would have been better placed to tell us the consequences and limitations of not walking. However, at the level of the spirit, we ourselves could by our foolishness; laziness and ignorance become the cause of our own lameness and or limitation.

Wait on the LORD; Be of good courage, And He shall strengthen your heart; Wait, I say, on the LORD! (Psalm27:14),

We are instructed to wait on the Lord. If the truth about waiting was what some Christians do today they would have grown beyond their wildest imagination. But it is not so. Quit waiting the way you have been waiting and start doing something. Wake up from sleep. Christians of today are tempted to abandon spiritual exercise in a way that they just end up being carnal religious people with one or two scriptures in their mouth hoping to just make Heaven. If you are like that, know you are falling from grace. So, wake up by asking real spiritual questions about your spiritual life. Again, if you have hope of seeing the promise, then you must purify yourself by walking in the spirit.

Therefore if anyone cleanses himself from the latter, he will be a vessel for honor, sanctified and useful for the Master, prepared for every good work. (2Timothy 2:21)

Do not sit down; purify yourself while waiting. As the scriptures declare: he that purges himself shall be fit for the master's use. In other words, you shall be fit for the Master's glory. Yet some just sit idling and expect the morning to come like magic. Stop deceiving yourself it is time to make your own morning come by sowing precious seeds in the period of patience and/or mourning. Remember it is what you sow on your way that you will harvest and rejoice with when coming back. Hear me if you have ears, I mean no harm but God's understanding of the word 'wait' is most at times misunderstood by some because of lust. In that same scripture 2 Peter 1:3-4 concludes this way: *having escaped the corruption that is in the world through lust.* Remember lust is the driving force behind the world of corruption in which we live. But we are not to be conformed to the world by being transformed through the renewing of our minds. God will not come down to renew your mind. You must discipline yourself to renew your own mind by hiding the Word of God in your heart like the psalmist and meditating on the Word like Joshua so when God comes, He will see you fit for Him and well prepared for His kind of glory. These then are some of the things you can do to keep growing spiritually.

1. **Prayer:** Ask yourself the question; am I praying regularly, if not then make a prayer plan to pray regularly. For those who are praying already, you must make sure you are speaking in tongues. If you do not pray in tongues know you are not being a true Christian because speaking in tongues is not given for pleasure. It was given as a tool. That's why a Christian who speaks in tongues will grow to become more spiritual while a Christian who does not speak in tongues at best will still be carnal. Also, when you pray, stop asking for carnal things, He knows you need them. What God does not know is how bad you want to be like Him or obey Him. So, ask spiritual things from a spiritual God and He will answer you. Also, you need to make plans to increase the length of your prayer time. If you are effectively praying one-hour increase to two, three, why not four. As you do that and challenge yourself, God will take you to new heights in Him always

2. **Bible study or reading:** If you do not study your Bible you are not ready to live the Christian life. So, spend time to regularly read the Bible and study new topics from the Word of God. If you have difficulty understanding the spirit of the word, pray about it and spend more time studying. Also, desire to learn new things when you read the Word of God because this might be the temptation of already established Christians. If you find yourself never learning any new thing from the Word know you are stuck in your spiritual past. It means the learning process that makes or transforms a man has stopped operating in your life. You are now like an abandoned spiritual factory that only tells people we use to make wonderful plates or automobile. So, what are you doing now? Nothing. Have you not seen Christians who glory only in their past? it's because nothing new is happening anymore. So, break from that evil and get your spiritual engines cranking again.

3. **Meditation:** Some people think that meditation is Bible study but nothing could be farther from the truth. Bible study gives an intellectual understanding of the scripture which is basically the letter that cannot save you. But meditation converts that Word into a spiritual knowledge that can save you. Meditation is the process where you spend time thinking and praying on one scriptural verse or a group of similar verses for a period of time ranging from minutes to hours, days, months and why not years. It is meditation that brings spiritual understanding to the Word of God without which the Bible will just be to you like a storybook. So, spend more time meditating. Practice the art of meditating which I define as the ability to keep the Word in your mind all day long.
4. **The voice of God:** In this 21st century, I can't imagine some people still doubt if God speaks to people talk less of true Christians who do not hear the voice of God but take it lightly. Please if you do not hear the voice of God you are doomed because God's guidance and comfort by His Holy Spirit are not active in your life. That is why many Christians today suffer from depression. So, if you must pray: pray. If you must fast: fast until you start hearing God talk to you. After that cultivate the relationship and practice listening to the Holy Spirit as part of your life. The Holy Spirit is a person who will not badge into your life; so, as you become friendly to Him, He will become friendly to you.
5. **Fellowship:** As a Christian, you must go to church. I do not care if you say church people treat you bad before, as though you never dealt anyone bad before; but still wanted your relationship to continue. So never use the excuse that you were treated badly to run from the church. It is the temptation of the devil eating the church and converting Christians into self-righteous individuals that will never be of any use to God. Don't you know that while you are running from church and saying those people are not Christians enough; those people you left in the church are also saying you are not a Christian enough because though we wronged you, instead to forgive us as Christ forgave, you left the church because of unforgiveness? It might shock you to hear this but all the people that hurt you are part of God's test in your life to find out what you have learned about Him and how far you

THE DIVINE NATURE OF GOD

are willing to go to practice those things you have learned. But when the test comes, some prove to God that they are just there learning nothing and are ready to practice nothing. So, if you think you are better than them then have compassion for them, go back there and help them to become like you. You will be surprised by how much God will use that process to also teach you. However, in a case where you must leave, ask God to lead you to another church or place of fellowship. Whatever you do, do not quit going to church.

"But let patience have her perfect work, that you may be perfect and entire, lacking in nothing." (James 1:4)
Patience in itself is not defined as waiting on God over time but it is the right attitude by which a child of God waits on God over time. But the waiting on God part for me is still an overstatement that can blur our realization of what is on the ground.

The real issue is stated in that verse we just read: that you might be perfect lacking nothing.

The only thing you and God are waiting for is your own perfection, not God's. You have all the potential but you must invest spiritually in yourself as you watch your growing process. At the end of the day when you become a grown up you will be perfect wanting nothing. So, by this, you can actually shorten or lengthen or even miss the entire promises of God for your life. For example: Let's say you have an earthly father who has a car willed to your name while he is still alive: like the famous prodigal son. Then he says to you, "the car is yours but I can only give you the keys when you show me your driving license." Then he says the car is yours anytime you show him the license within the next two years: for after two years, he will give it to your younger brother. Then instead of registering for the license, at once, you sit on the couch and watch TV and distract yourself with other things for all the time. Knowing fully well that the time period to learn and obtain a license is three months you only registered one month before the closing of the two-year period you were given. Then you will come like Esau and say is there no way you can get me the blessing? You see this is what happened with the elder brother in the prodigal story. Know that to be busy for God does not mean you are doing what is important. It is in this way that Martha was worried about many things but Mary sat down when she had found what was important for her training. So, the elder brother in the prodigal story was so busy that he even did not know what was his and the relationship he had with his father. So, he was angry when he saw the father giving his younger brother what he wanted. Do not be angry when you see others you started with being blessed. It is not favor isn't a fair issue. It is a favor that is fair. They have prepared themselves like the wise virgins and so the master has taken them in.

And so we have the prophetic word confirmed, which you do well to heed as a light that shines in a dark place, until the day dawns and the morning star rises in your hearts; (2Peter 1:19)

Child of God, do not chase the wind saying weeping endures for a night but joy comes in the morning. If you think it's a physical or probability morning then you will wait forever. But the morning I know is a spiritual one which comes after you have given heed to the word until that new creation man arises from within you and begins to shine-on in the world around you. Hence rather than get angry with God for blessing or increasing others, get angry with your laziness. Increase your prayer and Bible study time, give yourself wholly to the Christian vocation as it is said: let everyone that names the name of the Lord depart from evil. Live according to the Word which says study to show yourself approved unto God and the God who saw perfection in David while he was only seventeen years old will see it in you and remove you from the forest in no time. God has given you His nature but you have the responsibility to nurture it. If you do it well He'll pay you well. God bless you.

ABOUT THE AUTHOR

Emmanuel Efuetaka (Wiseman) was a regular Christian who met a ghost and lived. He is called by God to be his Apostle with tremendous insight into his word. His ministry is marked by deep revelation, faith in God and outstanding signs of healing and miracles. He is the founder of Kings Abode Church with a vision to perfect the saints of God. Married the best for a wife (Yvette) and has a wonderful baby girl for a daughter (Edrice).

REFERENCE

- Holy - Holman Bible Dictionary on StudyLight.org: May 20, 2017
- "Nature". Merriam-Webster.com. Merriam-Webster n. d. May 20, 2017
- Sanctification - Holman Bible Dictionary on StudyLight.org: May 20, 2017

www.ingramcontent.com/pod-product-compliance
Lightning Source LLC
LaVergne TN
LVHW051050080426
835508LV00019B/1802